THE BOOK
OF KASHRUTH

Seymour E. Freedman

THE BOOK

OF

KASHRUTH

*A Treasury of Kosher Facts
and Frauds*

To the women in my life who taught and defended the ritual of Kashruth:

My mother Dora, of blessed memory;
my beloved wife Rose Naomi.

To cherished friends who exemplified in their deeds the morality of Kashruth, Sam and Sarah Slepian

Contents

Introduction

In the beginning I undertook to write this kind of book because, after some research on the subject, I realized that there was no comprehensive study on Kashruth available in the English language. The usual work on this vitally important Mitzvah has either been directed towards the Jewish homemaker as an adjunct to a cook book, or planned as part of a text for the student of Judaism. I found two special studies on Kashruth—one a dissertation for a doctorate from Yeshiva University, prepared by Rabbi Sol B. Freedman; the second an encyclopedic text by Rabbi Jeremiah Berman, of blessed memory, entitled, *Shechita*, which as its title suggests, deals with many facets of Kosher slaughter. But I couldn't put my hands on one book that contained between its covers the many interesting issues which are included in the term "Kashruth." Therefore, I decided to write such a book.

As I delved deeper into the subject, new areas of interest kept me captive. For example, I found it especially important to learn that in practically every country where a dangerous program of anti-semitism reared its ugliness, the first avenue of attack upon the Jews was via the *mitzvah* of Kashruth, especially *shechita*. This was probably the

most potent weapon with which to begin the attack upon
the Jewish community because the blow was twofold—
physical as well as spiritual. Whatever else of his religion
might be denied the Jew, whether it were prayer or study,
Jews managed to practice it underground. But to deny him
his Kosher food was a much more devastating attack. The
Nazis added another dimension when they outlawed
shechita—that of ridicule, which struck a deep emotional
chord in the Jewish soul.

I was privileged to interview the old-timers in Kashruth,
those courageous men who struggled to establish Kashruth
in this country back in the early days of mass immigration
to America. They fought with great courage, often at the
risk of their very lives, to create an image of respect for
those laymen and professionals who were involved in some
manner in the growing industry of Kashruth. They believed in the sanctity of the *mitzvah* of Kashruth and its
centrality as a religious principle in the Jewish style of life.
They hoped to strengthen its observance in their new land
of freedom.

The Israeli rabbinate is the youngest Jewish community
to grapple with the many problems that confront the
Kashruth industry in a modern, traveling, and fast-moving
world society. They can learn much from the American
experience in Kashruth. Some of the problems that have
stymied American rabbis are frustrating Israel's sages today;
perhaps they will employ new areas of scholarship we
have missed, or that have not been available to us, in order
to resolve some very serious questions.

My hope is that those who will read this book will become excited anew about the meanings of Kashruth for
the Jew and for all men. Especially in times such as these,

when so large a section of the great Jewish ideas have been lost to our people, I trust in the potential of a modern approach to Kashruth to awaken renewed dedication to this ancient, spiritually uplifting, magnificent commandment.

The information contained in this book will prove to be valuable especially for students in food technology and hotel training programs. Should anyone of them decide to work in a Kosher food establishment, this text will be a valuable reference. Those employed in nursing homes and hospitals serving Kosher food will also have a better grasp of the importance of Kashruth.

Much thanks is due to all those who in one way or another contributed to the making of this book. Their numbers are legion and I could not possibly hope to thank them all. I know that they will find joy in the silent tribute that is given to them by these lines which tell their story. Yet, I find a compulsion to thank publicly those who helped so very much. My thanks go to Mr. Sidney Kahan, Chairman of the Kashruth Committee of the New York Metropolitan Region of the United Synagogue of America, for his advice on chemistry and Kosher foods; to Rabbi Sheppard Baum, director of the New York State Bureau of Kosher Law Enforcement for his interest in this work; to Rabbi Chaim Y. Hurwitz, executive secretary of the Kashruth Supervisors Union, Local #621, who led me to many sources of knowledge and introduced me to people who are still making Kashruth history.

BOOK ONE

The material contained in Book One represents a collection of basic information about Kashruth which has never before been presented in one volume. It is designed to provide an understanding and an appreciation of the history, the laws and the special food customs of the Dietary Code and of Judaism. The chapters in this section offer an explanation of the philosophic basis of Kashruth and focus attention upon some of the moral and ethical problems that have cancerized the very core of Kashruth.

Book One intends to answer the question, "Why is the commandment to keep Kosher important today?"

Kashruth Dictionary

Most people associate the Hebrew word "Kosher" with food—that which is permitted is Kosher, and foods that are forbidden are called *trayfe*. Much more meaning, however, is actually contained in the word Kosher. Therefore, if one is to grasp the full implications of the Kosher code of Judaism as a vital, dynamic religious principle, a broader knowledge is necessary. This excursion into the tradition of Kashruth requires a dictionary explaining the terminology that will appear throughout the book. The following definitions will provide a valuable guide to a better understanding of Judaism's application of the word Kosher as it appears in the sacred books.

1. AYVER MIN HA-CHAY—literally a "limb from a living thing," referring to a barbaric custom of slicing off a piece of flesh from a living animal and eating it. This custom was prohibited by the Torah.

2. BODEK—Literally, "a searcher," referring to someone trained to examine the insides of a beast following *shechita* to determine if the animal was healthy and thus Kosher.

3. CHALAF—Literally, "to change over," referring to the knife of a *shochet* which "changes the animal over" from a living thing to a dead carcass. (The regular Hebrew word for knife is *sakeen*.)

4. CHAYLEV—Literally "fat," referring to certain fatty portions of the animal which are forbidden. The prohibition of *chaylev* originates in the sacrificial code of the Book of Leviticus in which certain fatty portions and fats as such were designated as portions of the sacrifice and thus made holy. They were not to be eaten. This prohibition is still in effect.

5. CHOMETZ—Literally "leaven," referring to the prohibition of eating leavened foods during the period of Passover.

6. DAHM—Literal translation, "blood," referring to the biblical injunction against eating blood. This law of the Torah is the basis of the Kashering laws which require washing, salting or broiling of meats in order to remove the forbidden blood.

7. FLAYSHIG—Literal translation, "meat," referring to meat foods, dishes, utensils and silverware.

8. HADACHA—Literally, "washing" referring to the custom of washing meats. According to the Kashruth code, meats are washed or soaked under the following conditions:

   a) prior to salting or broiling in order to remove any surface blood or foreign substances.

   b) After salting or broiling to remove any surface blood which has been drawn out.

   c) Following Shechita, if the meat has not been koshered, then after every three days' period, it must be washed with water (or at least dampened) to keep it fresh so that the blood will not coagulate and resist salting. Should a period longer than three days pass without washing the meat, it can be koshered only through broiling.

9. HALACHA—A term applied to that section of the Jewish holy works which deals with the commandments that direct the life of the Jew. Literal translation, "to walk" implying that the commandments are a path upon which to walk in the ways of the Lord.

10. KASHRUTH—The totality of the laws and practices which are derived from the Jewish Dietary commandments.

11. KOSHER—Literally, something that is "fit" or "proper." While the term is commonly applied to Kosher foods it is not restricted in the sacred writings to foods alone. For example, the word Kosher is also used in reference to a completed Torah, Tefillin, or Marriage Contract, to indicate that the object is fit and proper for use at a Jewish religious occasion.

The term Kosher refers also to a thought process. In the Book of Esther, chapter 8 verse 5, Queen Esther beseeches her husband King Ahaseurus to intervene in behalf of the Jews of his realm whose lives the wicked Haman has endangered. Esther pleads, "If it please the king, and if I have found favor in his sight, and the thing seem right (Kosher) before the king . . ." Popular useage of term has also embraced this ethical meaning, i.e., "His objectives weren't Kosher."

12. KOSHER L'PESSACH—Literal translation, "Kosher for Passover," referring to food prepared in accordance with the special Passover Dietary Laws.

13. MASHGIACH—Literally "supervisor," referring to the person who is sufficiently familiar with the laws of Kashruth to be qualified to supervise the production of the foods in accordance with the Dietary Laws. A *mashgiach* need not be a rabbi.

14. MILCHIG—Literal translation, "dairy," referring to dairy foods, dishes, utensils and silverware.

15. MITZVAH—A divine commandment, a meritorious act, a good deed.

16. M'LEECHA—Literally "salting," referring to the Halachic requirement to salt raw meat as a means of Kashering it.

17. N'VAYLA—The carcass of an animal which died before it could be slaughtered in accordance with the Kosher slaughter laws.

18. PAREVE—Literal translation, "neutral" referring to foods which are neither meat nor dairy, i.e. vegetables, fish, eggs, etc. Pareve also refers to dishes, utensils and silverware.

19. PLUMBA—A tag which is affixed to something, such as food or a package of food, testifying to the fact that it is Kosher.

20. RAV HAMACHSHIR—Literal translation, "the rabbi who certifies Kashruth." A food plant producing Kosher products employs the services of a Rav Hamachshir who is an ordained rabbi and knowledgeable in the laws of Kashruth. The Rav Hamachshir guides the *mashgiach* in performing his work.

21. SHABBOS—Literally "the Sabbath," referring here to the laws that guide the preparation of foods for the Sabbath.

22. SHECHITA—The process of Jewish ritual slaughter of animals and fowl for food. Fish do not require *shechita*, according to the Torah.

23. SHOCHET—Someone trained in the laws of Jewish ritual slaughter.

24. TAHOR—Literal translation, "pure," referring to ritual purity as prescribed in the Torah.

25. TOMAY—Meaning, "defilement" referring to the defilement of body and soul when forbidden foods are eaten. The term *tomay* is used broadly in the Torah to depict a variety of situations in which a person may become *tomay* in addition to the defilement brought about by eating the *trayfe* foods.

26. TORAH—Literally, "law," referring primarily to the Five Books of Moses. However, the word Torah is used as an all-inclusive term encompassing all Jewish religious books and wisdom.

27. TRAYFE—Literal translation, "torn," referring to an animal that was attacked by another beast and torn apart in battle. The term has taken on a general meaning which is applied to all foods that are not Kosher.

28. TSAAR BALAY CHAYIM—Literal translation, "the suffering of living things," referring to the biblical commandment to be compassionate and not to inflict needless suffering, physical or emotional, upon God's creatures. As it relates to Kashruth, it refers to the prohibition of causing needless pain to an animal prior to or during *shechita*.

29. TRAYBERING—A Czechoslovakian word which entered the Yiddish language, meaning "to *porg*," to clean out the veins. This refers to the process of cutting away the forbidden veins or fat from a Kosher-slaughtered animal. In many countries *traybering* is still practiced as a profession, but not in America. Large slaughter houses in America find it economically impractical to employ a *trayberer*. It is much simpler to cut away that portion of the animal which contains the forbidden part and sell it to the Christian trade.

30. T'UDAH—The certificate which is given to a *shochet* upon completion of his studies and internship which testifies to his qualification as a Shochet.

31. VAAD HAKASHRUTH—Literal translation, "a committee for Kashruth," referring to the synagogue or communal committee whose task it is to safeguard the dignity and observance of Kashruth.

32. YAYIN NESSECH—Literally, "wine for pouring," referring to the pagan custom of pouring wine upon the altar as part of the idolatrous worship. Observant Jews refrain from drinking wine that has been handled by a non-Jew, fearing that perhaps the non-Jew while handling the wine might have thought of consecrating the wine to his own form of divine worship.

33. YOM TOV—Literal translation, "a good day," referring to the Jewish festivals which have their own special Dietary Laws.

Kashruth as a Moral Force

1 There is a story in the Medrosh[1] which relates that once Rabbi Yehuda Hanasi (Rabbi Judah the Prince) invited the Roman general, Antoninus, to his home for a Sabbath meal. The rabbi served his guest a meal of cold foods. Later on, Rabbi Yehuda invited Antoninus again to his home; this time, however, it was on a weekday. The rabbi served his guest a meal of hot foods. Antoninus surprised his host by telling him that he enjoyed the meal of cold foods served on the Sabbath more than he enjoyed the hot meal served to him on this day. Rabbi Yehuda answered that the weekday meal did not have a particular spice which the Sabbath meal had. Antoninus assured the rabbi that in the royal storehouse there was available any conceivable spice; he need only name the missing spice and it would be obtained for him. Rabbi Yehuda thought for a moment and then replied, "The name of the missing spice is 'Sabbath.' Do you have *it* in your storehouse?" The Medrosh concludes at this point with no further response of interest from Antoninus.

This story out of Jewish antiquity appears as the precursor of the new image recently given Jewish foods by modern, aggressive advertising, which declares, "You don't have to be Jewish to love Jewish foods;" like Antoninus the Roman, "You don't have to be Jewish to love Levy's Rye Bread" or "Vita Herring." Kosher wines are as good as any others, even though they are made in a special way. Even Christians and Buddhists can enjoy them.

This may well be true. You don't have to be Jewish for Jewish foods to excite your taste buds, if that is all that is desired. But Jewish cooking was traditionally prepared to *excite the soul!* The term "Jewish cooking" has for centuries been associated with the term "Kashruth," which is a soul-exciting spice; and to enjoy this special spice, we must emulate Rabbi Yehuda whose enjoyment of Jewish foods arose out of a commitment to Judaism.

The laws of Kashruth, which monitor the foods observant Jews may eat, are much like those of the Sabbath, which monitor the activities and thoughts of those Jews who appreciate its message and abide by its traditions. The laws of Kashruth create a spiritual atmosphere that lasts not only for the period of the meal itself, but also throughout the entire day, refining encounters with other human beings through an established and internalized *weltanschaaung* of compassion that encompasses all life. As such, the seemingly lifeless rituals that comprise the structure of the Dietary Code assume a meaningful aura which, when linked with the totality of Judaism, tend to make those who adhere to it "a little lower than the angels" because Kashruth is meant to be a rung on Jacob's dream-ladder, a vital segment of the Jewish mission to bring people along a path to the Godly life.

A Search for Meaning

Except in rare instances, the Torah does not give reasons for the observance of its commandments. Kashruth is one of those commandments for whose observance no reason is given. Although at first blush it appears that it would be very helpful to know the reasons for the observance of Kashruth, on further consideration it becomes acceptable to the mind that there is equal wisdom in not providing an explanation for the existence of these laws. For experience has shown that those who in the past have created reasons for the Kosher laws have unwittingly limited their value, making of them a temporary code and thus opening the door to their "legitimate" violation.

The great Maimonides [2] was one of those who sought to provide a rationale for the observance of the Kashruth laws. His purpose was to draw the loyalty of those who had abandoned them back to observing them once again. However, even he had to admit that when he wrote of the Kashruth code as being a means to enhance human health, he was merely offering a possible explanation rather than an accepted official interpretation. For those students of Judaism whose knowledge was at the introductory level, the initial discussion of Kashruth might be based upon a reason of health. But when this initial stage had grown to a broader knowledge and a deeper faith, one that could accept the fact that some Laws are to be observed wholly on faith alone, then the truth that Kashruth is without logical explanation could and should be told.

It is significant that, as a general rule, both the rabbinic and secular legalists determined that a law is to be obeyed

apart from any rationale that could be attributed to it.
"The generally accepted principle of jurisprudence and
legal philosophy in dealing with the motive of a given law
(*ratio legis*) . . . is that the binding force of a law is always
independent of its motive, whether directly expressed or
assumed." [3] This was especially true for the rabbis who
relied upon the Torah to guide their appreciation of some
of the more complicated laws that confronted them. They
understood the Torah's pronouncements of laws not as
mere suggestions of socio-religious patterns, but rather as
fixed laws that were binding upon all Jews and not subject
to changing times and conditions. Commenting on the Torah's statement, "This is the law (*chukas*) of the Torah,"
the Medrosh declares (in the name of the Almighty). "I
have promulgated laws (*chok*) and edicts (*g'zayra*) and
you have no right to transgress my edicts." [4] Based upon
this, the Franco-German school of Talmudists generally
opposed any investigation into the reasons for the Torah's
commandments. Medieval Jewish philosophers, beginning
with Saadya, who dared to study with a mind to discovering hidden meanings, did so hesitantly and somewhat cau-
tiously at first. Later, with Bahaya, Miamonides, and Nachmonides, such studies became increasingly significant.
Modern times, particularly in the Chassidic literature, with
its mystical excursions into Jewish legal statements, have
produced meaningful changes in the former reluctance to
discover the meanings of the commandments.

The Talmud provides us with the essential clue to understanding the reason for the laws of the Torah (including
the Kashruth Laws), by enveloping all 613 commandments
within the general statement that the *Mitzvos* are designed
to "unify people" in a spiritually uplifting manner. The

unity indicated here implies personal unity within oneself as well as social unity involving acts of brotherhood and compassion.

How It All Began

The Dietary Laws, as we know them today, are the result of centuries of living through moving spiritual experiences that brought forth these particular laws as a special category within the Jewish style of life. They represent our forefathers' conceptualization of the Divine Will which, according to the accounts in the Bible and the discussions of the Jewish sages in later sacred books, expanded until it was finally formalized into the canon of our tradition. For example, in the life of Abraham, centuries prior to the formal pronouncement of the Kashruth Laws, we read that Abraham set before his three angelic visitors who came to his tent a meal which no Kashruth-observing Jewish housewife would tolerate. In Genesis [5] it is recorded that . . . "he took curd, milk and the calf which he had dressed and set it before them and they did eat." This mixing of meat and dairy foods at the same meal, which is a clear violation of Kashruth, perplexed the commentators of the Bible. Rashi, one of the most famous commentators on the Torah, evidenced his disturbance by interceding with the cautious, somewhat forced explanation that the angels really didn't eat, but merely assumed the guise of men, and only appeared to Abraham to be eating. And, if in fact they did eat, says Rashi, they were careful to eat the dairy before the meat, as required by the Dietary Laws.

Generations later, the Patriarch Jacob established a basic Kashruth Law when he wrestled with a stranger who appeared suddenly out of the night. The contest ended in a stalemate, neither one vanquishing the other. However, in a final attempt to free himself from Jacob's grip, the attacker rendered Jacob a powerful blow on the thigh which caused him to limp thereafter. From this ancient experience came the prohibition that Jews do not eat the *Geed Hanasheh*, the sciatic nerve, in remembrance of Jacob's encounter.[6]

The high point for Kashruth was ultimately reached when Moses ascended Mt. Sinai to receive the Torah. Jews were commanded to be compassionate. They were permitted to slaughter animals for food, but only in the most humane manner. Other laws forbid Jews to eat raw blood. Animals, fish and fowl are divided into categories—those which may be eaten, and those which may not.

The sages of the Talmud who lived between the second and fifth centuries interpreted these laws of Kashruth and established guidelines for observing them. For example, they took the one passage, "Thou shalt not cook a kid in its mother's milk"[7] and built upon it the whole structure of laws separating meat from dairy in the Kosher kitchen.

In view of what has been said above, it would be an unfortunate mistake to assume that the mere ritual of Kashruth was the sole purpose of these special laws. The Jewish sages explain that the *Mitzvos* of the Torah were given for the specific purpose of refining the human nature of man. The use of foods throughout the Bible, therefore, was meant to provide opportunities for fulfilling divinely ordained rituals which could serve as provocative tools for cueing mankind's thoughts to God. Throughout the Torah there are stories which express this use of food as a means to accomplish a divine purpose. For example, Adam and Eve, the first human creatures, were given a spiritual challenge:

"From every tree in the garden you may eat thereof, but from the fruit of the tree of The Knowledge of Good and Evil you shall not eat." [8]

When they failed to comply with this single commandment, they were chastised by their Creator and were driven from the Garden of Eden to be buffeted about in a physically and spiritually indifferent world. This was their punishment for having eaten from the Tree of Knowledge, disobeying the will of God.

Their children were to learn from this to be more attuned to the divine commandments. When the redeemed Jewish slaves were in the desert, enroute to their Promised Land, God employed food once again as a means of discovering the nature of their commitment to His will. The children of Israel cried unto Moses for food, and God heard their plea and promised to grant them a miracle: food would descend from heaven for them; the Mana-Bread would be given to them daily. On the sixth day of the week, however, they were to collect a double portion in order that they would not need to collect it on the Sabbath, which would be a desecration of the holy day of rest. In Exodus,[9] the Torah explains the purpose for providing the Mana-Bread from heaven with the proverbial string attached to it: "Then said the Lord to Moses, 'Behold, I will cause it to rain bread from the heavens for you; and the people shall go out and gather a day's portion every day, that I may prove them whether they will walk in my law or not.' "

It is to the everlasting credit of Judaism that it took so plain a commodity as food and fashioned it into a tool for upgrading commitment to God. Its daughter-religions similarly employed man's daily bread as a means of drawing his attention to Heaven; for example, Catholicism prohibited the eating of meat on Friday; Mohammedanism prohibits the eating of pig's meat. The Torah, with its universal outlook, anticipated these actions by the founders of the later religions when it decreed that even those of the Gentile nations shall be required to obey certain minimal restrictions regarding food. These laws are contained in the "Seven Commandments For the Children of Noah," which are a basic guide given to the Gentiles. Among them is the commandment forbidding the ancient barbaric practice of slicing a piece of raw flesh from a living animal for food, a custom observed even today among certain primitive Arab tribes. The spiritual thread that seems to run through all of these precepts is the realization that man must eat each day the fruits of the earth, the produce of field and barn. These could speak to him of the creativity of God; his daily diet, therefore, could become a thing of reverence and an implement of worship. The Jewish way of eating is to bless God before and after each morsel of food and every meal. Before eating bread, the staff of life, which became a special symbol of holiness, Jewish tradition requires that the hands be washed ceremonially as a symbolic holy gesture in the manner of the *Kohayn*, the priest of Solomon's Temple, who washed his hands with much pomp and ceremony before approaching a sacrifice or blessing the congregation. The Jew does not merely sit down to eat a meal; instead, he selects the foods he will eat according to the Divine Will as expressed in the Kashruth Laws. Through this guidance the Jew is taught that the glutton lives each day so that he can feast himself without restraint. But the man of God eats so that he can have the strength to serve his God more fully each day.

By performing these God-inspired acts while eating, the Jewish heart and mind are focused upon God, and a particular psyche is being formed. The Jewish character, so widely praised in the writings of the prophets and sages as being fashioned "in the image of God"—compassionate, merciful, creative, and self-sacrificing—is taking shape daily. Judaism makes no mere pretense of being committed to these high ideals. It does not waste its energies on giving mere lip-service to such greatly desirable ethical values; it has from the very outset worked hard at making them real. But ancient men and women were not overly concerned with such fine conceptions of social relationships, and when our Jewish forefathers raised such issues for them to consider, their teachings were rejected as radical and were denounced as revolutionary. For example, the monotheism of Abraham was condemned as a revolt against the practiced religion of idolatry. His stubborn ridiculing of the idolatrous establishment of his day, however, was not only against the idols of wood or stone per se; his real purpose was to teach that when a man gives himself over to trust in a power outside himself to help him in his time of trouble, such a commitment of faith deserves some assurance that help will indeed be forthcoming. He chided his father's customers who came to purchase their household gods or to pray before a statue in his father's chapel. He drew the attention of old men and women to the fact that an idol that was but one day or one week old could not be more helpful in a time of trouble than they themselves, who had lived long and gained much wisdom about the ways of the world. He encouraged them to think about the fallacies of their misguided faith. He urged them to abandon the hypocrisy of a useless trust in idols. A portion of his spirit of realistic faith was implanted in the immortal Jewish soul.

Later on, Moses arose to challenge a different social miscarriage that was endorsed by the ruling power; he rebelled against the horror of human bondage. He taught both Egyptian and Jew that man was not born to be enslaved by other men. "The children of Israel are *my* servants," [10] saith the Lord, "and not the servants of servants." (The term "servants" used here refers to human beings who are viewed as being in perpetual service to God.) This basic lesson which Moses taught by his personal dedication to the principle of freedom was well learned by the Jew. Following in his paths has earned for the Jew the title, "stiff-necked people" because, neither as individuals nor as a nation, will they prostrate themselves before the despot who would enslave them.

Among the names of Jewish teachers who held out the brightest hope for a universal spiritual awakening of all men, regardless of religion, none captures the mind with greater magnetism than Isaiah the Prophet. He rejected the teaching that man and his universe are inherently evil. Instead, he foresaw a time when universal understanding would put an end to human animosities. He spoke for all men and women who would put an end to violence and war when he prophesied the future age of the Messiah:

"And the wolf shall dwell with the lamb
 And the leopard shall lie down with the kid
 And the calf and the young lion and the fattling together
 And a little child shall lead them
 And the cow and the bear shall feed,
 Their young shall not hurt nor destroy in all My holy mountain
 For the earth shall be filled with the knowledge of the Lord
 As the waters cover the sea." [11]

The charismatic effect which these early teachers had upon later generations of Jews who looked for guidance in times of oppression is revealed in the risks that were taken and the sufferings that were endured by latter-day heroes to keep the faith alive. During the Babylonian conquest (586 B.C.), for example, four young men who had committed their lives to the monotheistic faith taught by our Father Abraham refused to bow down to the idol of the man-god, Nebuchadnezzer, King of Babylon and Israel's conqueror. The Bible describes how these young men were cast into the fiery furnace for their obstinate refusal to comply with the command that required them to prostrate themselves in prayer before the great statues of the king. However, their God came to *their* rescue as He did to Abraham's, so that ordinary men and rulers alike might be shown once again the power of the true and one God, who will not countenance "other gods" before Him.

When the Greek-Syrians overran the State of Judea in 68 B.C. the tyrannical laws of the mad king Antiochus made it a capital offense to observe Jewish customs and ceremonies. Jewish mothers who were courageous enough to have their sons circumcised were hung from the gates of their towns; their babies dangled from around their necks until both were dead. When the oppression grew completely intolerable, the immortal image of Moses the redeemer was awakened in the hearts of the Hasmonian family of Mattathias and his sons. They raised the banner of revolt with the call to faith, "Who is like unto Thee, O Lord, among the mighty." Those who joined them in their heroic fight became part of the Maccabee guerilla fighters who hammered away at the invaders until they gave up and left the land.

The Roman conquest in 70 C.E. ended with the expulsion of the Jews from their land and began the years of exile which created the image of the "Wandering Jew" among the nations. Ruthless oppression followed upon ruthless oppression. Jews were expelled even from those countries which, at first, appeared to be hospitable. The most tragic of all these expulsions occurred in 1492, when Spain threw out all of her Jews. Few doors were opened for the refugees. Disease and hunger compounded their sufferings. But even this tragedy, which for centuries was counted as the most horrendous misfortune of the Jews, paled into mere historic record when the Nazi holocaust broke loose upon the world, and especially upon the Jew. Wherever the boot of the German armies marched, the Jews were herded together for special "consideration." They were "racked, twisted, burnt and broken and made to pass through every instrument of torture"; [12] yet, even in this nightmarish time, the stories that have survived this monumental brutality speak of the undying Jewish hope for a better world. Like Isaiah, they dreamed of a new age when the concentration camps and the crematoria would be gone from the earth, and mankind would awaken to a peaceful, happier world. Jews married according to the "laws of Moses and Israel"; babies were circumcized; Bar Mitvah boys and men put on *tefillin* even as they hid from the German S.S. Rabbis who were forced to work on the Sabbath prayed quietly and sang softly the Sabbath hymns as they worked under the menacing gaze of the concentration camp *Kappos*. By some miracle, many of the devout obtained matzos and celebrated Passover hoping for their own freedom through the intervention of a modern-age redeemer.

Today, attention of Jews throughout the free world is

focused upon the Jews of the Soviet Union, who have been silenced by the threat of the Communist tyrants. Mingled with deep concern for their safety is a feeling of pride because of the reports that even under the hard core of Communist domination, untold numbers of Jews remain steadfast in their faith. They wait, as Jews have waited under the most trying conditions, until God will appoint a hero who will rescue them. With this hope uppermost in their hearts, Jews continue to attend synagogue, even though they know that their sanctuaries are monitored by the secret police who play floodlights on the entrance to the synagogue in order to identify those who come at night. They are always under the surveillance of the quisling Jews who are in the employ of the enemy even as they pretend to worship God. To buy matzos in Russia requires that the purchaser sign his name and address in a register at the government controlled store. Knowing full well that this information will be turned over to the secret police, Jews nevertheless, go humbly but with determination to buy their matzos for the holy days of Passover.

The lives of all heroes of Jewish history have been stamped by the compelling pronouncement, " 'Ye are My witness,' saith the Lord." And, like dedicated and devoted children who serve their parents selflessly, heroic Jews continue to serve God with selfless devotion, and bear witness of Him among the nations. Often the scapegoat of a nation in economic or political trouble, the Jew nevertheless remained undeterred from the course his forefathers set for him. In every land wherein he has sojourned the Jew has brought with him the genius of his particular *weltanschaaung* and the blessings of his strong faith in the divine providence that graces mankind. In every land where he has settled he has made it better than when he first arrived there. This determination to "be a blessing" to the world society has motivated and sustained the Jew in every generation. It is this purposeful heritage that is passed on to the children in every generation, so that they too are indoctrinated with the concept, "How goodly are thy tents, O Jacob"; and they too become inspired by the heroes of our faith to continue this majesty of spirit which is at the very heart of Judaism.

In spite of all this evident spiritual grandeur, however, there are many Jews who are quick to cast aside portions, if not all, of Jewish tradition. Some choose to cast away the Sabbath, others discard daily prayer, and still others disregard the tradition of the Dietary Laws. What are some of the motivations that prompt Jews to cast aside these treasures of the spirit?

More than any other single commandment the code of Kashruth involves the Jew frequently each day in his religious heritage; therefore, by understanding some of the reasoning behind the rejection of Kashruth, an insight into the motives that prompt Jews to cast aside other religious precepts will be gained.

Why Some Jews Reject The Kashruth Code

One of the inevitable effects of anything that is special is that it is set apart from the ordinary. There are Jews who reject the special diet of the Kashruth code simply because it sets the Jew apart from the general non-Jewish community. There are those who fear the possible social consequences of anything "overly" Jewish, which might serve as a means of setting the Jew apart and imposing a self-inflicted ghetto. No alert Jew is ignorant of the horrible periods in Jewish history when Jews were segregated and deprived of their rights. Jews who were forced by the Nazis to wear the Star of David as a badge of shame are a living testimony to the horror of separate laws for Jews. If it was not the Star of David, then in other ages it was a special hat or some other symbol of separation that singled the Jew out for special and unfortunate treatment. The non-Jewish community is notorious for its failure to understand and appreciate the life patterns of the Jew. In view of this, what sensible reasoning can justify the Jews' continuing to observe such laws as those of Kashruth, which risk the widening of the breach between Jews and Christians? As hard as Jews have labored to establish a rapport with their Christian neighbors, there are still those who accuse the Jews of clannishness, of being overly loyal to the State of Israel, and of being unworthy of trust. And while it is true that the American Constitution guarantees freedom and equality to all, it is also true that laws are only what men interpret them to mean. The troubles that have befallen the Jew throughout history *can* happen here in America. Those who reject Kashruth as a threat, separating the Jew from the rest of the American community, undoubtedly feel that the tragedies that befell Jews in other lands can happen here and they will do nothing that might increase the possibility that it *will* happen here. To those who live with this fear of a hidden, underground anti-Semitism that needs only a good excuse to be revealed, Kashruth is an undesirable thing, a separatist element in Judaism which should be abandoned.

There are, of course, Jews who do not observe Kashruth (as well as other Jewish traditions) because they are untutored. They have never learned about it, so they do not comprehend its meaning or its importance for Jewish life. If, in the milieu in which we live, the wide publicity given Kosher foods through modern advertising has piqued an interest in the minds of the unlearned, that interest is usually transitory. Often the ignorant man who lacks knowledge of the spiritual meaning of Kashruth is confused when he is confronted by the pressure of this modern advertising. Especially is there confusion coupled with embarrassment if non-Jewish friends happen to inquire about Kashruth. The only escape from a display of ignorance is to relegate the whole business of Kashruth to ancient history. It is antiquated today, say the ignorant, because it was created originally in a time when sanitary conditions were poor and the knowledge of cleanliness was generally lacking. In those olden times, Kashruth served as a means of protecting the Jews, especially in the days when they were travelling through the desert. It helped them avoid the plagues and sicknesses which afflicted other nations that had no dietary laws. But today foods are sold to the public under the most rigorous codes of federal and state health inspections. Knowledge of sanitary procedures is widespread, and medicine has advanced so far that the old fears of disease no longer apply. Kashruth has outlived its value in these modern times. It no longer serves a real purpose in the life of the Jew.

In their ignorance of the wisdom of the Torah, the unlearned wonder what difference it could possibly make to God if a person eats Kosher or *trayfe*. Does God actually take account of such mundane things? It probably seems to them to be quite petty of God if, in fact, He does. But this charge against Kashruth is nothing new. The rabbis of the

Talmud wrestled with the same question more than a thousand years ago. But the laws of Kashruth were well-known to them, and they could not dismiss the recognition that God, in fact, had expressed His concern over what Jews eat; it is clearly stated in the books of the Bible. The answer which the rabbis gave, therefore, was that it does, in fact, make a difference to God what a man eats, how he lives, and how he works and prays. In all these activities of life the difference which concerns God is whether or not man brings a spirit of godliness into his life or not. The Book of Proverbs declares, "In all thy ways know Him." [13] Not merely when we pray should our thoughts be directed to God, but in *all* of life's activities there should be room for the divine spark in man to be operative. In this way the Kingdom of Heaven is brought down to earth to ennoble man's life and to create an atmosphere of peace and good will.

Finally, there are Jews who are involved in too many personal and communal activities to bother with what appears to them to be a trivial matter. Kashruth, they complain, tends to divert their energies and sidetrack them from their real purpose. They have no special objections to Kashruth as a matter of principle. It may be good for those who need or desire it. Others do not particularly need whatever religious values are involved in observing the Kashruth laws. They can, and do, get along fine without them; so why invite the extra bother and trouble which Kashruth observance entails? For very busy people, this attitude is pervasive of all of Judaism. Some Jewish customs must be observed because it is the thing to do in our society or because "it doesn't require that much" to comply with the tradition. But other precepts which require too much of a disturbance in the design of life that they have laid out for themselves are not included in their program of Jewishness.

The Values of Observance

We have considered thus far the reasons why Jews reject Kashruth. But what of those innumerable Jews who observe these laws with devotion and desire to pass them on to their children as a vital portion of their lives? What emotional and socially significant stirrings motivate them to adhere to the ways of Kashruth? And what good accrues to those who accept upon themselves the restrictions and discipline which Kashruth imposes? First, the observant Jew appreciates Kashruth in the same fashion that he enjoys the other traditions of the Jewish way of life. Keeping Kosher, like keeping the Jewish Sabbath or eating matzos, is a distinctly Jewish practice. Its obvious value is that it brings more Jewishness into life. The observant Jew, unlike his rejecting counterpart, does not fear the Kosher laws as a divisive force in his life, but appreciates them as a unifying power that brings him a greater purpose for living. He realizes that by observing Kashruth he is at one with his fellow Jews throughout the community, the nation, and the world who, like him, are *frum* (observant). Wherever he might travel in the world there is an immediate, deep communication between himself and other observant Jews. They all have a great deal in common because they live by the same Kashruth tradition. It is a sense of *K'lal Yisroel*— of Jewish peoplehood which is his because of his adherence to these Kosher laws. He belongs!

On the personal level, the Kashruth-observant Jew finds

that the laws of Kashruth are building blocks of emotional stability and strength. Every human life is lived in a number of emotional worlds at the same time. We play many varying roles each day that we live. We are men and women, and we are also businessmen, husbands, fathers, friends and taxpayers; we are wives, mothers, shoppers, etc. And we are also involved in being both American and Jewish at the same time. To live fully each strand of these parts of life gives us that greater sense of inner unity. An American Jew with a positive Jewish faith derives greater peace of mind as he blends the emotional lights that both cultures can reflect into his life. Kashruth-observing Jews see no conflict between what they want to accomplish in the secular world and what is demanded of them in their spiritual life. As with Jews who are Zionists, there is no problem of dual loyalties that insist upon a choice between devotion to America or to Israel. On the contrary, the recognition of the responsibility to support the historic homeland of the Jew strengthens his loyalty to America because both nations are of one democratic purpose. There arises a stronger conviction of loyalty to America simply because he does not deny his own spiritual heritage. To the Kashruth-observing Jew, the fact of his religiously ordained diet poses no special divisive ingredient between himself and the secular world. Insofar as its ritual requirements are concerned, it is something that he simply must do as a religious commitment and as a matter apart from his human relations with others. As a human being, it enhances his image as someone who is sincere and trustworthy because of his devotion to the principles of his faith.

In the Torah the first man to receive praise for his righteousness was Noah. He was given the cherished title of

Tsadik, a righteous man. Noah's age was an evil one, so much so that God saw the hopelessness of allowing that generation to continue. He flooded the earth to wipe it clean and permit a new, fresh start on it after the waters had subsided. It is significant that in calling Noah "righteous," the Torah added the adjective *Tamim,*[14] which means "whole," or "complete." Noah was a whole man, completely dedicated to righteousness, not living it some of the time and doing evil the rest of the time. As the first to be called *Tsadik,* Noah exemplified in his life that high standard to which all men should aspire, to achieve a sense of completeness in the pursuit of happiness in life. In this valuable sense, Kashruth is a cornerstone of Jewish faith upon which a Jew can construct a unity in his life. No one as yet has said it better than Shakespeare, whose immortal words are a challenge to every life: "This above all else, to thine own self be true." The Jew is truer to himself as a human being when he incorporates his religion into his life.

Every age has evidenced its emotional problems. The plague of our time appears to be a lack of meaning in life. Despite all our affluence in America, and all that has been achieved in the pursuit of material gain, we seem to have acquired little that is spiritually satisfying. We appear to have lost the anchor from out of modern life, and all is up in the air. But modern man is searching for a haven where he can settle down. Young Jews, like all moderns, have become familiar with the names of drugs and halucinatory stimulants as has no other generation before us in American history. It is said that these mind-releasing drugs help to unleash the hidden recesses of the conscious and subconscious and open up the mind for scrutiny and better understanding. The predicted results of such experimentation is that those who pass through it will have a more secure grasp upon the meaning of their own lives; they will know more clearly what their purpose ought to be. Thus far, the results of such experimentation have not provided the desired results. Less understanding, not more meaning, appears to have come into the lives of those who have gone on these psychic "trips." Greater, not less confusion has been the unfortunate "benefit" which these so-called "mind-expanding" drugs have given. Inevitably, in a time not too far distant, the pendulum of this searching for meaning in life will swing in another direction—hopefully in the direction of Judaism which for centuries has given the children of Israel emotionally healthy teachings to live by, and Jewish youth will find peace within the Jewish fold.

The recent hit musical, *Fiddler on the Roof*, provided many tunes that people all over the world sang, regardless of their ethnic or religious backgrounds. The lyrics of the song "Tradition" praise the worth of living by tradition. Tradition tells a person what to do in life, what his place in the world is. This is especially true of Jewish tradition because it is a dynamic tradition which directs the Jew at all times. At one time, because they followed their traditions (especially the tradition of Kashruth), Jews knew that they were Jews, and what was expected of them as Jews. Each day it reminded them of God and what He expected of them. It served as an anchor in their lives and provided a good measure of inspiration for them. They didn't have to smoke pot or inject weird liquids into their veins to discover the meaning of life. They simply imbibed the natural foods but added to them the meaningful obedi-

ence to the dietary code of Kashruth. The rabbis of an
earlier generation spoke of this same kind of search, but
they recommended another means of experimenting to find
out the mysteries of life. "Taste and see that the Lord is
good" [15] they said. If one is going to embark upon a search
for a meaning and purpose in life, channel that search, say
the rabbis, through the tradition of Kashruth that employs
food, not drugs, to help people find that God is good and
the universe He created can be good.

Secondly, Kashruth is a moral force. Its commandments
are a training program in discipline and self-control. In the
eyes of the sages of Israel, man's greatest conquests reside in
the victories of the spirit. "Who is a hero?" they ask. "He
who conquors his evil desires." [16] The prophet Zachariah
said it before the rabbis, "Not with an army and not with
brute strength, but with my spirit, saith the Lord." [17]

The world shall eventually come to learn that lasting
peace can only be won when the rulers of the nations will
have the wisdom to exemplify by their deeds the restraint
and mutual respect that builds rather than destroys men and
their territories. Through its code of voluntary discipline
Kashruth instills this very desirable trait in the human
heart. Its laws say, "This is permissible but that is forbidden. This meat you may have to enjoy freely but that meat
you must leave alone." Some foods are proper, others are
not. Thus, Kashruth begins from the very outset of life,
through the selectivity that goes on in a Kashruth-observing home, to teach restraint while at the same time encouraging the enjoyment of the permitted pleasures of life. It
trains through employing the socially neutral items such as
food, but its ultimate goal is the socially explosive "Thou

shalt not covet," which all men must learn to obey if the world is to endure.

With typical deep insight the rabbis asked, "Who is more worthy of praise, the man who says, 'I do not eat the *trayfe* food because I cannot tolerate it,' or the man who says, 'I would enjoy very much this or that forbidden food but what can I do since my Father In Heaven has forbidden it?' " And they respond that that man is worthy of praise who refrains from eating the forbidden foods because they are forbidden in the Torah. Thus, Kashruth is cast in the light of a matter of free choice and lauds the disciplined mind which resists temptation because of the right to choose freely. It is precisely because the choice is voluntary that it is most meaningful and settles deeply into the human personality structure.

The Talmud relates the tale of a rabbi who solved a mystery by applying the theory that we begin with little acts and move from them to the more important ones. It once happened that the rabbi was on a journey and stopped at an inn to rest for the night. During the supper meal an excitement arose among the guests. A robbery had occurred and a large sum of money was missing. The thief was clever enough not to leave any clues and the police were stymied. The morning following the robbery the rabbi was in the washroom refreshing himself. He noticed a man who had just washed his hands and, not seeing a towel to dry his hands with, proceeded to dry them on someone's coat, which was hanging on the wall. The rabbi hurried to the innkeeper and recommended that he call the police to interrogate the man who had performed this inconsiderate act. The police were called, and the suspect was questioned. In time he confessed to the crime. The innkeeper thanked the rabbi for his wise suggestion. In addition, he asked the rabbi if he was a prophet or the son of a prophet to know such things.

The rabbi responded, "I am not a prophet nor the son of a prophet. However, it stands to reason that a man who shows no regard for another man's coat has no qualms about stealing another man's possessions either." [18]

The rabbi's reasoning was sound. We begin to establish our system of values much the same as we learn to walk or to master any other activity of life. Our base is success in the small, insignificant challenges. Kashruth is for the Jew a training base that inculcates the discipline of self-control which distinguishes between the permitted and the forbidden. It begins with morsels of food, where people can succeed easily. It is because of this that in the Yiddish folk-expression of our people the words *Kosher V'yosher* (Kosher and honest) go together. The disciplined life is straightforward, proper and honest. Throughout the centuries Kashruth appeared as a very sure path to acquire these desirable social attributes.

It is very significant that in the Bible the destruction of the Jewish nation is connected with the eating of non-Kosher foods. The Torah warns us to avoid eating at the sacrifices to the idols of old. Through them, cautions the Torah, a fellowship is established between the Jewish family and the idolatrous hosts so that the children begin to intermarry, and Jews are tempted to drift away from their own heritage and follow after the pagan ways of the foreign gods. For this generation, intermarriage is on the increase between Jew and Gentile. While it is true that the freedom of a democratic society must inevitably bring with it a mingling of Jews and Gentiles, the question which disturbs the rabbis is whether it must also be true that such exposure must inevitably bring our youth to intermarriage? Jews are rightly concerned over the great increase in the number of intermarriages because in most instances of intermarriage the result is the loss of the Jewish party from the faith. The urgent need now is to revitalize the powerful identifying influence of Kashruth so as to affirm a strong, renewed pride in Judaism and to instill its compelling discipline so that Jew and non-Jew can continue to be friends without advancing to the further step of intermarriage, which neither Judaism nor Christianity favor.

The third major value which accrues to those who observe Kashruth is its power to create a sense of humaneness and compassion in the human heart. The rabbinic laws separating meat from milk are based upon the injunction, "Thou shalt not cook a kid in its own mother's milk." [19] This is not a prohibition to protect the slaughtered animal which no longer is sensitive to pain, but rather it is directed to men who are forbidden to be so callous as to cook the flesh of the young in the very milk of its own mother.

The Torah forbids the slaughter of a cow and its calf on the same day. It insists also that the mother bird be sent away from the nest before removing the eggs from it. Maimonides philosophises that motherhood does not differ between humans and animals in the intensity of its love for the young.[20] A mother cow suffers inwardly as much as the human mother when her young is taken away or hurt before her eyes. Acts of brutality, therefore, are not countenanced in the Torah, even though they are inflicted upon helpless animals that cannot express their inner feelings.

Man has been given the gift of speech and understanding

which affords him the opportunity of expressing himself about life as he meets it, according to the ethical values he has learned. The primary value which the Torah would like man to learn is a sensitivity to suffering. Man is urged to be compassionate, to be humane, to anticipate the sufferings of those creatures who are in his power and cannot tell him of their pain. It is to achieve this goal that the laws of shechita have been designed, They require of man that when he takes the life of another living creature, he do it in the most humane fashion.

This training in compassion which the Jew receives through these commandments has resulted in his voluntarily rejecting the brutal sport of hunting—killing a defenseless animal for the sheer joy of the kill. This Jewish abhorrence of violence is reflected in a Passover Haggadah printed in medieval times which portrays the Rasha (the Wicked Son) as a hunter, someone who is brutal and empty of any feelings of mercy towards the animal he stalks. The Jew who observes Kashruth knows that the only method by which animals may be killed for food is the method of *shechita*. He is also aware that Jews may kill another living creature for food or clothing but not for sport. Man was originally vegetarian according to the Torah, and only after the Flood in the time of Noah was man allowed to change his diet to include the flesh of an animal. In permitting man to eat animal flesh, however, the Torah set firm requisites of mercy, a matter with which the hunter is not usually concerned. From his earliest childhood, as he studies the Bible stories, the Jewish child inevitably learns that God desires mercy over stern justice.

He is taught the parable of the Medrosh which envisions God in the process of creating the world. The rabbis tell him through their poetic imagery that God first sat Himself in the seat of judgment symbolizing that He would direct the world along paths of stern justice. If man sinned he would be punished immediately. Then God saw that the world could not endure by such a plan, so He removed Himself from the seat of justice and established His reign over mankind from the seat of mercy. Thus, the Jewish appreciation of the universe and man in it, is that of a merciful design and kind understanding.

Finally, in the biblical Book of Deuteronomy the Torah forbids the eating of raw blood. "Thou shalt not eat the blood for the soul resides in the blood." It is not fitting for moral man to permit himself to be so hardened that he will consume the animal he has slaughtered, body and soul. Again, it is not the dead insensitive animal that is the Torah's concern but man himself. And the Torah is saying to him, "Train yourself in the ways of compassion, so that in the society of human beings you will live a compassionate life." It is through the ritual of Kashruth that the Torah seeks to teach men to live in peace and mutual respect, to personify in their lives the Torah's own image "Its ways are ways of pleasantness and all its paths are peace."

Humane Slaughter

> *"The commandment covering the killing of animals is necessary because the natural food of man consists of vegetables and of the flesh of animals; the best meat is that of animals permitted to be used as food. No doctor has any doubt about this. Since, therefore, the desire of procuring food necessitates the slaying of animals, the Law (Torah) enjoins that the death of the animal should be the easiest."* [1]

2   The rabbis of the Talmud described the Jews as being the compassionate grandchildren of merciful forebears. In the Jewish style of life this sensitivity is expressed with deep perception in the laws which govern the ritual slaughtering of beasts for food. The Torah and the Talmud repeated in a variety of laws Judaism's deep concern over the needless suffering of animal life. Commandments both positive and negative were ordained in order to alert humanity to its responsibility to watch and protect lesser creatures. Having been granted the blessing of a superior intellect, man was cautioned against abusing those creatures who could not match wits with him, and was commanded to be compassionate to them.

One of the first commandments of the Torah, a precept given to Noah, that early believer in monotheism, outlaws the primitive barbaric practice of eating a piece of flesh that has been cut from the body of a living beast. This commandment remains, even today, included in the proverbial Seven Commandments which non-Jews are expected to adhere to. When in later generations the Jewish Code of Laws was formulated, compassion for all living beings was capsuled in the phrase, *Tzaar Baley Chaim* (Beware of causing pain to living creatures). Merely proclaiming it as a law, however, did not automatically assure its universal acceptance. It was a law which remained on the books for centuries because illiterate, insensitive men did not comprehend its tender implications. On the contrary, man looked upon God's dumb creatures as having been created to receive the brunt of human frustrations, to bear the burdens of his labors and to be slaughtered for his food.

The Talmud relates that, "Once Rabbi Judah, the Prince, sat and taught Torah before an assembly of Babylonian Jews at Sepphoris, and a calf being led to the slaughter passed before him. It sought to hide itself in his cloak and began to cry as if to say, 'Save me!' Rabbi Judah, however, responded in a cold, objective fashion: 'What can I do since it is for that purpose that you were created?' "

The Talmud records the act of divine justice which resulted from Rabbi Judah's callous attitude by telling us that because Rabbi Judah was not compassionate, he was punished by a decree from heaven that suffering should come upon him until he should learn to be compassionate. And it is also related that "One day a weasel ran before his daughter and she wanted to kill it! He said to her, 'Let it be, for it is written, *His mercies are over all his works.* So it was decreed in heaven that 'because he had pity, pity shall be shown to him,' and his sufferings ceased." [2]

The majority of humans did not know the story of Rabbi Judah, his sufferings and ultimate healing, and went on abusing and beating their animals without the slightest thought of compassion or of doing wrong. This centuries-old problem of human lack of sensitivity toward animal pain and suffering has come down to modern times and is portrayed in the symbol of the American Society for the Prevention of Cruelty to Animals (ASPCA), which shows a man beating his horse. Were it not a readily understood scene, typifying the common practice of brutality to animals, it would not have become the symbol representing the work of this compassionate organization, which labors for enlightened, humane treatment of animals.

Judaism, with its respect for all created life, stood apart from these accepted attitudes of other men. From earliest times Jewish teaching surrounded the practices of slaughtering with strong controls which safeguarded the beast from needless suffering and established a psychology for the ultimate universal acceptance of humane slaughter practices. The code of *shechita*, the Jewish method of ritual slaughter, from beginning to end educates the *shochet* to the sanctity of his task. Life is God's gift to each living creature, even to animals; and the taking of it must be done with God's laws in mind. Compassionate, humane slaughter is the only acceptable method among Jews.

The person who becomes a *shochet* cannot be someone from the dregs of society who slaughters simply because he can wield a poleaxe, or thrust a sword coldbloodedly into the heart of a steer, or shoot it in the head. He cannot be someone who *must* do the work of a slaughterer because he can't find any other means of employment. A *shochet* is a scholar whose training is designed to make him sensitive and humble. He is a religious person whose commitment is to a life of sanctity. His is a profession, a high calling. He performs a holy task and offers a prayer before he begins his work, to alert himself to the presence of the divine spirit whose messenger he now is. Nachmonides wrote: "The reason for ritual slaughter is that the Torah forbids the infliction of useless pain on any living being. That is why before slaughtering the animal, the benediction is recited." [3]

In the community the *shochet* is respected for his service to people, providing them with Kosher meats as ordained in the Torah. His training is most exacting, so that when he is finally presented the *t'udah* (his diploma), he will represent in the market place and the community at large the highest standards of the Jewish ethic of compassion and humaneness. This is the spiritual image of the man who stands ready to slaughter an animal with God as his judge.

What are the wisdom-books used in the education of a *shochet* when he is trained for his profession? Like other Jewish clergy—rabbis and cantors—the *shochet* studies the *Shulchan Aruch* (Jewish Code of Law) in depth. From the specialized Talmudic Tractate of Hulin, he learns the anatomy of the cow and the chicken. He can distinguish between the healthy and the sick, as a doctor diagnoses the health and illnesses that beset human creatures. Although the area he will be most directly concerned with as a *shochet* is the neck, the windpipe, and the esophogus, he learns also about the damages to the brain and the body, as well as the infections that can enflame the internal organs.

Once he has mastered the required knowledge of the anatomical structure of cattle and poultry, he moves to study the preparation of the slaughtering knife, under the tutelege of an experienced *shochet*. He is shown how to prepare a blade properly, to understand the relationship of the knife to the honing stone, and how to bring out the correct sharpness. Too sharp a blade is unacceptable because it is so fine that it won't last out the day, and must therefore inevitably kill in a less than acceptable humane manner. Too dull a knife is equally unacceptable because it will not allow for a swift cut, and thus prolongs the process and inflicts needless pain and suffering. Judiasm categorically rejects any orgy of brutality. Jews do not countenance beheading an animal, or hacking away at it until it falls dead. The death must be swift and uninterrupted. The blade, therefore, must be sharp and smooth, without knicks, so that it will not catch the skin, and it must be the proper length so that the *shochet's* hand can move freely.[4]

In this phase of his training the novice *shochet* learns also how to relieve hand fatigue when the volume of those to be slaughtered exceeds the usual number. He becomes aware of the expectation that he will retire from his practice when, because of old age, his hand shakes with infirmity and interferes with his calling to slaughter in the quickest, most humane fashion.

The actual presence of the student *shochet* in the abattoir comes after he has mastered the theory and laws of *shechita*. It is here, on the very scene of slaughter, that he begins to understand his own inner makeup; he is either meant to be a *shochet* or he isn't. The words he has studied for months now take on reality before his eyes as he watches and then participates in the actual slaughtering process. The ideal of *shechita's* humaneness is revealed before him as he sees for himself that the animal loses consciousness just seconds after the ritual slaughter has taken place.

There are also contradictions to humaneness which the *shochet* observes, undoubtedly much to his regret. For while the act of *shechita* itself is humane, the method of restraining the animal prior to the slaughter (as has been practiced in the past and even today) is generally recognized as far from perfect. The *shochet* is the first to admit this. The method (known as "shackling and hoisting") currently employed in most abattoirs consists of shackling the back feet of the animal with chains, and then hoisting it off the floor so that its head hangs down awaiting the *shochet's* knife. It is presumed (with some justification) that hanging an animal of eight to fifteen hundred pounds from the ceiling by its hind legs is a painful, frightening experience for the animal.

This method of hoisting the animal off the floor of the slaughter house prior to slaughtering replaces a previous practice of casting the animal down on the floor, where it was held securely for the *shochet*. Government meat inspectors, however, were concerned that a slaughtered animal should not come into contact with the blood of a previously slaughtered animal, in order to avoid the danger of contamination. They therefore recommended that animals be hoisted off the floor of the slaughter house to avoid the spreading of disease.

In all fairness it must be said that shackling and hoisting, questionable though it is from the point of humaneness, is nevertheless an advancement in procedure. The non-Kosher slaughterer didn't have to concern himself with any *Halachic* infraction if the animal was not slaughtered ac-

cording to a stringent humane code. He could kill the
animal with an axe or a hammer. If it was clumsily wielded
it crushed the skull or smashed the face or mutilated the
head of the cow or steer until it finally dropped dead. A
chicken was not as troublesome. It was easiest to chop off
its head, or in smaller markets, to wring its neck, and stretch
it until it broke off, and then sever it from the body.

Even for Kosher slaughtering, shackling and hoisting is a
major correction over previously employed methods of
positioning the animal for slaughter. One *shochet*, whose
soul could not be at peace until he rid his abattoir of its
"practical brutalities," described his shock at the inhumane-
ness he witnessed. He reported that the heavy animals,
such as steers, cows, and bulls, were driven into a pen by a
cattle driver. Often if the animals did not walk fast enough,
they were then prodded along with the help of a heavy
whip or a shocking rod. This was standard equipment. A
shocking rod is an ingenious device which is used to
frighten the animal into obedience. It is a metallic round,
hollow rod containing electric batteries and a switch.
When a cattle driver has difficulties with a steer, he pushes
the rod against its hind part, including the rectum if necessary, and opens the switch, thus giving the steer a painful
electric shock. The steer was then made to face the wall.
Since normally an animal wouldn't stand still in this position, another very painful device was used to make him
obey. A long heavy stick was forced into its rectum by one
of the employees and pressed upward. This immobilized
the animal to the spot. His entire spine arched and his body
quivered with pain.

In recent years, however, times and attitudes have been
changing. As enlightened people became aware of the in-

humanities perpetrated against these defenseless beasts, the calls for humane laws to protect them become loud and clear. In September 1893, Switzerland became the first government to introduce humane slaughter legislation. It passed a law requiring that the animal be stunned and made insensible to pain before being slaughtered. The stunning device used was a hammer with which the animal was hit over the head. Later on, a bolt pistol was employed, which had the same effect of stunning the animal, but refined the procedure somewhat.

The Swiss move to insure humane slaughter was first introduced in the Canton of Aragon, in Switzerland. The Jewish Community accepted the humane intent of the proposed legislation, but not the procedure of stunning the animal. In most instances the inaccuracy of the stunning procedure broke the skull of the animal and pierced the membrane protecting the brain. This damage to the brain was sufficient to make the animal *trayfe,* as would any fatal accident. In addition, the legislation was suspected by the Swiss Jewish community as having sinister meanings because it was presented at a time when anti-Semitism was ascending in Switzerland. Further irritation to the traditional Kashruth-observing Swiss Jews occurred when two reform rabbis of the German *Haskallah,* which rejected Kashruth as a matter of principle, issued the unfortunate distortion that *shechita* was not a religious percept.[6] The Christian anti-*shechita* group in Switzerland seized upon this statement and urged that because *shechita* was not a religious rite, it should not enjoy the protection of federal laws. They won their battle.

Victory in the Canton of Aragon encouraged other anti-Semites so that they decided upon prohibiting *shechita*

throughout the entire Swiss republic. The matter was made
the subject of a National plebiscite.

To do this, they required 50,000 signatures. A campaign
to achieve this goal was organized which ultimately produced the far greater number of 82,000 signatures. On the
basis of this, the National Council arranged for a national
plebiscite to be held August 20, 1893. Jewish and liberal
gentile leaders worked hard to defeat the bill. The Catholic
Church stood solidly with the Jews in their attempt to
defeat the onerous bill. Catholic priests declared openly
from their pulpits that the intent of this law was anti-reli-
gious, a blatant attack upon the Jews. Yet, inspite of all this
strong sentiment, a law was put into effect prohibiting the
practice of Jewish ritual slaughter in Switzerland.

Other countries were soon to follow the Swiss pattern.
In most instances the tragic coupling of anti-*shechita* with
anti-Semitism was the condition under which the legislation
outlawing *shechita* was passed into law. For example, in
Germany the rise of Nazism brought an end to *shechita*. It
began by prohibiting it in Bavaria on January 29, 1930.
Prohibition spread throughout the entire Reich, so that by
April 21, 1933, the law prohibiting *shechita* throughout all
of Germany was passed, effective by May 1 of that same
year. It is ironic that under so inhuman a regime as that of
the Nazis, whose gas chambers and crematoria ruthlessly
destroyed millions of human lives, the law of prohibiting
shechita should be based upon the desire to avoid cruelty to
animals.

In Italy, until October 1938, Kosher slaughtering was
permitted. On October 19th *The New York Times* carried
a report from Turin, Italy, which read: "The Newspaper
Gazetta del Paplo today announced that Kosher killing of

animals for Jewish consumption had been prohibited in Italy." It said an order to that effect had been communicated by the government to local prefects in a "circular telegram." The order meant that henceforth all animals must be killed in accordance with the law of 1928, which provides that killing must be as speedy as possible, either by shooting or stunning with a blow. Hithertofore, exception has been conceded to Jews that they might eat meat according to their religious ritual.

The *Gazetta del Paplo*, without mentioning the government's anti-Jewish campaign, said the municipal officials and the Turin Society for the Protection of Animals had called the barbarous practice to the attention of the government.

"After tomorrow Jews who do not wish to become vegetarians must place themselves on the same level as all Italians as far as animal food is concerned." [7]

On October 21 *The New York Times* reported from Rome, Italy: "Official orders were issued by telegraph today to all prefects to see that no slaughterhouse in Italy tolerates Kosher slaughter of animals. Slaughtering of animals is regulated by law, which requires the most expeditious and painless method. Hitherto it has always been taken for granted that Kosher slaughtering did not conflict with the law. Now it has suddenly been discovered that such rites are, in the words of the *Gionaicle d' Italia*, a spectacle unworthy of a civilized race and such as to cause the most profound disgust. Therefore, the order has gone out that it is to be discontinued forthwith."

In Russia, *shechita* was outlawed in November 1917 following the Bolshevik Revolution, which continued the tradition of Russian anti-Semitism and added to it the intensity of its unilateral rejection of all religions. *Shechita* was permitted again, however, in 1922, under the new Economic Program, but suppressed again in 1927.

In Norway, in June 1929, a law was effected which required stunning before *shechita*, but which, as in the Swiss instance, rendered the animal *trayfe* because of damage to the brain, and thus in effect outlawed *shechita*. *Shechita* was outlawed in Hungary in 1938.

The country in which the outlawing of *shechita* was calculated to cause the greatest harm to the Jewish community was Poland. The Polish movement to abolish *shechita* arose at a time when anti-Semitism in the country was also on the upswing. It was calculated to attack the Jewish community on at least two fronts: first, to deny the three million Polish Jews the availability of the Kosher slaughtered meat, and secondly to deny the Jewish community the needed funds for its official offices, this money coming as it did from the special *shechita* taxes.

The anti-Semites complained that the practices of *shechita* gave the Jews many jobs in the meat industry which rightfully belonged to the Christians. It was argued that a considerable portion of the meats slaughtered by the *shochetim* was sold to Christians; therefore, Christians were justified in demanding a share of the meat-producing industry. The truth of the matter was that the charge was not isolated to the meat industry alone, but was part of a universal campaign in Poland designed to drive the Jews out of the professions and businesses.

As a result of the propaganda and its effects upon the emotions of the populace, a bill was introduced into the *Sejim* (Polish senate) on February 7, 1933, with the intent that *shechita* be abolished for humane reasons.

This original bill was not passed, and an amended bill was introduced in its place, which required that all animals except those set aside for Kosher slaughter be stunned before being killed. The apparent irony of the new bill was that the requirement of stunning did not apply to animals that were to be slaughtered for export. Apparently cattle going out of Poland did not require humane stunning before being killed. The law became effective in January, 1937. One month later the real intent of the law became apparent. Originally it was presumed that 60 per cent of the cattle slaughtered would be set aside for Kosher slaughter. However, by the end of the year only 23 per cent of all cattle slaughtered was allocated to Kosher slaughter. By 1938, one year after the passage of the law, only 20 per cent was set aside for Kosher slaughter.

The desired result, to increase the employment of Christians in the meat industry, did not materialize, however. In addition, the Polish economy felt the sting of this injustice because the sales of meat dropped off considerably. Polish leaders in the *Sejim* called upon the delegates, beseeching them to be patient. The law, which was in effect for a short time only, would eventually provide the Christian community with the desired positive results.

Matters did not improve, however, and out of desperation a bill was eventually introduced to outlaw *shechita* altogether.

The response of the Jewish community was to boycott the purchase of all meats. A period of sixteen days, from March 14–30, 1938, was to be meatless. Fish menus were publicized in the Polish newspapers by the Jewish community councils. The edict was widely publicized stating categorically that any Jew abrogating the edict would be excommunicated. Support for the Rabbinate in this cause was voiced by Jews throughout the land. Even the socialist Jews complied with the rabbinic pronouncement.

The economic effect of the Jewish boycott of meats hit hard upon the Poles. Yet, in spite of this, and against the protests of the Jewish and non-Jewish communities, the new law was passed to become effective in 1942. However, by September 1938, Poland fell into the hands of the Nazis, and the anti-*shechita* law never came into being. The Jewish cause, however, was not helped in the slightest by this; one evil was merely replaced by another. The Nazi Governor-General of Poland, Hans Frank, decreed on October 26, 1939, "In any territory under German rule, cruelty to animals of any kind is not permissible; effective immediately, Jewish ritual slaughter for Kosher meat consumption is therefore forbidden." [8]

These Jewish experiences in European countries established a fear psychology which mitigated against any acceptance of humane slaughter legislation in other lands. In America especially has this keen sensitivity against any legislation of the Kosher slaughter process been strongly felt. Because of anti-Jewish experiences with European *shechita laws*, the American rabbinic and lay leadership have fought vigorously to defeat any and all legislation which would tamper with *shechita* in any way.

Humane-slaughter legislation first appeared in the United States in 1958 in a federal bill which outlawed the shackling-and-hoisting preparations of conscious animals. The intent of this legislation was to reduce the potential of suffering for the animal. The animal was to be stunned by a hammer or bolt pistol prior to being hoisted. Senators Jacob Javits and Clifford P. Case introduced an amendment to this bill which limited its power to non-Kosher killing. Kosher-slaughtered animals were to be shackled and hoisted as before.

Other legislation introduced into state legislatures has followed this pattern of exempting Kosher slaughtering from any limitations or controls. In 1967, for example, bills were introduced in the New York State Legislature which aroused strong emotion and debate in the Jewish communities throughout the state. One such bill, sponsored by The Friends of Animals, Inc., and introduced in both houses of the New York State Legislature as Senate #2912 Adams, Senate #2333 Hudson-Adams; introduced by Assemblyman Mason and sponsored by Messrs Emery and Lins (print 2563-intro. 2547), required that non-Kosher slaughter be performed on animals that were rendered insensible to pain because this is humane. The wording of the bill, while conceding to schechita the privilege of continuing its method without change, implied that *shechita* is not humane slaughter because it does not permit stunning the animal prior to slaughter.

The Mason bill added further consternation by requiring the meat packer to label meats either "Kosher" or "humane," creating an obvious division between the Kosher and non-Kosher slaughtered animals which was uncomplimentary to Jews. The confusion in the public mind, as well as the embarrassment to the Jewish community which such a bill would create, was therefore, vigorously opposed by major Jewish organizations. They fought strongly against the bill about to come before the Constitutional Assembly, which was to convene that year, and the bill was defeated at the polls.

A bill favored by the New York State Humane Associa-

tion, and introduced into the state Senate by Senator Ron-
ald B. Stafford of Peru, New York, received the backing of
Jewish leadership because it did not single out *shechita* in
any derogatory manner, while at the same time it called for
more humane methods of preparation for slaughter in the
abattoirs in the state.

In America the campaign for humane slaughter legislation has been waged most vigorously by a group calling
itself Friends of Animals, whose director is Mrs. Alice
Herrington Schmidt. This group is located in New York
City and is one of many humane societies in the state of
New York. While presenting itself as dedicated to rescuing
animals from needless suffering prior to and or during
slaughter, the Friends of Animals have alienated the Jewish
community and most other humane groups by *its* militant
propaganda campaign, which has embarrassed the Jewish
community, and by its stubborn insistence that its program
alone can resolve the problem of humane treatment of
animals in the slaughter houses.

A full-page advertisement placed in *The New York
Times* in March, 1967, and repeated since then, declared in
bold type, "The Meat You Eat Is Seared With Pain"—explaining beneath this headline that cruelty to animals occurs
in both Kosher and non-Kosher slaughterhouses. This was
part of the propaganda campaign mounted by F.O.A. to
obtain community support for a bill, sponsored by Assemblyman Albert J. Hausbeck, which would outlaw shackling
and hoisting of animals prior to slaughter. As the time of
public voting on the submission of this bill to the New
York State legislature drew nearer, the intensity of the
propaganda campaign increased. Pictures depicting inhumane positioning of animals for slaughter appeared in the

press with accompanying testimony that procedures followed in Kosher slaughterhouses were brutal and inhumane. The following also appeared in a full page advertisement in *The New York Times:*

"In a Kosher plant I recently visited, the hoist was operated until the steer was hanging suspended by the leg with its face partly on the floor. The slaughterhouse worker then turned the hose on the animal's face and neck so that the animal got the full force of the water, and then I witnessed something I had read about as occurring in Kosher plants, that I could scarcely believe when I read it. The packing-house employee deliberately plunged both his hands into the steer's eyes until the eyes were displaced by being pushed back into the head. He then grasped the sides of the eye sockets and held the animal that way while the *shochet*, the man who performs the Kosher slaughter, stepped forward to cut the steer's throat." [9]

The response of the Jewish communities' leadership to this horrible charge of inhumanity was contained in statements issued by reknowned Rabbinic scholars. Rabbi Moshe Feinstein, Dean of Yeshiva and Mesivta Tiffereth Jerusalem in New York City and a member of the presidium of the Union of Orthodox Rabbis of the United States and Canada published the following reply:

"I and another prominent dean of a world reknowned Yeshiva spent a full day visiting the slaughterhouses in New York and New Jersey and we found that all claims of inhumane treatment levied against the slaughterhouses which are performing our sacred ritual slaughter are fabrications and utterly false."

The further charge was made in the press by Friends of Animals that shackling and hoisting of animals results in inevitable injury to the animal because of its fright, shown in the kicking and jerking of its body. To his allegation, Rabbi Pinchas M. Teitz, chairman, Committee for the Protection of Religious Freedom and Presidium Member Union of Orthodox Rabbis of the United States and Canada replied:

"I was shocked to read your advertisement in the New York Times . . . which is an unwarranted attack on Kosher slaughter, based on glaring inaccuracies and misleading statements bordering on religious bias . . . To cite some of the more obvious instances:

"It is absolutely false that injuries which render animals non-Kosher are an inevitable result of shackling and hoisting. In thirty years as a rabbi in America, visiting slaughterhouses several times a week, I have yet to see or hear of a single instance of an animal declared non-Kosher as a result of injuries sustained through shackling and hoisting . . .

"In general, the content and tone of the advertisements are so divorced from reality that they raise serious doubts that its writers have any firsthand knowledge of slaughterhouse procedures. Indeed, I have checked with every Kosher slaughterhouse in this (New York-New Jersey) area, and not one has any record or memory of having been visited by you or any member of your committee. I challenge you and all forty individuals who consented to lend their names to your advertisement to indicate the date and place of a visit to a slaughterhouse where the practices you describe occurred. . . ." [10]

There are those who stand apart from the battle over the presumed inhumanity in slaughtering, the charges and the counter-charges. They represent concerned people who have taken practical steps to bring about a new method of positioning the animal for slaughter—a method which is painless. Such a device now exists in the A.S.P.C.A. pen, which was invented after extensive research into the problem by the world-famous Armour Research Foundation. This research institution was employed originally by the Joint Advisory Committee, representing major Jewish organizations, to investigate the usefulness of the pen. Eventually the A.S.P.C.A. stepped into the picture, and at a cost of approximately $200,000, a large-animal restraining pen was invented and accepted by rabbinic authorities as complying fully with Jewish tradition. This pen replaces shackling and hoisting with a painless method of holding the animal, thus opening the way for complete compliance with the legislation, while at the same time meeting the public desire for a humane slaughter procedure.

The cost of the pen to the slaughterhouse is approximately $12,000, depending upon the structure of the plant. However, numerous benefits accrue to the slaughterhouse which ultimately overcome the initial cost. For example, the A.S.P.C.A. holding-pen immediately replaces one salaried employee who would normally be required to hold the animal during the shackling and hoisting method of preparation. Morale factors of employees are improved as well, because workers on the killing floor no longer have to fear the hazards of animals falling from their hanging position, and similar possible hazards from the animals which move along on a conveyor system.

In spite of the benefits of the A.S.P.C.A. holding-pen, only nine slaughterhouses had adopted its use by February, 1967. Most slaughterhouses have blatantly refused or found it too costly to change their previous patterns of slaughter preparation.[11]

With the development of the A.S.P.C.A. pen, the exemptions of *shechita* from humane slaughter legislation are no longer necessary. The Joint Advisory Council, therefore, has moved away from its former position of insisting upon exemption of *shechita* in all humane slaughter proposed legislation.

The pressure for humane slaughter legislation in Albany, however, continues. Every session of the legislature experiences a rash of bills proposing to alleviate the problems of conscience created by shackling and hoisting. None has survived the opposition from the Jewish community leaders. There is danger, nevertheless, that at some future session of the New York State Legislature a law will get through which will limit not only the practice of shackling-and-hoisting, but *shechita* itself as well.

If all interested rabbis representing the three wings of Judaism were to turn their energies to resolving the problems confronting acceptance of A.S.P.C.A. holding-pen, their united voice would result in a wider use of the humane device, and the turmoil over humane slaughter legislation would be a thing of the past. The threat to *shechita* would be gone forever.

A Short History of
Kashruth Organizations

3   The story of community involvement to control
the sale of Kosher meats dates back to the early period of
American history. In 1660, for example, Asser Levy, a
Jewish refugee from Portugal, came to these shores with
twenty-two other Jews seeking religious freedom. Shortly
afterward, he applied to the town council of New Amsterdam for a butcher's license to sell both Kosher and other
meats.[1]

In those pre-industrial days, control of the Kosher meat
business was a relatively simple matter because the *shochet*
was employed by the congregation and was subject to the
control of the rabbi and officers of the congregation. Infractions against the Torah's Kashruth laws were only occasional, and when violations did occur, they were dealt
with promptly. For example, on December 23, 1771, the
shochet Moses Lazarus was petitioned to appear before the
congregation's Committee on Kashruth to answer the
charge that he had been apprehended selling Kosher and
trayfe tongues in his Kosher meat shop. At his hearing
before the president and officers of the congregation, Lazarus was able to exonerate himself. He was warned, how-

ever, that his license would be revoked if ever a complaint
was lodged against him again.[2]

A second case involved a *shochet* named Hart Jacobs,
who had sold some Kosher meat to The Widow Hetty
Hayes, who filed a complaint against him for selling meat
that was questionable. In her charge against the *shochet*,
filed on October 17, 1774, Widow Hayes stated that she
had bought a forequarter from the *shochet*, and that a guest
in her home, a former *shochet* from Holland, had told her
that the neck of the animal did not show the usual signs of
Kosher *shechita*. The president of the congregation called
his officers together to sit in judgment on the issue. Sitting
with them at this special trial was one Rabby Samuel Bar
Isaac Keyser, a rabbinic scholar from London, who was an
authority on Kosher slaughtering. Rabby Keyser disputed
the charge against the *shochet* and proved to the satisfaction of the committee that the charge was baseless. Hart
Jacobs was acquitted. However, he was ordered to appear
at the residence of Rabby Keyser to be examined by him in
order to establish his expertise in matters of *shechita*. The
shochet, being a proud man, refused at first to submit to the
quizzing, but some weeks later agreed to take the test.
Ironically, and with much *chutzpa*, after successfully passing the exam, the *shochet* demanded that the congregation
pay him the wages he had lost while he remained out of
work because of his refusal to submit to the examination.[3]

Problems of another sort also confronted Kashruth during the colonial period because in many communities Kosher meats were sold to Jews from Christian-owned
butcher shops. In such situations, the *shochet* would perform the *shechita* in accordance with Jewish ritual requirements, and then place a metal tag on the meat so that the

Kosher meat could be easily distinguished from the non-Kosher meat. However, occasionally, an unscrupulous butcher would attempt to place counterfeit seals of Kashruth on *trayfe* meats. Two such cases were recorded, and they reflect the civil authority's concern that such fraudulent practices be punished. For example, on August 3, 1796, a complaint was lodged against the butcher Nicholas Smart who had fraudulently affixed Kosher seals to non-Kosher meats. He was ordered to appear before the municipal board to answer the charge against him. On August 15, 1796, the license of Nicholas Smart was revoked for a period of time as punishment for his dishonest act.[4] A second case involved a butcher, Caleb Vandenberg, who had also attempted to counterfeit the Kosher seals. Vandenberg responded to the charge against him by claiming that he had done so only as a jest. However, witnesses testified that he had actually offered the falsely labelled meats for sale to Jews. The congregations requested that Vandenberg's license be revoked. The municipal board honored the congretation's request and denied the butcher the privilege of the further sale of meat.[5]

The year 1813 was a fateful year because a serious and weakening change in this strict control of the sale of Kosher meats began to develop. The first step to break the pattern was taken by a *shochet* named Jacob Abrahams, who had been employed by congregation Shearith Israel of New York. Abrahams was employed on a yearly basis, and when time for renewing the *shochet's* contract came up, the officers took account of the many complaints against him and refused to rehire him. Abrahams, however, did not accept this verdict of the congregation's officers as being an end to his career. He took the radical step of establishing himself as an independent *shochet* and performed *shechita* for those who rallied around him. The congregation turned to the Common Council of New York, requesting that the Council give it exclusive authority to designate those butchers who should be allowed to sell Kosher meats. It requested also that only the *shochet* employed by the congregation should have the right to place the Kosher seals upon the meat that was to be sold to Jews. When the Council acceded to their demand, the trustees hoped that this action would put an end to Abrahams' rebelliousness. However, they did not fully reckon with his tenacity. Abrahams gathered his supporters around him and placed a counter petition before the Common Council, requesting that they reverse their original order because it encroached upon his religious rights and restricted those privileges to which he was entitled. The Council respected Abrahams' complaint against their action, and reinstated his right to be an independent *shochet* by reversing its original decision. This new ruling in effect denied the congregation exclusive rights in the sale of Kosher meats. The congregation requested that the matter be referred to a special committee, which would hear all the complaints against Abrahams and then judge the matter, but this request was denied.[6]

The position of the independent *shochet* was now established, and the tradition of congregational control of *shechita* began to decline. Secularized competition in its broadest expressions soon became part of what was formerly a wholly religious profession. For example, soon after the defeat which Shearith Israel suffered with Abrahams, another problem arose to confront the congregational leaders. A new *shochet* arrived in the community as an employee of the newly-formed congregation B'nai Jeshurun. The Congregants of B'nia Jeshurun pledged themselves to eat only from the *shechita* of their own *shochet*.[7]

From the year 1850 onward, the position of the synagogue *shochet* declined in importance, and that of the independent *shochet* gathered strength. As a result questions about Kashruth, which had never arisen before, began to plague the Jewish Community. For example, the independent *shochet* was now employed by a Christian butcher, who had complete control over him. The rabbi of the community in which the *shochet* practiced could not demand that the *shochet* show him his certificate authorizing him to be a *shochet*, nor could the rabbi require the *shochet* to appear before him for an examination of his qualifications. As a result of this anarchical situation, many complaints were soon heard about the reliability of the Kashruth of the Kosher meats offered for sale in the Christian butcher shops. It was often noted that no clear distinction was evident to the Jewish customer between Kosher and non-Kosher meats. The metal seals, which once gave silent but definite testimony that a piece of meat was Kosher, became a nebulous symbol of Kashruth because it was suspected that the Christian butcher was affixing them to the meat himself in a careless manner. Did the *shochet* apply it, or did the Christian butcher take it upon himself to apply the Kosher seal to the meat? In other instances no seal at all was used, and only the Christian butcher-boy who stood beside the meat stalls told the purchaser which meats were Kosher and which were *trayfe*.

In desperation over this scandalous situation, a group of synagogues in New York City gathered on April 24, 1863, established the Association of United Hebrew Congregations,[8] and appointed a special committee known as the

Shechita Board to deal with the Kashruth problems. The members of the *Shechita* Board were given the challenge of establishing standards for the testing of all *shochetim* who were practicing in the New York area, to pass upon and license all butchers who were going to handle Kosher meats in one way or another, and to develop a uniform lead seal that could be placed upon all meats to signify their Kashruth. The committee worked hard to achieve its goals. However, at the end of the first year's labors the committee reported that unfortunately, the majority of Jews were still buying their meats at unsupervised shops and were not inquiring as to whether the seal of the Association was attached or not.

By 1867 it was evident that the *Shechita* Board was not a practical solution to the problems of fraud confronting the Kosher meat business because, in addition to the previous complaints about those who patronized unsupervised butcher shops, it was found that Jews had purchased meats from those *shochetim* who did not pass the *Shechita* Board's examination. By 1870 the synagogue *shochet* was a thing of the past; most, if not all of them, were replaced by the independent *shochet*. Gone was the dignity, gone was the old respect for the scholarly *shochet;* gone was the security of his position, which once gave him the power to demand and receive recognition. Now the *shochet* was under the control of the butcher or the abbatoir owner who was his boss. He worked long hours for little pay under demoralizing conditions. In the bitter cold of winter, the *shochet* had to stand in unprotected places to perform his sacred tasks, warming his hands over a makeshift heater so that he could feel sufficient warmth in them to wield his knife. Finally in 1886, the *shochetim* made treir first move to better their lot by organizing into an association called *Zibhe Tamim*. (Righteous Slaughterers) The association did not accomplish much because it was short lived.[9]

From the year 1888 onward another serious problem arose to confront the *shochetim*. Slaughterers from Eastern Europe began to arrive in America. These new men worked for less money. As immigrants to a strange land, they had to content themselves with even fewer considerations than the already impoverished lot of the established *shochetim*. To complicate things even further for the immigrant *shochet*, the barriers created by the language difficulties between them and their employers often resulted in misunderstandings and arguments. The new *shochet* spoke Yiddish or Polish, while his employer was either an American gentile who spoke only English, or else he was a German-speaking Jew who usually had little regard for the "peasant languages." By 1892 the conditions under which the *shochetim* had to work became so unbearable that a revolt was attempted again, in a renewed effort to organize a union. Encouraged by leading rabbis, such as Rabbi Jacob Joseph and Dr. Philip Klein, the *shochetim* organized themselves into a group which they called *Melekhet Hakodesh* (Holy Work), and went out on strike demanding an improvement of their status.[10]

One of the policies of the *Melekhet Hakodesh* was that newly-arrived shochetim should not obtain employment in the New York City area. The officers of the organization would pressure the immigrant *shochetim* to seek employment outside the city and its environs. They assisted them in whatever manner possible to obtain a post elsewhere. One such instance was recorded concerning the *shochet* Feibish

Zevi Gross, who had signed an agreement that he would
not *shecht* in the New York City area either for himself or
for others. Later, however, Gross complained, and proved
before Rabbi Moses Weinberger that he had been coerced
into signing such a document. Rabbi Weinberger declared
the agreement to be void. Fate was with the shochetim,
however, because by the year 1900 all of the small slaughterhouses were taken over by the large meat-packing plants,
and the lot of the *shochet* improved considerably. As a result, the *Melekhet Hakodesh* dropped its militant attitude
and became primarily a social organization.

The *shochetim's* problems, however, were only half-
solved, for only the cattle-*shochet* was effected by the
take-over. The chicken-*shochet* was a separate matter. His
difficulties remained unchanged. Thus, in 1913 the first
attempt to organize the chicken-*shochetim* was initiated.
The members went out on strike to make known their
grievances and to appeal for surcease, but to no avail. Their
strike proved unsuccessful.

The following year brought for them another attempt to
alleviate their condition and to achieve some measure of
help. A wealthy Jew named Samuel R. Travis donated the
sum of $45,000 with the proviso that a Jewish *kehila* (com-
munity-type) organization be established in New York
City, with the task of establishing a *Vaad Hakashruth*
(Committee for Kashruth) as its first objective. The *Vaad*
would make the establishment of an organization of poultry slaughterers its first project, with an eye to regaining
for the shochet some of his lost dignity.[11]

The *Vaad* set about its task with conviction and vigor.
The leaders understood that so long as the butcher paid the

shochet his salary directly, the *shochet* would have little hope to free himself. Therefore, the *Vaad* decreed that henceforth the butcher would pay the *shochet's* salary to the *Vaad*, which would in turn pay the *shochet*. The purpose behind this was to provide the *shochet* with some freedom as a professional by guaranteeing his income, which the *Vaad* hoped to be able to do. The butchers refused to comply with this directive from the *Vaad*, insisting on their right to pay the *shochet* directly. The *Vaad* attempted also to raise the fee per slaughtered chicken, which would increase the over-all salary of the *shochet* This, too, the butchers rejected. The result of these rejections was that the *shochetim* went out on a strike that lasted for three months.

The butchers of New York City, who numbered by this time some five thousand, went to speak to Rabbi Velvel Margolies, who was a prominent figure in the rabbinate. They gained his sympathy. To further strengthen their stubborn refusal to comply with the *Vaad's* demand, the butchers imported *shochetim* from outside the city to do the necessary killing. The *shochetim* responded to this threat by placing large advertisements in the New York City newspapers proclaiming that the chickens being slaughtered by the scabs were *trayfe*. They appealed to the Jews of the city to stop purchasing such poultry. By the end of three months a compromise agreement was arranged so that the butchers agreed to the principle the *Vaad* was seeking to achieve. Instead of the *Vaad* paying the *shochetim*, however, the wholesalers of chickens paid them, which was a solution that was acceptable to all. The following year, 1915–1916, was a fatal year for the *Vaad*. The plan that the wholesalers pay the *shochetim* did not materialize, and the financial support for the *Vaad* dwindled so considerably that its office had to be closed.[12]

By 1918 the desired union of poultry *shochetim* had not as yet been organized. Nevertheless, local groups of *shochetim* in Harlem, the Bronx, and the East Side of New York came into being. In 1928 these small local groups marged into the larger Amalgamated Meat Cutters Union, and the chicken *shochetim* received their first charter from a national union. The rabbis of the city objected to the *shochetim* organizing themselves into a union. Rabbi Velvel Margolies ridiculed the *shochetim*, accusing them of surrendering their *shechita* knives to be inspected for possible imperfections by Christians. Cartoons appeared in the Jewish newspapers ridiculing the shochet as selling himself to his non-Jewish employers.[13]

The *shochetim* responded to this unwarranted abuse by the rabbis by explaining that they had no intention whatsoever of surrendering their professional dignity to the Christians. On the contrary, the officials of the Amalgamated Meat Cutters Union had no interest of any sort in their religious requirements or the inspection of their *shechita* knives. The only interest the Union had in the *shochetim* was to help them organize so that their conditions of employment would improve. The *shochetim* representatives pointed out to the rabbis and the Jewish community leaders that the *shochet* was the lowest paid of all functionaries in the Jewish community.

Soon after their affiliation with the union, the *shochetim* went out on strike to achieve higher standards of employment. By this time they had succeeded in convincing their former opponents in the rabbinate of the justice of their cause. Even Rabbi Margolies, who had previously ridiculed them, now joined them in their protest and worked to help them win. The result of the strike was that the *shochetim* became an ever stronger organization. All local union groups were united into one powerful local, No. 440, under the Amalgamated Meat Cutters Union. Mr. Kalman Shapiro was the first president, and Mr. Joseph Roseman was elected the first secretary.

The Jewish community rejoiced with the *shochetim* in the achievement of their goals, but all did not proceed well with the new *Shochetim's* Union. It was a deep shock to the Jewish community when it became known that a union organizer, with a reputation for using strong-arm tactics, was in charge of the *Shochetim* Union. He was a union man who used criminally brutal tactics to obtain his goals. The *shochetim* knew that there was danger in aligning themselves with such criminal elements, but they were a weak group and had to rely on strong men, whatever their reputations, to help them.

The tragedy inherent in joining forces with criminal elements soon became evident. This tough union organizer, together with his fellow-conspirators, hatched a plan for extorting a penny per pound of slaughtered chicken from the market men. Their weapon against those who would not cooperate was the walkout; the members of the *Shochetim* Union and those of the Trucker's Union would refuse to work for market men who would not pay the required tribute. The extortion ring adopted the impressive name "The Greater New York Live Poultry Chamber of Commerce." Eventually, however, their oppressive acts were brought before the courts.

The case against them opened on October 7, 1929 before

Judge John C. Knox in the United States Court for the Southern District of New York. The charge was that of organizing a conspiracy in restraint of trade, a misdemeanor under the Federal law. Israel B. Oseas was appointed Special United States Attorney to prosecute the case. There were eighty-four defendants to be tried simultaneously, which required that special bleachers be constructed so that all the accused could face the jury box.

Testimony against the defendants showed that threats of violence were used to compel market men to comply with the union's oppressive demands. The prosecutor summed up the evidence by declaring to the jury, "The conspirators made it as much as a man's life was worth to go down to the Washington Market in defiance of their regulations and attempt to buy poultry." It was unfortunate that the *shochetim* lent themselves to the conspiracy by obeying the orders of their corrupt union boss and stopping their work at those markets which resisted the extortionist tactics of the ring. During the trial it was shown that the racketeering activities netted the gang of conspirators between $13,000 and $16,000 each week.

Another method employed by the racketeers to extort money from the market men was to confine each market to a limited operation, either wholesale or retail. A *shochet* who was assigned to a market that was designated to sell retail was instructed to kill only fowl that was to be sold directly to the consumer and not to the dealer. The *shochet* cooperated in this unfair practice also.

On November 29, 1929 sixty-six of the defendants, including officials of the Orthodox Poultry Slaughterers of America, were convicted. The sentences imposed were light because the offense was only a misdemeanor. The *Shochetim's* Union and its president received suspended sentences. The union organizer was sentenced to serve two weeks in jail and to pay a fine of $500, which fine was suspended. Judge Knox said at the trial, "I hope that some day someone high in the Jewish community of this town will take the poultry industry in hand." [14]

In 1932 the Great Depression swept America. Caught up in this tragic occurrence were the *shochetim*, 150 of whom were suddenly without employment. These *shochetim* went to their union for assistance in finding employment. When the union could not help them, they organized themselves into a group and went to see Mayor Fiorello LaGuardia, who was then the mayor of New York City. The mayor appointed a committee and assigned to it the task of finding some solution to the problem of the *shochetim* who needed employment, and to investigate conditions in the poultry business generally. The committee was composed of local Orthodox rabbis and the *Vaad Hakashruth*. Their recommendations to the mayor included the following:

1. Establish a *plumba* system.
2. *Shochetim* should not work for a fixed salary, but they should be paid by the pound of slaughtered poultry.
3. Each *shochet* was to be limited to a maximum slaughter of 12,000 pounds per week. This figure, which was a low one, was decided upon in order to create more jobs for the *shochetim*.
4. Each slaughterhouse was to employ a *plumbirar* to make certain the *plumbas* were affixed to each

chicken. The salary of the plumbirar was to be paid through a tax of one cent per *plumba*, which the market men purchased.

The Jewish community was called upon to respect these recommendations which the committee had placed before the mayor. *Shochetim* were urged not to *shecht* in such poultry markets as did not purchase the *plumba* and affix it to their slaughtered chickens. However, the *shochetim* recognized that the rabbis had little power to enforce the *plumba* rule. They knew well that no one could help them except themselves. They called a strike in the hope of enforcing the *plumba* regulation at all poultry markets. Some of the market men complied; others responded to the strike by bringing in *shochetim* from outside the city in an attempt to break the strike. As a result, most *shochetim* gave up the strike and returned to work for the market men, even in those places where *plumbas* were not used.

The *Vaad Hakashruth* attempted to compel the *shochetim* to support the *plumba* rule without much avail. The *shochetim* replied to the pressures brought upon them by the *Vaad* by making a public statement that the *plumba* system was an unnecessary tax. In its formal reply to the *Vaad*, the *shochetim* stated the following:

"If the *shochetim* leave the markets at this time, other *shochetim* will be installed in their places, and the union will be powerless to prevent it because the agreement which the *Shochetim's* Union made with the marketmen would then be broken.

The *shochetim* recall the events of three years ago when they left their places at the behest of the rabbis. The *shochetim* dropped their work in all places where the *plumbas* were not used. What was the result? *Shochetim* lost wages and virtually suffered starvation, and at the end had to return to work in futility and embarrassment.

Let the world judge if we are not in the right when we protect ourselves against loss of our livelihoods.

We have always been on the friendliest terms with the rabbis and now stand ready to comply with all they request. They must, however, find some other means to accomplish the ends of Kashruth; one which will not expose the *shochet* to the danger of losing his livelihood. The *shochet* should not be treated as *hefker*, rightless, upon whom a ban, with which he has nothing to do is foisted. There is no basis in the Torah for disqualifying a *shochet* unless a flaw be found either in his slaughtering or in his conduct as a pious Jew. This may be established through trustworthy testimony.

No rabbinical power in the world may perpetrate such injustice. Had the *gaon*, R. Hayim Ozer of Vilna, heard the *shochetim's* side of the case, he would not have issued the responsum that he did. He was not apprised of all the issues involved, for he heard only the side presented by the rabbis. We stand willing, after having been given the opportunity to state our case, to hearken to the *gaon's* reaction.

After all, did not the rabbis eat of the slaughtering of the *shochetim* in the past, and was it not Kosher enough for them? Why now only overnight has it suddenly become *trayfe* and banned?

We declare publicly and without reservation that we *shochetim* have nothing to do with the general ban. We do our slaughtering in accordance with the religious law. The supervision is the most proper because the union sees to that. Under present arrangements a sufficient number of *shochetim* are provided for every market.

The *shochet* observes every regulation set down in the *Shulhan Arukh*, and the marketmen do not interfere.

Furthermore, it should be noted, all the *shochetim* are learned and God-fearing. Among them are found many rabbis who occupy positions in synagogues. Many of them are great scholars who would not, under any circumstances, disobey the religious law, and need not the judgment of the rabbis in this issue. We know, finally, that among the very members of the *Vaad Hakashruth* there are some rabbis who join in the opinion held by the *shochetim*." [15]

An added assist to the plea of the *shochetim* were the women, the housewives who came to the market daily to purchase their chickens and saw the birds slaughtered by the *shochet* according to Jewish custom. They, too, rejected the edict of the *plumba* because it added nothing to the Kashruth of the chicken. Everything before them was done in a very proper manner.

In 1936 George Lederman became the general manager of the *Shochetim's* Union. His father was a rabbi, and George Lederman's training was in a religious environment. He knew how to talk to the *shochetim* so that they trusted his decisions and cooperated with him.[16]

In 1938 the *shochetim* were reorganized into local No. 370 of the Amalgamated Meat Cutters Union. The great advantage to the *shochetim* of this action was that the salaries paid to the *shochet* for his services were sent to the office of the union, which in turn paid him his wages. This time the system was successful. It gave the *shochetim* throughout America their coveted independence and dignity. A program of savings was initiated which assured the *shochet* of half of his salary during periods of illness. A retirement program was also instituted.

In 1939 the *shochetim* went out on strike once more to demand an increase in pay. They desired to raise the fee paid by the marketmen for each chicken slaughtered from one-half cent per pound to one cent per pound. It was a long and bitter strike. Women joined their husbands on the picket line together with their little children, as a gesture to gain sympathy for their men, who were fighting to win greater benefits from their work. The settlement that was finally negotiated provided such benefits which would henceforth, hopefully, preclude the need for any further strikes. The *shochet* was to be paid two and one-eighth cents per pound at the wholesale slaughter plants. A minimum salary was established for the *shochet* in order to guarantee him a living wage at compaines which imported slaughtered fowl and thereby cut down on the poundage slaughtered by their own *shochetim*.

The *shochetim* in New York City complained against fowl imported from outside the city because their income was affected. In 1950 the matter was presented before Judge Max Dickstein, who decided that an equitable solution would be for Local No. 370 to provide the *shochetim* for the out-of-town slaughterhouses. The *shochetim* were satisfied with this solution to the problem because it provided many of them with much needed jobs.

In recent years new fads have arisen in the poultry industry. For example, women began to request "dressed poultry" (poultry that had been plucked of its feathers by the marketmen). Today 99 per cent of the chickens enter the Jewish home "dressed." Only a very small percentage of the Jewish housewives still want to pluck their chickens themselves.

Later on, still another fad arose to change a former pattern. The housewife now desired that her chicken be eviscerated (cleaned of its intestines) before it reached the home. In 1960 a new law was passed by the Federal Government, which required that all poultry must be eviscerated if it was to be packed for interstate shipment. The Commissioner of Agriculture had the right to permit exemptions where he felt it was necessary to do so. This was a necessary qualification of the law in order to accommodate the Orthodox Jewish housewife who felt bound by religious scruples to see the chicken opened in her presence in the event that some defect in its intestines raised the question of its Kashruth. In 1967 the poultry slaughterhouses began a lobby in Congress to pass a new law which would require all chickens to be eviscerated. No exemptions were recommended for Kosher poultry. The Union protested the new law, and were joined in their action this time by the prestigious Union of Orthodox Rabbis of the United States and Canada. The exemption for Kosher poultry was retained in the new law. Membership in the Poultry *Shochetim* Union today numbers over two hundred. Eighty retired *shochetim* are enjoying their latter years on pensions provided them by the Union.

Control of Kashruth in Community Food Shops

The concerns for upgrading Kashruth observance was by no means limited to assisting *Shochetim* gain recognition. The problems of supervising Kashruth in butcher shops, restaurants and food manufacturing plants that represented themselves as Kosher posed another kind of challenge to the leaders of the Jewish community. Unfortunately, like the early attempts to stabilize Kashruth in the poultry industry, here too initial moves to elevate the standards of Kashruth were met with crushing defeats.

The hopelessness of the situation surrounding Kashruth ultimately drove the leaders of the Jewish community to seek the aid of the civil authorities. Serious efforts were made to have Kosher laws passed by the various states.

After years of protest by dedicated Jewish leaders, Kosher laws were written into the civil statutes of many states. The following states are a few of those which enacted Kosher laws: New York—1915; Massachusetts—1929; Pennsylvania—1929; Wisconsin—1935; Michigan—1939; Rhode Island—1937.

The frustrating reality of the lack of funds, however, alerted the leaders of the Jewish community soon after the passage of the Kosher law that little would be accomplished by the civil authorities. In New York City particularly, a delegation went to see Mayor James J. Walker to apprise him of the hopelessness of the situation and to request that he take practical steps to limit the corruption in the Kashruth industry. Mayor Walker responded by appointing a special committee composed of sixty-eight rabbis and laymen who would investigate the conditions of Kashruth and report back to him. Their findings only verified further the need for the city government to step in and implement the Kosher laws so recently written into the statutes of the state. The committee found that only a small number of butcher shops were supervised by a rabbi. Those that had a rabbi supervising their Kashruth were, in most cases, receiving superficial interest. The rabbi usually was supervising more than one butcher shop and was too busy to spend much time at any one place. The customary pattern of the rabbi was that he would merely stroll casually through the premises. The major complaint of the committee, however, was that the rabbi was not independent. He was an employee of the butcher-shop proprietor where he was supervising Kashruth, and was dependent upon him for his livelihood. "Such a relationship cannot possible be productive of very strict discipline."

The Committee recommended that in view of the State's current inability to act in a practical way because of a lack of funds, a voluntary Kashruth board be established, consisting of every Orthodox rabbi affiliated with a congregation, or at least with some rabbinic association. The Kashruth board would employ its own Kashruth supervisors who would be independent of the butcher-shop proprietors. Monies to pay the supervisors, as well as the other costs of the Kashruth board, would come from the sale of lead seals (*plumbas*) to the butcher shops. Unfortunately, however, once again, little practical gain came out of the recommendations to correct the frauds and other abuses that prevailed. The only meaningful result of the Kashruth Board's activities was the creation of the Kashruth Association. The new body took upon itself to enforce the ruling of its predecessor, the Kashruth Board, and made it mandatory that a *plumba* be attached to all fowl by the *mashgiach* who represented the Kashruth Association; to give force to their ruling, the rabbis of the Association pronounced an *issur* (a rabbinic prohibition) on all Kosher fowl that did not have a *plumba* attached. This *issur* was pronounced with much pomp and ceremony at a special convocation of rabbis who were solemnly assembled for this auspicious moment at the prestigious Beth Hamedrosh Hagadol Synagogue on Norfolk Street on New York's lower East Side. They declared, in addition, that any *shochet* who would slaughter without the required rabbinic supervision or refuse to affix the *plumba*, would immediately be deprived of his status as a shochet, and no longer enjoy the privilege of practicing his profession.[17]

A significant court trial took place during that year which had far-reaching effects upon the Kashruth industry. No

sooner had the *issur* been pronounced than it was challenged. For example, the S.S. and B. Live Poultry Corporation declared the *issur* to be an infringement upon its rights.
It claimed that the *issur* was a special superimposition upon
the Kosher industry because it was not required by the
Torah. The case came before Judge Philip J. Cooke, who
decided in favor of the Kashruth Association's *issur*, ruling
that those who were in the Kashruth industry had to expect
to assume special obligations that are determined by the
proper religious authorities.[18]

Another Kashruth case that came before the courts was
much greater in its far-reaching consequences and much
more dramatic in its intrigue than the case involving the
S.S. & B. Live Poultry Corporation. It was the trial of the
managers of the Branfman Kosher Provisions Company in
March, 1933. At that time, this company was considered by
all to be the paragon of the Kosher provisions industry. Its
name and reputation as a Kosher provisions producer were
impeccable. In fact, prior to the scandal, it was said that
the company's directors were offered a million dollars for
the use of its name on another food product, so high was
the esteem in which the company was held. However, in
time the company was turned over to others, who apparently were not as interested in Kashruth as their pred-
ecessors. The record of the case brought against them
discloses a detective-story sleuthing. A group of rabbis, ac-
companied by officials of the District Attorney's office,
maintained surveillance some distance from the Branfman
plant on the Sabbath when the plant was presumed to be
closed in observance of the Holy Day. In time, however,
the sleuths were shocked to see a truck pull up to the load-
ing dock of the plant, and barrels of meat rolled from it

into the plant. The rabbis and the officials went into the plant and confronted those who were receiving the meats on the Sabbath. The barrels were opened, and the meats were found to be *trayfe*. The charge against the Branfman concern was that of fraud—presenting to the public non-Kosher meats as Kosher.[19] The shocking impact upon the general populace, and the Jewish community in particular, was devasting enough to focus attention upon the urgent need for a realistic solution to the problems of corruption in the Kashruth industry.

Prior to the Branfman case, the State's interest in Kashruth enforcement was superficial. It was the responsibility of the District Attorney to prosecute only such cases of violation of the Kosher law as were brought to his attention. Knowledge of but a few such violations ever reached him. As a result of the scandal of the Branfman case, however, a new Kosher Law Enforcement Bureau was created in New York State's Department of Agriculture, which had as its sole responsibility the control of Kashruth throughout the State. Rabbi Sheppard Baum, together with Mr. George Ringler, was appointed in 1934 and given the responsibility of visiting all establishments dealing in Kosher meats to investigate to what extent the Kosher law was being respected and where violations, if any, existed. Two years later, in 1936 the Bureau was given heightened stature by establishing it as an independent department under the Department of Agriculture, with Rabbi Baum at its head. The Bureau employed ten inspectors, who were expected to cover the entire state. In addition, the original responsibility of the Bureau which was limited to matters involving only the sale of meats, was now expanded to cover the sale of all Kosher foods. This broadening of responsibility was in response to the growth of the Kosher foods industry. The new State office, known as the Kosher Law Enforcement Bureau of the Department of Agriculture, functions as a watchdog. The Kosher Law Enforcement Bureau's inspectors investigate plants where Kosher foods are manufactured, and businesses where Kosher foods are sold. These inspectors for the Kosher Law Enforcement Bureau need not be rabbis, although such a high calibre of Jewish scholarship would be preferred. Some inspectors are rabbis, others are former Kosher butchers, while still others are laymen who themselves observe Kashruth. All new inspectors are given training in this specialized field of work.

The basic responsibility of the Kosher Law Enforcement Bureau, as prescribed by the laws of the State of New York, is to protect the consumer from being misled by fraudulent advertising of Kosher products. The laws of the State of New York which pertain to Kashruth enforcement are contained in the latest publication, "Circular No. 811 of the State of New York, Department of Agriculture and Markets," dated 1961, and in "Document No. 2563 Intro., 2547," dated January 18, 1967. The principles enunciated in "Circular 811" provide that the Kosher Law Enforcement Bureau "will investigate, inspect, and supervise the sale of Kosher meats." In addition, the Bureau will make such rules and regulations that will be necessary in order to enable it to carry out its responsibilities. In addition to the Kosher Law Enforcement Bureau, the Commissioner of Agriculture appoints a lay Kashruth advisory board of nine members, one of whom is their elected chairman. These members of the Kashruth advisory board are distinguished members of Jewish communities throughout the State of

New York. They serve voluntarily and without pay, except for travel expenses to and from places where their committee meetings are held. The advisory committee meets upon the call of the Commissioner, or whenever the members feel that there is a special need to meet. It is the responsibility of the advisory committee to advise the Commissioner on matters related to Kashruth administration and enforcement, and to recommend to the Commissioner such changes in the Kashruth law as will make it more effective in achieving its goals, and to consider all matters that shall come before it.[20]

The Kosher law is very explicit in its protection of the consumer. It requires that any foods that are prepared for sale as Kosher must conform to the "Orthodox Hebrew religious requirements." "Fraud" includes any representation of food as being Kosher, regardless of the manner or language of representation, when such food is in fact not Kosher. An extension of this requirement to remove the possibility of fraud prohibits the mere possession of non-Kosher food products in an establishment which represents itself to the public as being Kosher. The *plumba* tag must be clearly evident on all meats that are "exposed for sale" as being Kosher. Prepared foods that are sold as Kosher must not contain any questionable ingredients.

Violations of the Kosher laws today are dealt with in a variety of ways. For example, the law allows that violators may be fined up to $500, or sentenced to a year in the county jail or the penitentiary. If the violation is a basic contradiction of the law, the Judge may impose both the fine and the jail sentence. Violations of a technical nature, such as labelling of Kosher meats in an unclear or questionable way, may result merely in a warning from the inspector, or a minor fine. Such cases do not go to court for trial. Some of the more prominent cases that did come to court for trial challenged the very fundamental principles of the Kosher law. In the case of the Hygrade Provisions Company vs. Sherman, who was then New York State Attorney General, Hygrade was accused of presenting to the public non-Kosher meats as Kosher. Hygrade pleaded innocent, contending that the Kosher law was unenforceable because the meaning of the word "Kosher" was subject to a broad variety of interpretation—so much so that no clear meaning could be unequivocally applied to the term. Hygrade claimed further that because of the ambiguity of the meaning of the word "Kosher," anyone could violate the law without realizing it. Hygrade lost the case in the lower courts and appealed it to the Supreme Court.

The presiding judge denied the plea of the defendant, saying that the term "Kosher" does, in fact, have a definite meaning. He reminded the defendant that people engage in selling food that is called "Kosher"; therefore, the word does have a very definite interpretation. "Kosher" food is an item that is marketable, and people understand what the term signifies when they are shopping for food. The ambiguities which may surround the word "Kosher" are neither more nor less confusing than the ambiguities that surround any other legal terminology.[21]

Another case of great importance to come before the courts was a second action brought by the S.S.& B. Poultry Corporation against the Kashruth Association of New York. The S.S.& B. Poultry Corporation complained that the edict of the Kashruth Association requiring that Kosher meats must have a *plumba* gave the Kashruth Association monopolistic control over the sale of Kosher chickens. The

judge ruled against the complaint of the S.S.& B. Poultry
Corporation. He noted that Kashruth was purely a rabbinic
function to be administered by the rabbis, who were the
sole arbiters of what Kashruth requirements were. Therefore, by the very nature of the laws of Kashruth, they had
to be under the direction of the religious body most qualified to assure that the requirements were met. The claim of
monopolistic control, therefore, did not apply in this instance.[22]

The case of the People vs. Goldstein, which was tried in
1951, added another dimension of strength to the effectiveness of the Kosher laws. Goldstein Meat Packing House
was visited by the inspectors of the Kosher Law Enforcement Bureau, who found *trayfe* meats on the premises. The
Defendant claimed that the law did not apply to him because the *trayfe* meats were not "exposed for sale"—a
condition which the law stipulates as constituting a violation. The meats were in Goldstein's plant; this could not be
denied. But they were not there for the purpose of sale,
merely for storage.

The judge did not accept Goldstein's plea of innocence;
nor did he accept the lawyer's interpretation of the law's
use of the phrase "exposed for sale." With keen legal insight, the judge pointed out that if the phrase "exposed for
sale" was to be interpreted strictly, it would be limited only
to those meats in the first row of the meat stand because
these were truly "exposed," in the strictest sense of the
terminology. Consequently, only the first row of meats
would have to be Kosher. The remaining meats in the rear
rows, not being fully exposed, would not then be in the
jurisdiction of the law if the inspector found them not to be
Kosher. By such clever interpretation of the law, the un-

scrupulous Kosher meat dealer could sell non-Kosher meats as Kosher and be free of any punishment from the law. The only way in which a Kosher meat dealer could then be prosecuted was to apprehend him selling non-Kosher meat which he was holding in his hand.

The intent of the law, the judge pointed out, was to remove the possibility of the Kosher meat dealer's holding *trayfe* meat on his premises which might be sold as Kosher. For a Kosher meat dealer, the mere possession of *trayfe* meat is a violation of the law. Therefore, the judge denied Goldstein's plea of innocence and held him for court action.[23]

Many other similar attempts to circumvent the law have been apprehended by the inspectors from the Kosher Law Enforcement Bureau, and the successful prosecution of each instance has added strength and deepened the power of the law, as well as sharpened its clarification. An example of the further sharpening of the law is the appearance in the windows of food stores selling both Kosher and non-Kosher foods signs bearing in large, prominent, letters the notification that both Kosher and non-Kosher foods are being sold.

Another very significant step in removing misleading, fradulent advertising from the Kosher foods industry was the restriction of restaurants serving food cooked in the traditional Jewish fashion from advertising "Kosher style," which was confusing to the public, who through ignorance, read the word "Kosher" in the phrase "Kosher style" and thought that this signified properly supervised Kosher cuisine.

The areas of Kashruth that are still to be corrected through more careful surveillance by the Kosher Law En-

forcement Bureau are many. The recent revelation of the
scandalously unsanitary conditions in some of the Kosher
meat packing plants and provision houses is indicative of
the urgent need for increasing supervision. The hotels and
resorts remain a separate problem, as do the catering establishments, which very often advertise Kosher foods without the presence of a mashgiach to insure adherence to the
Kashruth law.

The high pricing of Kosher meats as compared to non-
Kosher is a problem which both the religious and civil
authorities have been grappling with for many years without a solution. And the demand for some reasonable control
of this corrupt situation is heard daily because, in addition
to the abuse which such unfair pricing of Kosher meats
represents, its harm to the Jewish community goes even
deeper when it results in discouraging young married people from keeping Kosher because of their inability to pay
the high prices.

Although the Kosher meat industry is only a fraction of
the total concerns of the state departments that are established to protect the consumer from fraud, yet if the job is
to be done effectively at all, the work of the Kosher enforcement bureaus in the various states must be upgraded.
Funds to employ sufficient staff must be given these departments, and their budgets be increased so that they can function in the manner that is required of them.

New York City Kosher Law Enforcement Department

In a large city such as New York, the work of the State
Kosher Law Enforcement Bureau is supplemented by a
city department of Kashruth enforcement. The New

York City Kosher Law Enforcement Department is attached to the Department of Markets. Its function is limited to maintaining inspection of the food shops in the local areas of the city to protect the consumer from fraud. The Kosher Law Enforcement Department of New York City came into existence in 1923 as a branch of the Department of Health, transferring in 1965 to the Bureau of Weights and Measures, and finally in 1966 moving into the Department of Markets as a division of the section on Consumer Law Enforcement. The investigators of this department differ from those who are employed in the State Kosher Law Enforcement Bureau in that city inspectors are required to investigate not only Kosher food products, but also sales of a general nature such as coal, fuel, oil, and ice. Violators of the Kosher foods' law are prosecuted under charges of mislabelling and misrepresentation. Cases of such fraud are turned over to the District Attorney's office for prosecution. Guilty parties are fined, and in some instances may be forbidden to operate a Kosher business again within the boundaries of the city.

One such case occured in April 1963, when Judge T. Vincent Quinn fined the United Rabbinical Supervisors of America, Inc. $500 for Kashruth fraud. The directors had represented themselves as a Kashruth supervising agency while, in fact, they were not. The charges placed against them by the investigators from the New York City Department of Kosher Law Enforcement included finding shrimp (a non-Kosher fish) in a refrigerator that was supposed to contain only Kosher foods; a Chinese chef preparing the Kosher meal without the supervision of a mashgiach; and the catering of Kosher weddings and Bar Mitzvahs without a mashgiach to supervise. Judge Quinn agreed to set aside the fine on the promise that the directors of the United Rabbinical Supervisors of America would dissolve their organization, which they agreed to do.[24]

The city department of Kosher law enforcement employs sixty inspectors whose qualifications include a high school education plus two years in some commercial activity. They are trained for a month at the foods'-testing station of the City's Department of Markets. Following this, they spend approximately another month in the field under the guidance of an experienced supervisor who instructs the novice investigator in the practical procedures of investigation.

The early days of the Kosher Law Enforcement Department were a period of trial and error for the inspectors. A typical problem revolved around the apprehension of the guilty. For example, an inspector would discover that a delicatessen was selling *trayfe* meats as Kosher, and the inspector might then casually purchase a corned beef sandwich as evidence. When he was served his sandwich he would confront the proprietor with the fact that he was defrauding the public by selling *trayfe* meat as Kosher. The inspector would then proceed to a telephone booth to report his discovery to the Bureau office and request further instructions. Often to the surprise and regret of the inspector, when he returned to his table to pick up his evidence he would find that the proprietor had used the time while the inspector was in the phone booth to remove the *trayfe* sandwich, altogether or to change it to another one that was Kosher. The inspector was embarrassed, for he no longer had a case.

Today's detection procedure is much wiser. Now, when evidence has been discovered that a storekeeper is selling *trayfe* food as Kosher, the inspector's first act is to place the evidence in a plastic container and to mark it as evidence of mislabelling of Kosher food. He keeps the evidence with him at all times until he reaches his office, where he files a report and initiates proceedings against the proprietor.[25]

Another problem confronting the inspector who has apprehended an unscrupulous businessman selling *trayfe* meats as Kosher has to do with establishing a violation so that the case can be successfully prosecuted. For example, an inspector might discover that a Kosher delicatessen is selling *trayfe* food as Kosher. He will seize the evidence and proceed to issue a notice of violation to the proprietor. The case will eventually come to trial in court.

In the meantime, the guilty party will be working to establish his innocence. One of the most successful defense mechanisms that he can produce, of course, will be some proof that the accusation against him was false; that the meat he was selling was indeed Kosher. To accomplish this end, the unscrupulous proprietor will search out someone who, like himself, is dishonest enough to be willing to sell his soul for the right price. Such a person will come to court and present himself to the judge as a rabbi. He will testify that the meat sold by the accused was Kosher. The judge now finds himself in the peculiar position of trying to decide whether the investigator's testimony or that of the supposed rabbi is to be believed. Most judges will avoid such an embarrassing position, feeling unqualified to decide the religious qualifications of the defense witness, and will dismiss the case for lack of conclusive evidence.

The typical tricks-of-the-trade employed by storekeepers to try to hide evidences of fraud from the inspectors have all become basic to the training program given the novice inspectors. They are taught to recognize when the labels of Kosher or *trayfe* meats have been altered, and when metal tags that are placed upon processed meats to identify them as *trayfe* have been switched so that *trayfe* meats are tagged as Kosher. A popular ruse practiced by the unscrupulous is to pack a barrel of meats that is being sold as Kosher with Kosher meats near the top of the barrel, and the *trayfe* meats, which comprise the bulk of the contents, below them. A host of other established machinations have become known to the inspectors over the years, and by now are of little value in attempts to defraud the public. The unscrupulous, however, still try to use them and sometimes manage to find new ways.

A case of Kosher-front fraud occurred in Brooklyn, New York at a restaurant advertising Kosher-for-Passover meals. A brochure that was distributed as an advertisement had on its cover the picture of a man wearing the vestments of a cantor. He was surrounded by a smiling woman and children. This scene was advertised so as to give the image of a typical Jewish family at Passover time.

When the inspector from the city's Department of Markets went to the so-called Kosher restaurant, they asked if they could meet the cantor and his family whose picture was on the brochure cover. The inspector was informed by the manager quite candidly that the restaurant did not employ a cantor; the picture was only to draw the public to the restaurant. The Passover meals, however, were strictly Kosher.

The inspector then asked the manager to take him on a tour of the kitchen where the Passover meals were being prepared. It was during the tour that the inspector found that not only was the picture on the brochure phony, but that the claim of "strictly Kosher" Passover food was equally fraudulent. The inspector found that the chickens that were being served to the unsuspecting public were *trayfe* which, of course, meant that the entire meal was *trayfe*, in addition to being unacceptable as Passover food.[26] Such, and many similar instances of attempted fraud are sought out by the inspectors of state and local Kosher law enforcement agencies in an effort to keep Kashruth honest.

The Communal Organizations for Kashruth

Throughout this tumultuous period in the growth of Kashruth in America, along with attempts to dignify Kashruth by making its enforcement a matter of concern for the legal authorities, there were always certain private citizens who were interested in strengthening the observance of this sacred Jewish tenet. One such person was Abraham Goldstein of blessed memory, a chemist by profession, a committed Orthodox Jew by faith. Abraham Goldstein believed that if processed Kosher food products were made available to the Jewish housewife to make her work easier in the home, as processed non-Kosher food products are available to non-Jewish housewives, more of the Jewish women (especially Jewish brides) would give serious consideration to the possibility of keeping Kosher.

Putting prepared Kosher foods into the hands of Jewish housewives became for Abraham Goldstein a life-long crusade. He devoted endless hours to research and correspondence with food manufacturers in attempts to have them produce Kosher foods. Already in 1918 he managed to import from England a Kosher product called Rennet, which is basic for the manufacture of cheese. His next project was to find a company that was producing crackers which were so popular a treat in the Jewish home throughout the week and especially on the Sabbath. He hoped to be able to induce some baking company to put a Kosher cracker on the market. To achieve his goal he negotiated with the Sunshine Biscuit Company, which followed Goldstein's advice and began to manufacture a Kosher cracker. Goldstein himself received no remuneration for his professional guidance to the companies with whom he was working, nor was he awarded any royalties from the new Kosher products that were appearing on the shelves of the grocers. Through his unselfish efforts, and without realizing it, he began creating a whole new market of catering to the "Kosher trade." [27]

In 1924 the Union of Orthodox Jewish Congregations, the major national body representing the Orthodox wing of Judaism, entered the field of Kashruth supervision. Established in 1892 as a spokesman for Orthodoxy in America, the Union was an organization that had the impressive title and important stature in the Jewish community to accomplish the gigantic task of organization which the burgeoning Kashruth industry represented. Together with its rabbinic arm, the Rabbinical Council of America, it established its Kosher Certification Service (KCS). Abraham Goldstein was chosen as the first director of the KCS. The immediate task which confronted him was to devise a symbol that could be placed upon a food package which would represent the food item to the housewife as Kosher. The choice of a proper Kosher symbol was of extreme importance to the company producing food for consumption by Christians as well as Jews. The symbol chosen should not convey the impression that the food in the package was for Jews only, which might be the case if Hebrew lettering or the Star of David were chosen as the Kashruth symbol. After exploring numerous suggestions of the kind of symbol that would be acceptable, Goldstein and his committee realized the futility of attempting a distinctly Jewish symbol and devised the "U," which signifies the first two letters of the words "Orthodox Union," referring to the Union of Orthodox Jewish Congregations.

Although the genesis of the KCS was prompted by concern for the Kashruth of a few small bakeries, butcher shops, and some of the canned products that were already in the small grocery shops and modest self-service stores, the foresight of the members of the Committee envisioned the possibilities of the growing food industry. The early records of their deliberations show that they agreed that Kashruth certification in manufacturing should be divorced from profit considerations. Their goal was to create a communally directed program capable of steady expansion both geographically and in variety of commercially produced Kosher foods. Time and the rapid expansion of the food industry generally into what is today known as the "food revolution" bears testimony to the wisdom of their planning. In the forty-year period since the KCS came into being, the average housewife's kitchen has been converted from a steamroom where the housewife slaved to prepare personally every morsel of food that went into her family's menu, to the pleasant kitchen area where the housewife's work is made infinitely easier, thanks to the prepared foods that come out of cans or a host of other containers.

With this growth of the food industry, however, new foods became available which created special problems for the observant Jewish housewife. For example, the American invention, the TV dinner, may include meat, fish or fowl, several vegetables, etc. On the label of such a dinner the housewife might find such items as beef, shortening, whole milk solids, oil, salt, flavoring, potatoes, carrots, string beans, onions, vitamin D, gelatin, monosodium glutamate, wine, spices, and leavening. While for the non-Jewish consumer the TV dinner would be attractive as a delectable meal, for the Jewish family that observes Kashruth, such a dinner would be fraught with so many problems that they would simply pass it by. For example, the beef would not be Kosher, and if it were Kosher, mixing it together with whole milk solids in the same meal would make it unacceptable. The vitamin D may be drawn from a fish such as the shark, which is rejected because it is *trayfe*. Similar problems surround the shortening—is it an animal or vegetable derivative? Gelatin is almost always of forbidden origin, unless specified as Kosher gelatin. And overriding the whole syndrome of these questions, should all of the foregoing queries be resolved, is the problem of the Kashruth of the manufacturing plant itself. Does it manufacture Kosher and non-Kosher foods? If so, is there a clear separation between the two processes? Did Sabbath-observing Jews handle the wine that went into the meal, or was it handled by Gentiles? Is there a *mashgiach* at the plant? But, thanks to the U, the observant housewife need not deny herself or her family the pleasures of a TV dinner, or some other desirable packaged food because all of the above questions have been resolved for her by the U. There are at present more than 2,500 food products (representing 475 companies) under the Kashruth supervision of the U, and the number and variety of foods under U supervision is growing continually.[28]

The system of investigating a company before providing certification has been established by the U, and involves the following procedures: The company which seeks Kashruth supervision from the KCS must first file a formal application in which are listed all the ingredients of the product for which supervision is desired. Ingredients that are compounds of a number of separate items must be broken down to their units so that every particle of food going into the final product will be made known to the KCS. In addition, certain ancillary facts must be declared, such as any other food-producing plants which may be owned by the candidate company, their location, and the products that are manufactured in them. Once the information contained in the application has been accepted by the U as representing a possibility of certification, the next step is a formal visit by a committee of rabbis, members of the Rabbinical Council of America, who are well-versed in food technology as well as the Dietary Laws. A thorough inspection of the plant is made by the rabbis, who report to the KCS their findings and recommendations. While in most cases whatever changes in production are recommended involve only foods going into the product, occasionally the report of the rabbinic committee is such that the company must undertake extensive structural revisions, such as adding a new wing, before the KCS will grant the product U certification.

Once a company has been fully approved for Kashruth certification, the supervisory fee is set by mutual agreement between the company and the KCS. The fee is kept low in accordance with the non-profit policy of the KCS. Often, in a large production, the fact that thousands of pieces of the product are produced makes it possible for the company to absorb the minimal cost for the Kashruth supervision without substantially raising the market price of the item. The observant housewife can keep Kosher without depleting her budget any more than does her non-Kosher neighbor who buys processed foods.

A vitally important feature of the KCS program of supervision is the status of dignity which the *mashgiach* has. The KCS has dogmatically insisted that the mashgiach must be paid by KCS and not by the company itself. In this way it has freed the *mashgiach* from the control of the management so that he can perform his duties with the highest standards of professional integrity. He cannot be threatened or coerced to overlook violations of the Kashruth rules out of fear that he will lose his employment. The *mashgiach* is an employee of the KCS and is assured of his livelihood, even if he should declare the product *trayfe*. His only concern is that his supervisory functions be performed honestly. The ⓤ has become a symbol of Kashruth that is accepted by the most scrupulous Kashruth-observant housewives because its high standards of supervision are widely known throughout the Jewish community. The appearance of its letters on a food package is a guarantee of unimpeachable Kashruth. The current director of the ⓤ is Rabbi Alexander Rosenberg.

The OK Laboratories

Mr. Abraham Goldstein, as noted earlier, was the first director of the KCS. His relationship with the KCS was terminated after approximately nine years because of disagreements between Goldstein and his superiors about the purposes and goals of Kashruth supervision. However,

Goldstein's dedication to Kashruth remained undiminished. In 1935 he established a non-profit Kashruth-supervising agency known as the "OK Laboratories"; the letters "OK" referring to the words, "Organized for Kashruth." As in the past, he worked in his free time to broaden the possibilities of observing Kashruth in the Jewish home by inducing manufacturers of foods to accept the requirements of Kashruth. In the beginning, his services to manufacturers were given freely and without any kind of remuneration. Ultimately, the number of companies seeking his Kashruth supervision grew to such a number, and the demands on his time by the Jewish community so increased, that he was compelled to devote his whole time to the growing Kashruth field. In March 1935 he published his first Kashruth Directory at his own expense. In it he expressed his hope that his labors would enable Jewish housewives to enjoy the blessings of the expanding food industry and still keep Kosher.

"The rapid changes in the process of manufacturing new articles of foods made it necessary to investigate the ingredients as well as the method of fabrication to ascertain if they do not contain a *trayfe* substance in itself, or come in contact with such during the manufacturing process. Such investigations were unfortunately entrusted to chemists who, while proficient in some fields, were not acquainted with the research of food articles, or were misled to state that the articles in question conform to the Jewish dietary laws. . . . To remedy this abuse and the great damage it has done to the strict observance of our dietary laws, the OK Laboratories have been founded. Their object is to provide a reliable and unbiased source of information for Rabbinical organizations or private rabbis if a certain article contains ingredients not permitted by the dietary laws." [29]

The first issue of the pamphlet (48,000 copies) was distributed nationally, also at Goldstein's personal expense. The response to it was phenomenal. Letters poured in from all over the country congratulating the author and encouraging him to continue to publish his findings about Kashruth. But a cloud soon arose to shroud this first flush of success. The rabbis who read Goldstein's work objected vigorously to the intrusion of a layman into their official rabbinic domain of responding to *shaylos* (questions of religious matters). Goldstein was not deterred by this outburst of clerical censure. He stood firm in his conviction that he was performing a much needed and valuable service to the Jewish community. His courage remained undiminished.

The next publication of the Kashruth Directory appeared as a July–August 1935 issue. In it Goldstein discussed the pressing question of the Kashruth of a gelatin dessert called Junket. He debated the Kashruth of eels and sturgeon, which were being advertised in a rabbinic journal as being Kosher. The rabbis who declared eels to be Kosher claimed that they could do so on the basis that there were actually two different species of eels—one which swam in sweet water, the other which inhabited salt waters. The sweet-water eels were Kosher according to the editor of the rabbinic journal. Goldstein rebutted this statement that there were two separate species of eels by pointing out that, in fact, there was only one specie of eel. It spawned in salt water, but swam in sweet waters. This peculiar trait of the eel might have caused the rabbis to assume that there were two separate species of this fish. Nevertheless, the fact is that there is but one specie of eel. The major objection to the eel, Goldstein pointed out, was not whether it swam in sweet or salt waters, but the fact that it did not have fins and scales as required by the Torah, and therefore could not be considered Kosher.

As a result of Goldstein's relentless insistence upon the religious and scientific facts regarding the eel, the rabbinic journal was compelled to retract its advertisements of eel as a Kosher fish. Goldstein achieved similar results in the case of the sturgeon, declaring it to be a non-Kosher fish.

The questions of Junket and Jello remain unresolved even to this day. Although some rabbis will sanction Jello and Junket as Kosher products, the OK Laboratories' bulletin retains its own attitude that these products are *trayfe* because they are manufactured from non-Kosher ingredients.

The OK Laboratories today are managed by Rabbi Bernard Levy who recently acquired the accounts of the Laboratories.

Kashruth Supervisors Union, Local No. 621

The Kashruth Supervisors Union, Local No. 621, has been the center of controversy from the time of its inception. As a union organization, it was part of the violent era when unions were fighting to gain a hold on American industry, attempting to put an end to the many tragic abuses which management was guilty of perpetrating against its hapless employees. Rabbi Chaim Yudel Hurwitz, who has been the Executive Secretary of the Kashruth Supervisors Union since its inception, was the founder and originator of the idea that Kashruth supervisors, who were religious functionaries, had the right to dignified conditions of employment. Rabbi Hurwitz was particularly suited for the difficult role he was to play, having been involved in his European home town in radical political activities.

Soon after his arrival in America, Rabbi Hurwitz met the girl who was destined to be his wife and became engaged to be married. Assuming the traditional patriarchal role, he set out to find a suitable wedding hall for the momentous occasion of his marriage. He arrived at one such catering wedding hall and made his inquiries. One question which was vital for him was the presence of a *mashgiach* on the premises to insure Kashruth. When the proprietor told him that the Kashruth was of the highest caliber, under the supervision of a rabbi, young Rabbi Hurwitz asked permission to meet the rabbi. The proprietor called to the rabbi to come out of the kitchen to meet the prospective customer. Rabbi Hurwitz was shocked at the appearance of the rabbi who came to greet him. Out of the kitchen came a stately-looking gentleman with a beautiful full white beard, wearing an apron and holding in his hand a partially peeled potato. Following a brief conversation between the two rabbis, the owner of the wedding hall dismissed the rabbi-*mashgiach* and ordered him back into the kitchen to resume his work peeling the potatoes. This tragic scene gave Rabbi Hurwitz no peace because he soon found that the unfortunate status of the one *mashgiach* he had met was actually typical to that of most rabbis in this important profession.[31]

Investigation of the status of the *mashgiach* revealed to Rabbi Hurwitz that most *mashgichim* were old Jewish scholars who were abused and tightly controlled by the proprietors of the delicatessens, restaurants, and catering halls who employed them. As he toured the lower East Side, for example, visiting various Kosher eateries, he noticed that in front of a number of such places the owners had stationed patriarchal-looking old Jewish gentlemen (the longer and whiter the beards, the better) to act as fronts for the Kosher operations. The appearance of such religious-looking old men in front of these places was intended to convince the naïve passerby that the food inside was Kosher. Often, the food served inside was not Kosher, but the old men probably were not aware of the tragic role they were playing. Their pay for the day was usually their supper meal.

This was the unfortunate lot of Kashruth and of the *mashgiach* in those unsophisticated days. He was completely under the control of the proprietor. His primary function was to give an air of Kashruth legitimacy to the place where he was employed. His salary varied according to the number of menial tasks he was willing to perform in the kitchen, the cellar, or some other area of the establishment. Strange as it may seem, the only task that the *mashgiach* was forbidden to perform was the supervision of Kashruth, the very job for which presumably he was hired. When Rabbi Hurwitz set himself the monumental goal of organizing the *mashgichim* so that they would have the collective strength to protest against their sad lot, he expected to incur opposition from the owners and managers of the Kosher food shops. To his surprise, however, he found equally strong opposition arising from the *mashgichim* themselves—the very men who were being abused and whom he was trying to rescue. Their objection to being unionized was based on the idealism that the *mashgiach* was a *Talmid Chochom* (a wise student of the Torah) and should be able to deal with his fellow Jews (or Gentile employers) on a personal, moral and ethical basis.

It was a breach of Jewish professional etiquette for a *mashgiach* to stoop to the level of the business world by joining a union in order to achieve his aims. The tragedy of the situation which confronted the rabbis made Rabbi Hurwitz all the more determined not to be deterred from his purpose. He would find a way. Somehow, he ultimately managed to convince the *mashgichim* that to organize into a strong union with the power to improve their working conditions was a legitimate enterprise for Jewish scholars.

Once he had persuaded the *mashgichim* to accept the idea of a union to achieve new rights for them, the courageous young rabbi set about the task of organizing his new union. Luck was with him, and he was able to convince the truckers' union to cooperate with him in his work. When a stubborn proprietor refused to accept a *union mashgiach* as his Kashruth supervisor, Rabbi Hurwitz, in typical union fashion, would station pickets at the shop. When a truck driver who was delivering supplies to the same place saw the pickets marching in front of the store, he would turn away and not make the delivery. It wasn't long before a union *mashgiach* was employed.[32]

A short time later the waiters' union officials also appreciated the justice of Rabbi Hurwitz's cause, and they too joined in the movement to clean up the Kashruth field and to stop the degradation of Jewish scholars. Waiters refused to serve at restaurants that did not hire a union *mashgiach*, and this action was sufficient to compel the proprietor to accept the *mashgiach* sent by Rabbi Hurwitz.

Rabbi Hurwitz did not win his fight without great personal risk, however. One incident vividly points up the dangers that confronted him. In one establishment that he was visiting in an attempt to convince the proprietor to accept a union *mashgiach*, the rabbi was standing for a moment of meditation when suddenly he heard something whizz by his ear. It was a meat cleaver which someone had thrown from behind and which barely missed the rabbi's head.

Rabbi Hurwitz began his efforts to organize the *mashgichim* in 1933.[33] On February 10, 1940, the *mashgichim* who had accepted his invitation to unionize were gratified when the American Federation of Labor awarded them a charter as a branch of the Meatcutters and Butchers Union. Later, on March 8, 1941, the United Hebrew Trades conferred a charter upon the *mashgichim's* union, designating them as the Kashruth Supervisors Union, Local No. 621, the title which is still its designation today.

The intervening years saw the growth of the membership. In August of 1951 Rabbi Baruch Katz was elected president. His associate, chosen by the board of trustees, was Rabbi Lemel Steinberger. A rabbinical advisory board was appointed which was headed by Rabbis Rubin Levovitz and Moshe Pollack. Rabbi Chaim Y. Hurwitz, known to his many friends, and enemies alike, as "Chaim Yudel," was elected secretary. While other officers have been replaced in the normal course of the organization's functioning, Rabbi Hurwitz has succeeded in retaining his important post.

The Kashruth Supervisors Union now proceeded to grow in both numbers and power. In June 1952, contracts for Kashruth supervision were written with many companies producing Kosher delicatessen. In a few short months, however, the same manufacturers who had signed the contracts agreeing to employ only union *mashgichim* reneged and refused to honor their commitments. Rabbi Hurwitz responded to this immediately with courage. He called the owners of the provision plants to a meeting to mediate the matter. While they discussed the consequences of broken contractual agreements, Rabbi Hurwitz's union members were picketing the plants to give emphasis and reality to his power to punish those who defied him. By December 1952 all the companies who had revolted against the Kashruth Supervisors Union had accepted fully the terms of their contract and were hiring only union *mashgichim*. A major achievement of the union was the decision to deny Kashruth supervision to places where Kosher and *trayfe* foods were served, even if separate departments were maintained. A decision such as this meant the loss of many potential hotels and catering services which, under other circumstances, might have accepted the Kashruth supervision of the Union. Rabbi Hurwitz, however, saw the acceptance of such Kosher places as a compromise of Kashruth standards, and refused to accede to the lowering of his Kashruth standards.

His zeal in protecting the high standards of Kashruth observance has made Rabbi Hurwitz a lone champion. He alone has used the power of his organization to make the Jewish community aware of the negligence of certain Jewish communal organizations who hold *trayfe* banquets annually. His persistent picketing of such *trayfe* affairs given by large Jewish communal organizations whose official policies require Kosher affairs has publicized their disregard for this basic Jewish tenet. It is to his everlasting praise that he has compelled such Jewish organizations to increase the number of Kosher affairs under their sponsorship. Perfection has not yet been achieved. Many Jewish organizations continue to pay mere lip service to their announced commitment to Kashruth. But with continued irritation of the issue by Rabbi Hurwitz and his union members, Jewish communal groups will ultimately be compelled to honor Kashruth fully and unequivocally.

Within the Kosher meats and catering industries, many strategic posts are held by Union mashgichim, giving the organization tremendous power and control over the distribution and sale of Kosher meats. There is little doubt that because of this control, Chaim Yudel can stop the flow of Kosher meats into the butcher shops of New York City should he desire to do so. The methods employed by Chaim Yudel for achieving such vast power have been criticised by many. But often he has awakened the Jewish community to its responsibilities to observe Kashruth rather than desecrate the commandment. The picket line has been one of his most potent techniques for punishing a Jewish group which does not take his warnings seriously. In many instances he has compelled Jewish communal organizations to increase the number of Kosher dinners they sponsor, and by elimination, to reduce the number of *trayfe* ones.

Unfortunately, however, amid this noble labor is the regrettable abuse of his power. More than one synagogue has been picketed, not because they were serving *trayfe*, but simply because the congregation did not elect a union *mashgiach* to supervise their Kashruth. Ultimately, the congregation was forced to knuckle under.

As a union, the Kashruth Supervisors Union has intimate contact with other unions in various fields; i.e., the waiters, musicians or teamsters unions. Chaim Yudel has been known to use the tactics of calling upon these other unions not to service a synagogue which will not comply with his demands. The other unions have always respected the call for help from the Kashruth Supervisors Union.

However, as the ledger of achievements is read, and in spite of these pressure tactics employed by Chaim Yudel, the Kashruth Supervisors Unions through the zeal of its executive secretary, has in the main enhanced greatly the dignity of Kashruth in America.

The Kashruth Department Of The United Synagogue Of America

The newest organization in the Kashruth field is the Kashruth Department of the United Synagogue of America (Conservative). Established in 1966 [33] it was immediately questioned by rabbis and laymen alike. Many felt that the Conservative movement had no legitimate cause for entering the Kashruth field. The Orthodox groups appeared to be performing the necessary services to maintain Kashruth in the Jewish community; to introduce a new organization would only add a divisive element. Yet, in spite of these protests the Conservative movement proceeded to establish a beachhead in Kashruth through its own program of Kashruth supervision.

Significant steps were taken in vital areas to correct some of the existing problems and abuses of Jewish tradition under the guise of Kashruth. For example, the United Synagogue became the first institution supervising Kashruth to look at this tenet of Judaism not as a separate entity unto itself, but as a segment of the totality of Judaism. The practical application of this principle introduced a revolutionary approach to Kashruth supervision. While the existing Kashruth supervising agencies were willing to accept catering places for Kashruth supervision, even where the Sabbath and holy days were violated, on the principle that so long as the food was Kosher the violation of other commandments of the Jewish tradition were not their immediate concern, the leaders of Conservative Judaism refused to accept this kind of reasoning. Kashruth, they claimed, must not be the handmaiden of American economy. It cannot be used to excuse the violations of the more vitally important Jewish Sabbaths and holy days. As a representative of Judaism, although in a limited way, a Kosher catering hall must not permit violations of the sanctity of Jewish life so that those who come to celebrate an occasion of life there will not be given reason to think that so long as the place is Kosher, all other irreligious and unsavory activities may go on under the protective umbrella of Kashruth. The Kashruth Department of the United Synagogue does not accept for Kashruth supervision any Kosher catering which is served on the Sabbath or on holy days.

The moral issues of Jewish life which were intertwined with Kashruth were of equal concern to the rabbinic and lay members of the Conservative Kashruth Department. They established a pay scale which would provide a living wage to a *mashgiach* so that he did not have to seek "side money" to supplement his income. For example, no *mashgiach* who is supervising Kashruth under the sponsorship of the Conservative movement is permitted to take food or liquor home from the catering place that he is supervising, a practice which is countenanced by other Kashruth agencies. He may not officiate at any other religious function, such as a wedding or Bar Mitzvah, in addition to being a *mashgiach* on the premises; he must devote his entire attention to the specialized task of Kashruth supervision. He dare not accept any gratuities from the suppliers of food to the catering establishment as the result of his having approved the purchase of a Kosher product. On one occasion, a *mashgiach* who was employed by the Conservative movement as a supervisor wrote to the suppliers of the catering hall where he was supervising Kashruth, asking them to make contributions to a charity in which he was interested. Those suppliers who did not respond to his appeal were denied further business from the catering establishment by order of the *mashgiach*. When knowledge of this extortive practice became known to the Kashruth Department, the *mashgiach* was suspended immediately from further service to the Kashruth Department.

The Kashruth Committee has also turned its attention to the growing problem of extravaganza Bar Mitzvah celebrations which have, in many instances, deteriorated into vulgar orgies. A strong statement was issued to all Conservative congregations reminding them that the Bar Mitzvah experience, whether in the temple during the worship, or at the catering hall where the reception is held, must at all times retain the sanctity of a religious occasion.

While there are a number of committees for Kashruth throughout the Conservative movement, only the New York Metropolitan Region of the United Synagogue maintains an office and employs a Director of Kashruth. Created in the late Spring of 1961, the Kashruth Department of the New York Metropolitan Region was given the mandate of fulfilling the following resolution:

"Whereas we are vitally interested in furthering the observance of Kashruth, be it resolved that we will . . . work in cooperation with the Rabbinical Assembly of America (the rabbinic arm of the Conservative movement) and welcome the cooperation of other organizations and individuals interested in furthering Kashruth and raising the standards in United Synagogue congregations."

The following goals were designated for the Kashruth Department:

1. To enter all areas of Kashruth problems and standards;
2. To cooperate with all bodies interested in Kashruth and work towards fostering a community-wide organization to further Kashruth;
3. To enter into negotiations with any establishment desiring Kashruth supervision which is not supervised by any other organization;
4. To conduct such surveys which will discover the standards, rules, and practices of Kashruth in the Conservative congregations and recommend upgrading them wherever necessary;
5. To search for ways and means of strengthening Kashruth in our congregations and also in the community;
6. To publish and publicize information about Kashruth.[34]

The Conservative leadership is unique in its attitude towards other organizations involved in Kashruth. Its expressed purpose is to strengthen Kashruth within the community as well as within its congregations. To achieve this end, rule No. 2 expresses the willingness of the Conservative leadership to cooperate with all groups, institutions, and organizations involved in Kashruth supervision. Such a desire to work with others who are interested in Kashruth is found as a positive precept within the Conservative Kashruth program, but unfortunately, is not often reciprocated by a cooperative attitude emanating from the other Kashruth groups.

In spite of the fledgling image which the Conservative Department of Kashruth represents because of its newness in the field of Kashruth, the United Synagogue has made significant contributions to raising the standards of Kashruth. Several flagrant violations were uncovered and reported to the proper agencies. The report of the Kashruth Committee, dated March 1966, relates the respect which this new body was able to achieve in the short time of its existence.

"One by-product of our campaign to eliminate dishonesty in the area of Kashruth was recognition by law enforcement agencies of our reliability. On four occasions we were consulted by the New York City Markets Commissioner and the District Attorney in preparing cases against violators of the existing ordinances. Our experience in this area has revealed that both New York State and New York City have inadequate enforcement procedures. Twice we have been requested to introduce remedial legislation. We are prepared to undertake this important area of activity and have volunteered lay leadership willing to assist in this neglected field." [35]

The Kashruth Department of the United Synagogue, like other Kashruth supervising agencies, has accepted catering establishments and congregations where catering services are provided, and is maintaining Kashruth supervision in them. Its future plans include entering those areas of the Jewish community in America where a sizable demand for Kosher foods presently exists, but is not yet being met. Such places as colleges where a large number of Jewish students are enrolled; airlines' arrival and departure points; ship lines and small communities where no Kosher butcher shops are in operation, are some of the areas for which the

Conservative movement has begun programming. A special project of providing vending machines which would dispense Kosher foods at many of these places has been under careful consideration, and already steps have been taken to provide such a service.

In the spring of 1969, despite the enthusiastic plans and noteworthy successes, the New York Metropolitan Region's Department of Kashruth was closed by the region's officers. The reason given for concluding the Kashruth department's activities was a lack of funds to continue its operations.

The Dietary Laws

4   The denominations of Judaism have varying views on the value of the Dietary Laws as eternally relevant religious teachings. Orthodoxy does not waver in its complete acceptance of the total Mitzva of Kashruth. It is part of the Torah given to Moses on Mt. Sinai, and as such is immutable. Reform Judaism, on the other hand, set the laws of Kashruth aside when the founders of the movement established their constitution of religious practice and belief. Among the articles drawn up in November 1885 in Pittsburgh, known as the "Pittsburgh Platform," there appears the following statement regarding Kashruth: Article 4: "We hold that all such Mosaic and rabbinical laws as regulate diet, priestly purity, and dress originated in ages and under the influence of ideas entirely foreign to our present mental and spiritual state. They fail to impress the modern Jew with a spirit of priestly holiness; their observance in our days is apt rather to obstruct than to further modern spiritual elevation." [1]

Conservative Judaism arose as a means of curtailing the spread of Reform Judaism in America. In 1824 the first Reform Jewish congregation was already established in

Charleston, South Carolina. It was essentially a way of Judaism that expressed dissatisfaction with Orthodoxy. As the voice of protest against Orthodoxy grew stronger, the leaders of the Jewish community who wanted to see change brought about, but were not so radical in their thinking, established a new standard of Judaism called "Conservative," which as its name implies, was intended to "conserve" Orthodox Judaism while allowing innovations so that it would become more palatable to the Jew living in America. In his initial report, as president of the newly established Jewish Theological Seminary of America, the first representative institution of the new Conservative trend, Rabbi Sabato Morias stated the underlying principles and purposes of Conservative Judaism.

"At the basis of our Seminary lies the belief that the Pentateuch was in all truth inspired by the Living God to promulgate laws for the government of a people sanctified to an imprescriptible mission; that the same laws embodied in the Pentatuech, have unavoidably a local and general application. Those comprised in the first category lose their force outside of Palestine, the others are obligatory elsewhere; but both the former and the latter, being of necessity broadly formulated, needed in all ages a formal interpretation. The traditions of the forefathers are therefore coeval with the written statutes of the five holy books. That these truths have not been denied by any of the prophets who succeeded Moses, that our sainted seers laid the greatest stress upon moral injunctions, simply because ceremonial observances were mistakenly regarded by many of their contemporaries as an exemption from the principles of social rectitude, the founders of the Jewish Theological Seminary hold as their credo." [2]

The elaboration of the thinking expressed by Rabbi Morais detailed the commitment of Conservative Judaism to the traditional patterns of observance. "Judaism must stand or fall by that which distinguishes it from other religions as well as by that which it has in common with them . . ." they declared. There could be no compromise with any acts which would ultimately end in the abandonment of the Torah. Thus when the United Synagogue of America was founded by the Conservative congregations already in existence, as a "union of congregations for the promotion of traditional Judaism," the preamble to its constitution explicated that Conservative Jews would be dedicated to the historic traditions of Judaism, among them especially the observance of the Dietary Laws.

Reconstructionism, the newest denomination in Judaism, began to take shape with the publication of Rabbi Mordecai Kaplan's book, *Judaism As A Civilization*, in May 1934. The principles of Reconstructionist Judaism may be summed up in the following statement from this original work: "Reconstructionism holds that previously enunciated programs or patterns of Jewish life are inadequate to solve the problems that confront the Jews in the modern world. It therefore suggests a new approach, which accepts from Orthodoxy its emphasis upon the need for the maximum of Jewish life and from Reform, the method of change and development. Reconstructionism conceives of Judaism as a civilization with its own language, land, history, tradition, laws, religion, and art. It maintains that Jews can find a deep satisfaction in the knowledge and the cultivation of that civilization. It maintains that adherence to Judaism should no longer be judged by the acceptance of a creed but by participation in the total life of the "Jewish people."

The leaders of Reconstructionism were deeply concerned over the alienation from Judaism of so many modern Jews. Their solution, however, differed from any already recommended by the other branches of Judaism in that they stressed the esthetic, rather than the religious elements of Judaism. The creative arts, music, drama, and literature took on new dimensions of importance for Judaism. The stablization of observances so urgently desired by the traditionalists was avoided by the Reconstructionists, who recommended a reevaluation of existing Jewish practices by each generation. Thus, Kashruth, as well as other Jewish traditional activities, was left open and without the force of support by the movement. Reconstructionism, by its very nature, did not comment specifically upon the value of Kashruth as a desirable precept that was fixed in the roster of Jewish practices. It remains for each generation and congregation to decide upon the place of the Dietary Laws in the Jewish life style of the time.

The Jewish Tradition of Kashruth

The *Mitzvah* of Kashruth began to evolve with Noah and his Ark.

"Noah was a righteous man in his generation," [3] says the Torah. This implies that Noah was a God-fearing man. And according to our sages, he anticipated the commandments of the Dietary Laws centuries before they were presented to the Jewish people at Mount Sinai. The Bible records that he took into his ark "clean" (Kosher) animals and those that were "not clean" (*trayfe*). As it is written, "Of every clean beast thou shalt take to thee seven and seven, each with his mate; and of the beasts that are not clean two and two, each with his mate." [4] Our sages interpret the words "clean" and "not clean" as references to the animals which in the future would be labelled as Kosher and *trayfe*.

How did Noah distinguish between those animals which were Kosher and those which were *trayfe?* A Kosher animal has two characteristics which separate it from all the other animals in the world; it has a cloven hoof and it chews its cud. An animal having just one of these signs is not Kosher. Therefore, the pig, which has a cloven hoof, is not Kosher because it does not chew its cud. A camel is not Kosher, even though it chews its cud, because it does not have a cloven hoof. Horse meat is forbidden to observant Jews because it neither chews its cud nor has a cloven hoof. Noah became involved in the Dietary Laws without really comprehending the significance of them except to know that such was God's will. However, for us who have an overview of the lives and deeds of all the forefathers mentioned in the Bible, there arises an awareness that the Dietary Laws were part of the Divine Plan from the very beginning. Ultimately, man was to learn that all of life possesses that which is "clean" and that which is "not clean," and wise men learn to distinguish between the two for their peace of mind.

There are fish that are Kosher, and those that are *trayfe*. Kosher fish display two signs also: they bear fins and scales. Jews are forbidden to eat any form of sea life which does not display these two signs of Kashruth. Therefore, any hard-shelled sea foods, such as lobsters, crabs and shrimp are excluded as *trayfe*. Examples of Kosher fish are pike, carp, bass, and sable.

Birds are in a category all their own. Those which are wild and birds of prey are *trayfe*, while those which have been domesticated are Kosher. This rule produces the anomaly that one specie of bird may be both Kosher and *trayfe*, as for example the pheasant or turkey. Those which are raised on a farm are Kosher. Turkeys or pheasants which are wild are *trayfe*.

Insects are also classified as Kosher and *trayfe* by the Torah's specific selection. "All winged swarming things that go upon all fours are a detestable thing unto you. Yet these things may ye eat of all winged swarming things that go upon all fours, which have jointed legs above their feet, wherewith to leap upon the earth; even these of them may ye eat: the locust after its kinds, and the bald locust after its kinds, and the cricket after its kinds, and the grasshopper after its kinds. But all winged swarming things are a detestable thing unto you." [4]

Fruits and vegetables are Kosher without qualification. There are no *trayfe* fruits or vegetables.

The Prohibition of Eating Blood

The Torah established the prohibition against eating blood by declaring, "Thou shalt not eat blood; thou shalt pour it out upon the ground as water." [5] This negative commandment is repeated a number of times throughout the Bible. The Torah reasons that the soul resides in the blood, and it is unbefitting for human beings to be so insensitive as to devour an animal for food completely—to consume the flesh and the blood together.

The method of removing the blood from the animal, however, became a matter of rabbinic law. The Jewish method of slaughter, *shechita*, removes the major quantity of blood by the cutting of the veins in the throat. In the home, the remaining blood is removed from the meat that has been brought from the butcher shop by the following process: *First,* the meat is soaked in cold water for a half-hour in order to soften the meat so that the blood will come out easily and, in addition to remove any surface blood on the meat. *Second,* the meat is carefully salted on all its sides and in its crevices. The salt that is used must be coarser than ordinary table salt so that it will not deteriorate before the task of removing the blood has been completed. *Third,* the salt that has become saturated with the withdrawn blood is washed off by soaking the meat momentarily in cold water and pouring the water off. This soaking and pouring-off process is repeated three times with fresh, cold water each time.

An alternate method of withdrawing the blood is broiling the meat. Meat that is broiled need not be Koshered by salting.

Because of the concern over eating blood, certain special laws were promulgated. For example, liver is so filled with blood that salting is considered to be insufficient to withdraw all the blood from it. The rabbis ordained that broiling is the only method acceptable for Koshering liver because only such intense heat is strong enough to draw out the blood and burn it up (a precaution to be observed is to rinse off the blood that has come to the surface of the meat or liver after it has been broiled.) Similarly, the heart is an organ through which a massive amount of blood passes. Therefore, before Koshering the heart by the process of salting, the housewife is required to cut it in criss-cross fashion so that the salt can penetrate more readily into all areas. (For blood on eggs see ques. 21, Chap. VI)

The Separation of Meat and Milk Foods

The Kosher Laws require a separation of meat and milk foods. This practice arose from the repeated statement in the Torah, "Thou shalt not cook a kid in its mother's milk." [6] This verse appears in the Torah no less than three times, and because it is repeated, the rabbis drew from this emphasis a broader interpretation than they might normally have. Their explanation of this verse resulted in the structure of the laws separating meat from milk foods. They said in essence, "The Torah forbids not only the cooking of a kid in its mother's milk, but the cooking of any meat in milk." The Torah forbids, in addition, eating meat and milk together, cooked or cold, during the same meal. An observant Jew waits a bit of time between the eating of meat and milk because the flavor of a meat meal lingers in the mouth. While it is true that customs vary as to the amount of time that one should wait between eating meat and then milk, most Jews wait six hours after eating meat before they eat dairy; other Jews (German Jews, for example) wait three hours. The reverse procedure, however, does not apply. There is no requirement to wait any length of time after eating dairy foods before eating meat. One need only rinse out the mouth to remove any particles of dairy that might have remained in the mouth before eating meat. This law of not waiting between dairy and meat does not apply to dairy foods which are sharp and have lasting flavor and therefore require the usual waiting period before eating meat. For example, a sharp cheese that has been aged for a long time is assumed to have a lasting flavor, and therefore requires waiting six hours before eating meat.

Other laws which are related to this prohibition, require two sets of kitchenware, dishtowels, separate tablecloths, napkins, etc.

The Dietary Laws and Health Precautions

One of the accepted premises regarding the laws of Kashruth is that they are basically laws of cleanliness and health. While this idea might be challenged as not representing the official basis for the dietary laws of Kashruth, there are in the Dietary Code, nevertheless, laws which determine the diet of observant Jews and which are concerned primarily with health. An example of this is the law which forbids eating meat and then fish. This law is based on the belief that doing so can be injurious to health. The reverse, however, eating fish before meat, is permissible provided the particles of fish are thoroughly rinsed from the mouth first.

The Special Dietary Laws of Passover

The holiday of Passover places special dietary demands upon the observant Jew. The basic law of Passover, which controls the diet on these holy days, forbids eating foods that are considered *chometz* (leaven). The Torah declares: "Seven days shall there be no leaven found in your houses: for whosoever eateth that which is leavened, that soul shall be cut off from the congregation of Israel, whether he be a sojourner, or one that is born in the land. Ye shall eat nothing leavened; in all your habitations shall ye eat unleavened bread." [8] *Chometz* includes various kinds of grains such as wheat, barley, oats, rye and spelt which ferment, other forbidden foods include baking-powder, yeast, starches and rice. Because of this law of chometz, bread, cake, biscuits, all liquids which contain ingredients or flavors made from grain alcohol, unsupervised canned and processed foods, jellies, shortenings, and relishes are examples of forbidden products.

Because of the intricacies of the Passover dietary laws, some confusion inevitably exists in the minds of some people regarding the idea of prohibiting fermented foods. It should be clearly understood that fermentation per se is not forbidden by the Torah, as is evidenced in the use of wine, which is fermented, in the Seder home service. It is only the grains enumerated in the Torah which are forbidden when they are fermented. In order to assure the observant housewife that her home is properly prepared for the Passover, there is a large amount of foods which are now manufactured under rabbinic supervision, testifying to the fact that no *chometz* is contained in them.

Most vegetables are permitted on Passover, but peas and beans are forbidden. While many observant families do not eat string beans on Passover, considering them beans, others who are observant do eat string beans, because in the case of the string bean, the bean remains within the pod and is not evident.

Some of the foods which are permissible when they have rabbinic supervision are matzos, cakes, candies, noodles, beverages, dried fruits, liquors, bottled milk, butter, cheeses, etc.

There are foods which do not require any rabbinic supervision, and may be eaten on Passover. Such foods are fresh fruits and vegetables (except those mentioned earlier). Fruits and vegetables normally permitted in their

natural state are permitted when frozen provided no questionable additives have been included, and if the fruits and
vegetables have not been pre-cooked or processed so as to
create a Kashruth problem. Coffee, tea, sugar, salt, and
pepper do not need rabbinic supervision if they are taken
from packages that are opened first on Passover. This requirement that the package not be opened prior to its use
on the Passover assures that no ingredient of *chometz* has
fallen into the package.

A brief explanation is appropriate here regarding the
permissibility of eating dairy foods on Passover, because a
change of attitude has created a creditability gap between
the practice of the previous generation regarding dairy
products, and the current tradition of most American Jewish families. There is a debate in the Talmud concerning
the use of dairy products on Passover. One opinion holds
that inasmuch as the milk which the cow manufactures
derives from the food that the cow eats, if that food was
chometz, then the milk is forbidden as a derivative of
chometz and may not be used on Passover.

The other opinion holds that it is of no consequence
what food the cow has eaten because the food has been
digested and absorbed into the blood stream, which in turn
has manufactured the milk. Therefore, dairy products as
such are permissible on Passover.

The previous generation of European Jews generally
respected the first opinion and therefore preferred not to
use dairy products on Passover unless it could be ascertained that the cows producing the milk for Passover had
not been fed the forbidden grains which were *chometz*.
Current practice, however, follows the second, more lenient attitude, and therefore permits the use of dairy products

provided they have been processed under rabbinic supervision at the dairy plant.

The Koshering Process
Preparing the Home for Passover

Like the foods eaten on Passover, so too do the dishes and utensils used for the holiday require special attention. Only such that are reserved for Passover use, or have been "Koshered" especially for use during the festival, are acceptable. The same process of Koshering silverware, pots, pans, and glassware which applies at all times during the year, pertains to Passover as well. Theoretically, it involves a simple principle of the science of physics—metal will expand when heated sufficiently, and will contract when cooled. Therefore, to Kosher a pot or piece of silverware that has been made *trayfe* by putting it into a hot food (as for example, a dairy spoon that was used inadvertently to mix a boiling meat soup), the following steps are necessary:

1. Scour and clean carefully the spoon that is to be Koshered.
2. Set the spoon aside and do not use it for twenty-four hours.
3. Immerse the spoon in boiling water for a few moments.
4. Remove the spoon from the boiling water and place it in cold water for a few moments. The spoon is now a Koshered piece of silverware, and can be used again.

(Incidentally, the spoon is now neutral and can be used for meat or dairy.)

The foregoing procedure may be used to Kosher metalware. Certain exceptions to the Koshering process, however, are mentioned by the rabbis. For example, a metal knife or fork with a handle of wood, plastic, or some other material that has been glued on, may not be Koshered. This is because the rabbis feared that because the glued-on handle might come off when the knife was dipped in the boiling water, the person Koshering the piece would be afraid to immerse it completely in the boiling water as required, and the piece of silverware would not be Koshered properly. In such a case, if the item is an especially valuable one, the owner of it should consult a rabbi for guidance. Table glassware may be permitted for Passover use after soaking for seventy-two hours, changing the water every twenty-four hours. Fine, translucent chinaware, if not used for a year, may be permitted for Passover use as well as for use during the rest of the year.

Metalware, such as spits and wires, that is used for broiling during the year may be Koshered by the procedure outlined above in steps 1 and 2, except that instead of immersing it in boiling water, it must be placed upon the fire and allowed to become white-hot before immersing it in cold water.[9]

Special Food Customs In Judaism

In addition to the formal legalism of the dietary laws, there exists in Judaism a group of informal customs which involve foods. These customs of eating special foods and not eating certain other foods have to do with the unique observances of Judaism, and therefore are special dietary laws in that they are observed only at the various holidays.

For example, the cycle of the Jewish year begins with Rosh Hashanah, the Jewish New Year. Traditionally, on this most important of holy days, a bottle of honey appears on the festive table. Custom bids the Jew, after having pronounced the blessing over the bread, to dip a piece of *challah* in the honey to symbolize the hope that the coming days of the New Year will be filled with the sweetness of God's blessings. In addition to the *challah*, a piece of apple may also be dipped in the honey. The reason for apple being chosen rather than some other fruit is that Rosh Hashanah, according to Jewish tradition, marks the time of the creation of the world. It is a time to recall the purity of the earth, and man's life at the dawn of time. The apple, on the other hand, symbolizes man's fall from grace when Eve disobeyed God's commandment not to eat from the tree of knowledge. Traditionally, it was the apple tree from which Eve was given fruit to eat by the serpent. The custom of dipping the apple in honey is a symbolic act expressing the hope that this original sin will be forgiven, turning the bitter wrath which it incurred into the sweetness of God's forgiveness.

Carrots are eaten on Rosh Hashanah because the Yiddish word for carrots is *meren* which means to "increase, or to multiply." Thus, the Jew reiterates the hope that the Jewish nation will increase greatly in numbers during the coming year—so much so that Jews will no longer be a small people, an oppressed minority. This is a hope that is based upon the promise stated in the Bible as part of the covenant which God made with Abraham, our forefather, as it is written: "And he brought him forth abroad and said, look now toward the heaven and count the stars if thou be able to count them. And he said unto him, so shall thy seed be." [10]

The Jew hopes for that day when he will be so large a people that no other nation will dare to oppress him. It is a hope, each year, that at last the Jew will know peace and an end to his suffering as a persecuted nation.

A similar hope is revealed in the presence of the cooked head of a fish on the dinner table. This symbol expresses the hope that the New Year will see the Jewish nation redeemed and at the head of the nations of the world rather than at the tail as a small, downtrodden people.

The vision of our prayers rising heavenward is expressed in the special way that the *challah* is prepared for Rosh Hashanah. There are two traditions which effect the making of the *challah* for Rosh Hashanah. One custom is to make the *challah* round, with the center section tending upwards. The other is to design the top of the *challah* in the shape of a ladder. Both of these symbolize the hope that our prayers will ascend to God on high and be acceptable before Him.

Spicy foods are avoided on Rosh Hashanah because they are usually bitter, and this holiday is one on which sweetness is the thought of the day. In addition, bitterness is reminiscent of harsh judgment and of difficult, bitter experiences. Jews do not approach God on this holiday of judgment with the fear that God will condemn them during the coming year to suffer bitterness in their lives. Our faith teaches us that God will administer his judgment of us with much mercy.

On Yom Kippur, of course, there is no food eaten during the twenty-four hour fast. However, in order to facilitate and lighten the burden of the fast, the rabbis established certain guidelines for the afternoon meal preceding the holiday. Thirst-inducing foods are avoided during this meal, and the foods that are light and without spicy embelishments should be eaten. One food in particular is avoided at the meal which introduces the fast. Nuts of any kind are not eaten. The reasons for this prohibition is that nuts induce an abundance of saliva in the mouth and create a thirst which should not be induced. Also, the mystics point out that the Hebrew word for "nut" has the same numerical computation as the Hebrew word for "sin." For this reason also, nuts are not eaten on the eve of Yom Kippur, the day when we hope to atone for our sins. We do not choose to awaken any thought of sins, even through so small a symbolism as eating nuts.

The Festival of Sukkos is related to the days of Rosh Hashanah and Yom Kippur because it is said that the period of judgment, in some of the more difficult cases, continues until Hoshanah Rabbah, the last day of Chol Hamoed Sukkos. Therefore, at the meals of the festival, the symbolic honey, with its message of sweetness, is still found. While no other symbolic foods are customarily eaten on Sukkos, it is recommended that a new fruit, not yet eaten during the new year, should appear on the table as part of the meal on the second night. Often this new fruit is a pomegranate.

Most unique, however, is the Sukkos law which requires that during the festival meals be eaten in the Sukkah booth. On the first two nights especially, even in the event of rain, observant Jews will eat some part of the festival meal in the Sukkah.

The next major holiday on the Jewish religious calendar is the Festival of Passover. Unlike Rosh Hashanah, which emphasizes sweet foods, this holiday focuses upon the eating of bitter foods as a reminder of the bitterness of slavery which our forefathers experienced in Egypt. As already noted in the chapter which discussed the Dietary Laws, the

primary symbolic food of the Passover observance is matzoh. There are other foods, however, that are similarly
important. These appear on the Seder plate, and are employed during portions of the home Seder service. For
example, there is the mixture of nuts, cinnamon, apples, and
wine called, "*Charoseth,* which symbolizes the mortar used
by the Jewish slaves in building the cities of Pharaoh. The
salt water symbolizes the tears which our forefathers shed
because of the tortures visited upon them by their taskmas-
ters. The bitter herbs are eaten to give the participant a
symbolic taste of the bitterness of a slave's life. The roasted
shankbone of a lamb on the seder plate is not eaten. It
symbolizes the outstretched arm by which the Almighty
redeemed His children from slavery. The roasted egg is a
reminder of the ancient sacrificial offering which was burnt
on the altar in Solomon's temple. A green leafy vegetable is
eaten during the course of the evening to remind everyone
that Passover is also a spring-harvest festival.

While telling the story of the Exodus from Egypt, four
cups of sweet wine are drunk. The sweet sacramental wine
often appears in Jewish rituals because it is symbolic of the
sweet joy which every Jew should feel as he hears of the
miracles which the Divine Power performed in order to
rescue the oppressed. Therefore, during the reading of the
Passover story from the Haggadah, as the ancient promise
of redemption is repeated in its forefold expression, the
traditional four cups of wine are raised and blessed, and
each person drinks from them as a sign that even we, who
are not enslaved, rejoice in the freedom granted our forefathers. The Haggadah reminds us, "For if the Holy One,
blessed be He, had not redeemed our forefathers, then we
and our children and our children's children would still be
enslaved unto Pharaoh in Egypt." [11]

The final morsel of matzo which is eaten at the conclusion of the Seder service is taken as the *afikomen* (the ceremonial dessert).

The last of the biblical holidays observed during the cycle of the year is Shavuos, the Festival of Weeks, which commemorates the time when the Jews received the Torah on Mt. Sinai centuries ago. On Shavuos it is customary to eat dairy products. Cheese blintzes are traditional because the wisdom of the Torah was compared by our sages to "milk and honey." Tradition suggests that on the eve of this holiday, special sessions on the study of Torah and other Jewish books of sacred knowledge be undertaken. Those able to do so spend the entire night studying, completing their learning in time for a sunrise morning worship service. Following such an intense experience of study and worship, the tradition takes us one step further, replacing the customary holiday meat meal with a dairy one, providing a special climax to our excursion into the wisdom of Torah, which, it is presumed, was a spiritually sweet experience.

The rabbinic holidays have their own special dishes which enrich the observances of the period. For example, on Chanukah, the Festival of Lights, it is customary to eat potato pancakes called *latkes*. These are eaten to commemorate the dedication of the women in the towns, hamlets, and cities of Judea who shared in the battle for freedom in their own special way by providing the Maccabee guerilla fighters with batches of potato pancakes as their staple food. The Maccabees had raised the banner of revolt against the Greek-Syrians who had invaded their small country, and successfully drove the foreigners from the soil of the holy land.

The methods of warfare employed by the Maccabees in many ways set the pattern of guerilla warfare employed by future freedom-fighters. The Maccabees lived in the forests and the mountain caves, which gave them excellent concealment, but made food very scarce for them. The women of Judea, therefore, hit on the idea of giving them the kind of food which could be quickly prepared, readily carried, and did not spoil easily, in addition to being satisfying. The potato pancake or *latke* was the solution to the Maccabee food problem. It has been enjoyed by generations of Jews ever since.

On Purim, the Festival of Lots, the traditional food is a cake called *Hamantaschen*, which is like a popover cake. It is usually filled with prunes or poppy seeds. The *Hamantaschen* is triangular in shape, symbolizing to many people the hat worn by the tyrant Haman who plotted to destroy the Jews of ancient Persia. Others have it that the shape of the *Hamantaschen* originated with Haman's ears, while still others are of the opinion that the design of the festival cake came from the shape of Haman's pockets.

The minor holiday of Hamisha Asar Bishvat, popularly known as *Tu Bishvat*, observes that occasion called the "New Year of the Trees" which is recorded in the Talmud. During the period of the year marked by *Tu Bishvat*, all plant life is judged by the Almighty for the rest of the year. On this day, therefore, children in the Hebrew schools are given fruits to eat so that they may pronounce the blessing over them and pray to God for a good year of plentiful harvests. The fruits of Israel are especially popular for the holiday of *Tu Bishvat*.

During the summer months the Three Weeks are observed as a minor period of mourning in commemoration of the siege of Jerusalem and the destruction of the temple. The last nine days of this period of mourning, which culminate in the Fast of Tisha B'Av, the Ninth Day of the Jewish Month of Av, the day upon which, according to tradition, both the first and the second temples were destroyed, reflects a spirit of national sadness. As a symbol, during these nine days, observant Jews abstain from drinking wine or eating meat except on the Sabbath, when chicken meat only is permitted. Weddings are also forbidden on these days, beginning with the onset of the Three Weeks. These personal sacrifices of not eating or drinking foods that "gladden the heart," among other acts of self-sacrifice, express the sadness of the Jewish people over the destruction of their temple and homeland, but more than this alone, man's evil design is memorialized, and the hope for the coming of a new day of universal brotherhood is expressed.

It is traditional to serve hard-boiled eggs to those who mourn the death of a loved one at their first meal upon returning from the funeral. The symbolism of the egg is that it is without an opening—or "without a mouth." So too are the mourners who are speechless with grief over their loss and therefore need to be consoled by friends and neighbors.

An almost forgotten custom is the eating of *arbes* (chick peas) at Jewish family celebrations such as a wedding, briss, or Bar Mitzvah, to symbolize the hope that the joys of life will continually increase.

On the Sabbath, Jewish tradition bids us to take two *challahs* at the Sabbath meal reminiscent of the double *challah* which graced the altar of the Temple in Jerusalem.

Glatt *Kosher Meat—*
Jewish Milk

5   In recent years a new title—*"glatt Kosher* meat"—
has become popular among both the observant and non-observant Jews. Many have used the terminology without
quite fully understanding its meaning. To some, the words
"glatt Kosher" have implications of a whole new set of
commandments related to the Dietary Laws. This is not so.
Glatt Kosher is not a new law of Kashruth. The great stress
upon the observant housewife to purchase only *glatt* Kosher meats arose in recent years in the Chasidic community,
particularly with the *Satmer Rebbi,* and from that vantage
point spread to other Chasidic and non-Chasidic Orthodox
Jews. There is a long, exciting history to the variations of
Jewish practice that have arisen over the centuries between
Chasidic and non-Chasidic or *Misnagdic* Jews, not only
in the areas of foods but in the overall style of Jewish life
which both communities of Jews accepted upon themselves. Chasidic Jews are given to a much more emotionally
charged Judaism, and follow their *Rebbis* with much
greater awe and dedication than do non-Chasidic Jews.
During the height of some of the quarrelsome years which
shook both Chasidic and *Misnagdic* communities, life and

limb were in danger when devotees of both sides clashed.

Between the years 1770–1790, one very volatile difference between the Chasidim and *Misnagdim* developed around the method of sharpening the *shechita* knives. The Chasidim adopted the custom of burnishing their *shechita* knives and at the same time honing the blade to an extremely fine sharp edge. They claimed that only by preparing the blade in such a fashion could the *shochet* inspect his knife carefully enough so that any imperfection could be easily discovered. Rabbi Shneor Zalman, b. Baruch of Liady, Lithuania (1747–1812), clarified the position of the Chasidim with the following statement: [1]

"Most of the *shochetim* at the present time employ a blunt and heavy knife. They are obliged to sharpen it much in order to eliminate every knick from the cutting edge and to make it keen enough to cut without pausing. Even then most of the *shochetim* do not obtain satisfactory results; for it is difficult to produce a flawless edge on a dull knife. We therefore favor the fine and highly polished blade.

"This decision of ours should not be taken to reflect upon the Kashruth of meat slaughtered by those who use the heavier knife." [1]

The *Misnagdom* objected to the use of the highly polished knives because, they complained, such a finely sharpened blade was easily prone to denting, which is forbidden by Jewish tradition as a *shechita* knife because it tears rather than cuts the flesh. They argued that a blade so finely sharpened became knicked with the very first cut into the tough skin of an animal that was slaughtered, and this put a special burden upon the *shochet* to sharpen his knife after each killing. What's more, they contended, the knife blade might become damaged even during the first act of *shechita* itself, and thus the very first animal could become a *nebelah*. The *Misnagdim* found support for their cause in a response written in Egypt by a Rabbi David, b. Solomon ibn Zimra (1479–1589). The case placed before Rabbi ibn Zimra concerned a *shochet* who tested his blade before *shechita* and found it to be perfect and without blemish. Following the *shechita*, he tested it again, but this time he found that the blade was dented. He questioned the rabbi regarding the Kashruth of the *shechita* and the condition of the slaughtered animal. Could it be sold to Jews as Kosher meat?

The rabbi responded to the question by declaring the animal a *nebelah-trayfe*. He added that the *shochet* was to be held responsible for the financial damage incurred by the beast's owner because "he (the *shochet*) should have taken heed not to slaughter with a knife that was too sharp." [2]

The Chasidim admitted that the response of Rabbi ibn Zimra was known to them, but nevertheless, the value of achieving a near perfect blade outweighed the fear of a possible dent in the blade. In the event such a thing came about, then the animal would be declared a *nebelah*. The *Misnagdim* countered by arguing that such an eventuality could and should be avoided by using a less highly sharpened blade.

The *Misnagdim* emphasized their position in this matter by threatening excommunication upon anyone who ate from the *shechita* of the Chasidim. The ban upon Chasidic *shechita* was announced publicly at the fair in Brody, Poland, on the 20th of Sivan, 1772. It declared:

"They make for themselves polished *shechita* knives not called for by the Talmud or the rabbinical authorities, knives which all the *shochetim* say cannot be used without "burrowing," "cutting outside the prescribed area," and "tearing." These burnished knives may not be mentioned in all the borders of our *kehillas* and their environs, they are of a certainty blemished with the taint of heresy. Meat slaughtered by these burnished knives are *nebelah* and *trayfe*. All the people of the *kehilla* are warned against eating such meat.

When one of our community chances to be in a strange town, let him inquire whether they employ these burnished knives there. If this is so let him not partake of any meat course, for even their dishes are *nebelah* and *trayfe*.

We command our *shochetim* sternly, let them not produce their knives for any stranger but only for a known rabbi, of a known community, and with the approval of the monthly administrator."[3]

In the community of Zelve, Poland, the Vilna ban was read to the entire populace with the following additional punishment:

"We place them (those who employ the burnished knives) in extraordinary excommunication: they shall not count toward a quorum in the synagogue; none shall give them lodging; their *shechita* is forbidden; none may transact business with them, marry with them or take part in their burial"[4]

Other European communities followed suit in declaring the meat of animals slaughtered by the Chasidim to be *nebelah*. In 1784 prominent *Misnagdic* rabbis issued a summarizing edict which accused the Chasidim of haughtiness in their insistence upon using the highly burnished knives. The edict said in part, "Why should they (the Chasidim) invent a new mode which our forefathers never knew, and by it stamp Jews as eaters of forbidden meat? What has led to this foolishness if not that they do it to glorify themselves before the masses, who themselves are innocent and scrupulous in the observance of the commandments." [5]

As the gap between the Chasidim and the *Misnagdim* widened, the Chasidim retaliated by acts of harassment against their *Misnagdic* rabbis in order to get rid of them. After the year 1815, especially in Galicia, Poland, Chasidim began to employ their own *shochetim* with the express purpose of compelling their local *Misnagdic* rabbi to leave the congregation. For example, one specific incident, involving a *shochet* named Hayim, came before Rabbi Joseph Saul Nathanson. Hayim, the *shochet*, acted in defiance of an opinion written by the recognized scholar, Rabbi Solomon Kluger, who forbade a *shochet* to pass as Kosher any animal found to have rotted and blistered lungs. In an effort to check Hayim's rebellious actions, the community hired a second *shochet* and ordered Hayim to slaughter only in the presence of the second man. Hayim refused to obey the ban on him, claiming that the new *shochet* did not know how to prepare the *shechita* knife properly.

The rabbi called the new man to his study, examined his qualifications in the preparation of the knife, and found him to be quite competent. When Hayim heard this, he declared that the rabbi and his congregation were "stuffing themselves with *trayfe*."

The rabbi hesitated to take direct action against Hayim. Instead, he sought a compromise solution in which both *shochetim* agreed not to slaughter except in each other's presence. Hayim requested the opportunity of asking a *shayla* of his Chasidic rabbi before agreeing to such a thing, but in reality he had no intention of asking his rabbi, as the facts later indicated. He simply continued to *shecht.*

As a last resort, sixty families joined their rabbi in his attempts to contain the rebellious Hayim. They signed a manifesto that they would not eat from Hayim's *shechita* until he yielded. Ultimately, Rabbi Nathanson stepped into the picture and called for Hayim's dismissal as community *shochet.* Rabbi Nathanson wrote harshly of Hayim in his decision, declaring, "It is a wonder to me how a Jewish community can countenance such a wicked, brazen, libelous, and untrustworthy man. He should be straightaway discharged from his post. Better to eat meat from gentile shops, which is but *trayfe,* than eat the meat of this man's slaughtering, which is both *trayfe* and the work of a man who violates his oath." [6]

The recent popularity of *glatt* Kosher meat is another incident of Chasidic independence from Misnagdic practice. There are many Jews who are confused by this sudden emphasis on *glatt* Kosher meat and consider it as if it were a whole new set of dietary requirements. The fact of the matter is that the concept of *glatt* Kosher meat is not a new phenomenon. It is discussed in the Talmud. Clarification of the *glatt* principle is as follows:

The word *glatt* means "smooth." As is generally known, the cow eats a good portion of its daily food requirement in the field. Often the grass which it eats is mixed with foreign objects that have a tendency to puncture the lungs as they pass down the esophagus of the cow into the upper stomach. A punctured lung raises the question of Kashruth because if the puncture is such that it does not heal, then the animal is *trayfe.* The Talmud states that if the punctures of the lung are covered over with scabs, however, then the animal may be accepted as Kosher.

After an animal is slaughtered by the *shochet*, it is opened, and the *shochet* places his hand inside the animal and feels the lungs. If he finds that scabs have formed on the lungs, he will have the lungs removed and examined or blown up so that he can test them and see if the punctures have been covered by scabs or not. If the scabs have healed the punctures of the lung, the animal is declared Kosher; if not it is declared *trayfe*. The Chasidic Satmer Rabbi and his followers recently began insisting upon *glatt* Kosher meat, that is meat which comes from an animal whose lungs were smooth (*glatt*) and without scabs of any kind. Such choosing of *glatt* Kosher meat only is commendable as a superpious requisite since non-*glatt* meat is also Kosher if the scabs have sufficiently healed the punctures. However, the unfortunate aspect of this new phenomenon in Kashruth is that it has been carried to an extreme by many Orthodox Jews, who naïvely have come to accept only *glatt* Kosher meat as really Kosher, and all other meats as questionable.

Jewish Milk

The Dietary Laws forbid Jews to eat the meat or drink the milk which comes from non-Kosher animals. In former times, when farms were small, and farmers had a limited number of milking cows, it was feared that in the event a farmer found the weight of the milk given by his cows insufficient to meet his quota for sale in the market place, he would milk a pregnant horse or a pig in order to obtain his full measure. Such mixing of milk from a non-Kosher animal made the entire batch *trayfe*. Therefore, as a precaution, the rabbis required Jews to drink only milk that was purchased from God-fearing Jews so that they could be certain that their milk was unquestionably Kosher. Hence comes the term "Jewish milk," which implies that the milk has been bought from reliable Jews. Although today Chasidic and very Orthodox Jews scrupulously purchase only *Chalav Yisroel* (Jewish milk), it is not likely that the same fear which prompted the rabbis of old to declare such an edict still has a basis in fact. Like the *glatt* Kosher meat, it is a matter of super-piety which is important only to those who observe it.

Questions that are Asked about Kashruth

6 1. What is the rationale for the Kashruth laws?

Answer: In the Torah there are two categories of law. One group of laws is known as *Din*, which means "justice." The laws that come under this category are laws of social justice, such as the laws found in the Ten Commandments, "Thou shalt not kill," "Thou shalt not steal," "Honor thy father and thy mother" etc.

The second category of laws is known as *Chok*, which means "law." The laws found in this group are without apparent rationale. They have no obvious meaning, and are accepted purely on faith alone. Examples of *Chok* laws are —the prohibition of wearing wool and linen in the same garment; the law of the Red Heifer which both purifies and defiles when the ashes are sprinkled. The laws of Kashruth are in the category of *Chok* laws. While it is true that health and moral reasons have been given as justifications for the observance of the Kashruth laws, these are unofficial, and superimposed upon the Kashruth code. What scientific reason can in fact be given for designating one animal as proper for food, and another as unfit for food?

A philosophic explanation of the acceptance of such

Chok laws is given by a contemporary who compares the Jewish people to the soldiers of an army. When a soldier receives an order from his commander to proceed along a certain line of action he need not understand every detail and reason of the necessary action. He must, however, follow the command with confidence in the wisdom of his commander and the faith that he would not order his soldiers into needless dangers. Observant Jews perceive these *Chok* laws in the same light. The Torah is replete with laws that are wise and just. Its overall wisdom has won the confidence of those who have drunk deeply of its sagacious words. The observant Jews are prepared to follow without question the few commandments which have no apparent reason because of the overall rational spiritual majesty of the Torah's teachings. (*See* "Kashruth As A Moral Force," page 1).

2. We were having a discussion at a friend's home, and during the course of the conversation someone mentioned that at one time tuna fish was not accepted as a Kosher fish. Is this true? Why?

Answer: Yes, it is true. Some years ago tuna was considered *trayfe* because it did not have any scales when it was sold in the market. However, as the science of ichthyology progressed and improved its methods of research it was capable of observing marine life in their natural habitat. It was then that it became known that the tuna fish did, in fact, have scales while it was in the water. On the basis of this new information the rabbis declared the tuna to be a Kosher fish, quoting the verse in Leviticus II:9 which states: "And these shall you eat from all that is in the water. All that has fins and scales in the *water*; in the *oceans*, *rivers* and *streams*, these may you eat." [1]

The rabbis interpreted this verse in the Torah which stresses the phrase "in the water" to imply that so long as the fish has scales while it is in the water, even though it loses them upon being drawn forth from the water, it is still to be considered a Kosher fish.

3. Is swordfish a Kosher fish?

Answer: The question of the Kashruth of swordfish is a hotly debated issue between the Orthodox and Conservative halachic authorities.

A careful study of the materials that have been published regarding the question of the Kashruth of swordfish leads to the conclusion that the dispute between the Orthodox and the Conservative regarding swordfish revolves around two questions: (1) Whether the scales of the swordfish are, in fact, scales, and not mere spiny protrusions from the body of the fish, and (2) Whether the fact that these "scales" are shed during the fish's growing process is a deciding factor whether the fish is either Kosher or *trayfe*.

The Orthodox position, headed by Dr. Moshe Tendler, who is a rabbi and Associate Professor of Biology at Yeshiva University, is that the scales which the swordfish has as a juvenile are not real scales, but merely "bony tubercles or expanded compressed platelike bodies." Rabbi Tendler declared such growths to be bony plates, and not the scales referred to in the Torah as the identifying symbol of Kosher fish.

Secondly, Rabbi Tendler challenged the Conservative movement's position permitting swordfish, stating that even if we accept the protrusions as real scales, the swordfish has them as a juvenile but loses them as an adult fish. According to Rabbi Tendler, there is no Jewish halachic authority who permits a fish as Kosher which is such a deviant that it loses its scales before reaching full mature growth.

However, the Conservative position headed by Rabbi Isaac Klein of Buffalo, New York, quotes the basic statement in the Torah which specifies that a fish, in order to be considered Kosher, must have fins and scales in the streams or rivers. Rabbi Klein quotes a letter from the Assistant Laboratory Director of the Bureau of Fisheries, the United States Department of the Interior, Mr. Bruce Collette, who refers to a fishery leaflet prepared by Isaac Ginsburg and published in 1951 which states, in part, ". . . as you can see from these references, swordfish do have scales as juveniles. They retain the scales until they are approximately four feet long. This means that most swordfish found in the markets no longer have scales although they once did." Having established the first requirement that swordfish do have scales, Rabbi Klein then quotes numerous rabbinic sources which in the past and present have permitted swordfish. For example (Darchay T'shuva),² "It is the widespread custom in all *Israel* to eat the swordfish called 'fish *ispada*' even though it has no scales when it comes out of the sea, because it is said that as a result of its excitement, it shakes and sheds its scales."

4. Is sturgeon a Kosher fish?

Answer: The question which surrounds the Kashruth of the sturgeon is similar to that of the swordfish, for this, too, is debated by the Orthodox and Conservative rabbinates. The Orthodox forbid eating sturgeon because, like the swordfish, it sheds its scales in the water while yet a juvenile. The Conservative rabbinate, on the other hand, considers the fact that the sturgeon fish once had scales is sufficient to make it Kosher. As in the case of the swordfish, the matter remains inconclusive between the two halachic bodies and, it becomes a matter of personal choice as to which of the two to follow.[3]

5. Is all caviar Kosher?

Answer: No. Only the caviar coming from Kosher fish is acceptable as Kosher. The questions about proper scales noted above played a major role in a recent court case involving caviar. A fish packaging company was recently fined by the New York State Kosher Law Enforcement Bureau for selling caviar as Kosher because it came from a fish which did not have proper scales. The caviar in question came from the lumpfish, which according to Dr. Tendler, does not have scales, only the questionable tubercles. Based upon Rabbi Tendler's decision, the court fined the company for misrepresenting the caviar of the lumpfish as Kosher.

6. Why don't Jews eat sirloin steak?

Answer: One of the basic laws of Kashruth is the prohibition of eating the *geed hanasheh*, the sciatic nerve, which runs along the back of the cattle from the middle downward. This *geed hanasheh* [4] must be removed from the body of the cattle in order to leave the rest of the meat Kosher. In countries like America, however, where Kosher and *trayfe* slaughtering are performed at the same abattoir, it is not economically wise to employ a trained person who can *traiber* the *geed hanasheh* from the body of the cattle, because it is an expensive and time-consuming procedure. It is much more to the advantage of the company to direct the lower portion of the cattle to the *trayfe* market. Because of this economic consideration, Jews in the United States do not eat sirloin steak which resides in the lower portion of

the body. In other countries where the slaughtering of
Kosher animals is completely under the jurisdiction of the
Jewish community, the profession of *traibering* is practiced. Jews in countries such as Israel enjoy sirloin steak
because the *geed hanasheh* is removed, leaving the rest of
the carcass Kosher.

7. Why aren't kidneys available in a Kosher butcher
shop?

Answer: The reply above applies to the kidneys also.
They are situated in the lower portion of the cattle's body,
and therefore are sold with the rest of the lower portion of
the animal to the non-Jewish trade.

8. Why do some Jews wait for six hours between eating
meat and dairy, while other Jews wait less time?

Answer: There are a variety of opinions presented in the
Shulchan Aruch [5] as to the required time to wait between
eating meat and dairy foods. Some sections of the Jewish
world adopted one tradition, while others accepted another. The Jews of Western Europe accepted upon themselves the more stringent requirement of waiting six hours
between eating meat and dairy. Other Jewish communities
accepted a lesser time requirement.

9. May liver be Koshered by salting?

Answer: No, liver may not be Koshered by salting. The
liver is the unique organ in the body which cleanses the
blood which is constantly passing through it so long as the
animal is alive. Therefore, because of the vast amount of
blood contained within the liver all the time, and particularly at the moment of shechita, the rabbis say, "the liver is
full of blood" and requires a more potent method of Koshering. Because of this, only broiling is accepted as the
proper method for Koshering liver. The Sefardic Jewish

tradition is an exception to this rule. Traditionally, the Sefardic rabbis have permitted their congregants to Kosher liver by salting as they do for the rest of the meat.

10. Is the letter "K," which appears on many food packages, acceptable as a symbol of Kashruth?

Answer: While the "K" may be accepted generally as being a symbol for the Kashruth of a product, and in most cases is in fact such a reliable symbol of Kashruth, the "K" is not a copyrighted symbol for Kashruth, and because of this may be misused. It is, therefore, wise for an observant Jew to make a careful inquiry when a doubt exists by writing to the rabbi whose name appears along with the "K" on the package. If no such rabbinic name appears on the product accompanying the "K," then it is best to write to the manufacturer to obtain the name of the supervising rabbi, and then to correspond with the rabbi directly to obtain an answer from him.

11. May I use the same dishwater for both meat and dairy?

Answer: Yes, a dishwasher may be used for both meat and dairy utensils. The following precautions should be taken, however:

(a) Meat and dairy dishes should not be washed at the same time;

(b) Hot water should be allowed to run through the empty dishwasher after it has been cleaned and before washing another set of dishes;

(c) Most authorities require separate trays (racks). There are some who do not require separate trays if they are metal. All, however, agree that if the trays are plastic, there should be one for meat and another for dairy.

12. What about separate sinks for meat and dairy dishwashing?

Answer: Meat and dairy dishes should not be washed in the same sink. It is well to have two separate sinks, if possible. However, if this is not available, the dairy dishes should be placed upon a tray or in a dishpan used *only* for this purpose, and meat dishes should be handled in the same manner, with a separate tray or pan for meat only.

13. Why must detergents have rabbinic testimony that they are Kosher?

Answer: Soaps and detergents have animal fats as a basic ingredient; therefore, in order for a soap or detergent to be acceptable for use in a Kosher home, it must have a rabbinic endorsement testifying to the fact that no *trayfe* animal fats have been included in its preparation.

The concern over the Kashruth of a soap or detergent arises over the fact that some of the detergent or soap might leave a residue on the dish. If such soap or detergent is not Kosher, then the residue on the dish, not being Kosher, can make the food served on it *trayfe*.

14. Is there a difference between the notation on the label of a food package reading "Vegetable Shortening" or "Pure Vegetable Shortening?"

Answer: According to the Department of Markets of New York City, when a food label carries the inscription "Vegetable Shortening" it is assumed to be pure, without any mixture of animal fats in it. However, it is wisest to purchase vegetable shortening that has rabbinic supervision.

15. Does all manufactured food require rabbinic supervision?

Answer: No, natural foods such as salt, sugar, coffee, tea, and the like do not require rabbinic supervision to guarantee Kashruth. These are usually free of any questionable mixtures. Other foods that are the result of more complicated processes do require rabbinic supervision to verify the fact of Kashruth. Foods such as cooked vegetables, fruits, breads, and cakes require Kashruth supervision because they may contain preservatives or flavorings that are questionable as regards Kashruth.

Other questions that could arise regarding cooked foods involve the utensils in which the food is prepared. For example, one food-producing plant could manufacture both Kosher and non-Kosher food products. The supervision of a *mashgiach* at the plant would insure the fact that the Kosher food product was not cooked in the *trayfe* pots. It is best to have the assurance of rabbinic supervision in order to remove any doubts. This can be readily noted by looking for the Kashruth symbol or notation on the package. If such a notation does not appear on the label, then it is wise to write to the company to inquire about the Kashruth of their product.

16. It is generally accepted that glass is not porous; therefore, may one set of glass dishes be used for both meat and dairy foods?

Answer: While it is true that glass does not absorb, and therefore, should be permitted for both meat and dairy, it has not been the practice in observant homes to actually serve both meat and dairy in the one set of glassware. Rabbis have not recommended the use of one set of glass dishes for both meat and dairy because of the fear of confusing the Kosher Jewish family as to the need for separating other dishes, that are not glass, for meat and dairy foods.

Pyrex dishes are in the same category as glass dishes, as regards the use of one set of dishes for both meat and dairy.

17. Is there a question about the Kashruth of cheeses?

Answer: Yes. A question of Kashruth applies to all hard cheeses, as for examples American, Muenster, Swiss, and Gouda. Most hard cheeses are made with a curdling agent called "rennet." This ingredient causes the milk to solidify so that it can readily be manufactured into a hard cheese. Rennet is a secretion found in the inner lining of the stomach of a pig, calf, lamb, or any other mammal. When this liquid is mixed with milk, it coagulates the milk readily, enabling the cheese manufacturer to make the cheese rapidly, rather than having to wait for the milk to sour. In order to be used in the process of making cheese that is to be eaten by Kashruth-observing Jews, the rennet must come from Kosher animals that have been slaughtered in accordance with the Jewish laws of *shechita.* Any cheese which does not conform to this requirement cannot be considered Kosher.

18. Why is gelatin considered to be *trayfe?*

Answer: Gelatin (or gelatine), unless specified as being Kosher, is usually *trayfe.* It is manufactured from the bones and skins of animals. Therefore, unless the bones and skins used in the manufacturing process are procured from Kosher animals, the gelatin is *trayfe.* (However, there appeared recently a statement from the Conservative Rabbinic Law Committee permitting Jello).

19. Is glycerine Kosher:

Answer: The problem with glycerine is similar to the problem noted above regarding the manufacture of gelatin. Glycerine is also usually derived from an animal source; therefore, unless it is manufactured from a Kosher animal it must be considered *trayfe*. (The same is true for glycerides and glycerin.)

20. Is it true that certain vitamins are *trayfe?*

Answer: Yes, some vitamins are derived from non-Kosher sources which, of course, would make them *trayfe*. For example, Vitamin D is a common additive to fortify milk, and can be derived from two sources; one of them is the liver of the shark. In such a case, it is derived from a *trayfe* fish and is, therefore, *trayfe*.

21. I have heard that special care must be taken when breaking open whole eggs for cooking. Is this true? If so, why?

Answer: Yes, it is true that when breaking raw eggs special care must be taken. This is so because Jews are forbidden to eat blood, and eggs may sometimes have blood in them. If the blood is on the yolk or white of the egg and cannot be removed without breaking the yolk, then the whole egg must be discarded. If the egg has been put into a batter or some preparation of food before the blood spot had been noted, then, if the whole egg (*yolk and albumen*) can be removed from the mixture, it should be taken out; if it cannot, then the whole mixture must be discarded.

22. Does condensed milk contain any ingredients that are *trayfe?*

Answer: No. There is nothing in condensed milk which is questionable.

23. Is Anchovy paste Kosher?

Answer: Yes, Anchovy paste is usually Kosher. However, because production procedures are prone to change, it is desirable to purchase Anchovy paste that has rabbinic supervision.

24. Recently I was eating at a Kosher restaurant, and in

a bowl on the table there were packets of saccharin marked
pareve. Why was such a marking necessary?

Answer: It was necessary to mark the packet of saccharin *pareve* because saccharin may contain lactose, which
is a milk derivative. If the saccharin is served with a meat
meal it should be free of lactose. Therefore, the packet on
your table was designated as *pareve* to assure you that it
contained no dairy products.

25. Is there such a food as "Kosher bacon"?

Answer: The term "Kosher bacon" is a commercial gim-
mick. The food referred to as "Kosher bacon" may take
either of two forms: It may be corned beef sliced thin so as
to resemble the strip of bacon and can be fried with eggs as
is bacon and eggs, or a vegetable product called "Baco
Chips," which may be available.

26. Recently I was shopping in a new Kosher butcher
shop that had just opened in my neighborhood. The
butcher had a special on sirloin steak. I understood that
sirloin steak is not Kosher. Is this new Kosher butcher
selling *trayfe* meats, or am I wrong about sirloin steak?

Answer: You are right about sirloin steak not being
acceptable here in America (see answer to question No. 6).
However, butchers who sell "sirloin steak" to the Kosher
trade are using the term "sirloin steak" loosely, in order to
attract customers. The truth of the matter is that the meat
which is being sold as "sirloin steak" is simply a slice of
meat cut to look like a sirloin steak, but is in reality a slice
of meat from the upper, Kosher portion of the cow.

27. I was with an Orthodox friend the other night. I
ordered a Manhattan cocktail. The friend told me that the
drink was not Kosher. Is this true?

Answer: Yes, it is probably true. A Manhattan is made of

whiskey and wine. The wine is the problem. Observant Jews do not drink wine that has not been made and bottled under rabbinic supervision. The possibility is that the wine mixed with the whiskey in your Manhattan was not Kosher wine, i.e., wine that was not bottled under rabbinic supervision.

28. I travel a great deal both for business and pleasure. A business acquaintance and I were discussing a recent trip, and he mentioned to me that whenever he flies he orders a Kosher meal. Do airlines provide Kosher food? If so, what must I do to get a Kosher meal on my next trip?

Answer: Yes, Kosher meals are available on airlines and ships. They are easily obtained by simply instructing your ticket agent to order a Kosher meal for you when making your reservation.

29. My children love candy, as do most children. Recently they were at a birthday party where Kosher candy was served. What is the question of Kashruth in candy?

Answer: Candy, like any other food product, might contain ingredients which are *trayfe,* such as gelatin or glycerine. Therefore, Kashruth-observing Jews will be careful to purchase only such candy as has rabbinic certification, which insures them that all products included in the manufacture of the candy are Kosher.

30. Is there a question of Kashruth related to ice cream?

Answer: Yes, there can be a question of Kashruth in ice cream because gelatin may be used in the production. It is best to inquire from the manufacturer to be sure.

31. When I buy chopped meat from a Kosher butcher, do I have to Kosher the meat?

Answer: This depends upon your butcher. Kosher butchers will sell both Koshered (salted) and non-Koshered chopped meat. It is necessary, therefore, to inquire if the chopped meat had been Koshered beforehand.

32. If I want to freeze my meat, are there any rules that I need to bear in mind?

Answer: Yes. Meat must be Koshered before it is frozen. This is done because Jewish tradition forbids allowing meat to remain un-Koshered (that is, still retaining the blood) for more than three days, because after this period the blood will no longer be removable by salting. This rule need not apply to such meat that is definitely to be broiled, such as liver or steak.

33. The apartment I live in has electric cooking. Is an electric broiler acceptable for broiling Kosher meats? Has it the same status as fire broiling? [11]

Answer: Yes. An electric broiler has the same status regarding Kashruth as a fire broiler. It may be used for broiling Kosher meats in the same manner as a fire broiler.

34. My job requires that I travel a great deal and often I find myself in a community where there is no Kosher eating place. Can you help me solve this problem of what to do about Kosher food? Are there foods that I can eat even in a non-Kosher restaurant?

Answer: This is a very difficult question. There are those who are very strict regarding matters of Kashruth and will not eat any morsel of food that is not strictly Kosher regardless of the burdens placed upon them. It is, however, the view of some who observe Kashruth (Conservative Jews) to permit eating broiled fish, baked potatoes, raw vegetables, canned fish, hard boiled eggs, fruit salads, and the like in a non-Kosher restaurant.

35. I recently attended a wedding which was catered by a Kosher caterer. Along with our coffee we were served a

liquid cream which was, I was informed, *pareve*. Is there such a product presently on the market as *pareve* cream?

Answer: Yes. There are available today a number of coffee creams which are vegetable compounds, and which are *pareve* and Kosher and may be served at a meat meal.

36. Are all so-called non-dairy creams that are sold in the markets *pareve?*

Answer: No. Non-dairy creams may, in fact, be dairy according to Jewish Kashruth standards. The difference arises from the secular law which accepts the idea that a dairy product loses its character of being a dairy product if the atomic composition has been totally changed. Non-dairy creams often contain casein, which is derived from milk. Judaism does not hold to this theory, for the present at least.

37. I've heard that dressed Kosher chickens are not as completely cleaned as non-Kosher chickens. Is this true, and if it is so, why is it so?

Answer: It is true that dressed Kosher chickens may not be as free of little feathers called "pin feathers," and this is so because when a chicken is Kosher-dressed, it cannot be placed in water as hot as the water used in dressing *trayfe* chickens. The rabbis set the upper limits for the heat of the water in which the freshly-killed chicken is placed in order to loosen its feathers because they were concerned lest the chicken be partially cooked in the over-heated water, and the blood would no longer be flowing out of the veins by salting. The result is that the chicken would be eaten with its blood still in it, which is forbidden.

38. When I was growing up we had a Christian maid in our home. I remember her as being very scrupulous in her

own faith and in respect to ours. By that I mean that she was very strict about Kashruth, about Shabbos, and such. However, I remember that when we ordered meat from the butcher shop, Mary (our maid) was not allowed to go and pick up the meat herself if the butcher could not deliver it. Often my brother or I would have to go and fetch the meat. Why is this necessary?

Answer: The law which required such action is not generally known to many Jews. There is a Jewish law which forbids meat going to a Kosher home to "disappear from sight." The rabbis were afraid that a careless attitude toward the handling of Kosher meat could lead to problems of switching Kosher meat with *trayfe*. For this reason, you or your brother had to go after the meats.

39. Many people associate Kashruth with cleanliness. Does this mean that a Kosher butcher shop which is not meticulously clean is not Kosher?

Answer: It is true that Kashruth as a *Mitzva* must maintain the highest standards of dignity as well as Jewish religious principles. Therefore, it may be rightfully assumed that at a Kosher butcher shop cleanliness is maintained. Where, however, there is a laxity of cleanliness, Kashruth is not jeopardized, except where, the meat may become rancid or spoiled. Then the meat becomes forbidden because it is injurious to health.

40. What is the custom of "taking *challah*" in a Jewish home when a woman bakes bread:

Answer: The custom of "taking *challah*" is derived from the temple order of sacrifices. It was customary to have *challah*, called "Show Bread" daily on the altar. Since the Temple's destruction it became customary to take a bit of *challah* from the bread that is baked, whether in the home or in the Kosher bake shop, and cast it into the fire and destroyed in commemoration of the Show Bread of the Temple.[12]

41. Why are marshmallows questionable regarding Kashruth?

Answer: Marshmallow is made with gelatin. Therefore, if it is not made under supervision to be certain that Kosher gelatin has been used, it must be considered *trayfe*.

42. A friend of mine told me that grape juice is also questionable because of Kashruth. What is your answer?

Answer: Grape juice is Kosher. It is not in the same category as wine. However, some observant Jews extend the restrictions on wine to grape juice.

43. Is striped bass a Kosher fish?

Answer: Striped bass has fins and scales and is Kosher.

44. Is custard pudding Kosher?

Answer: Custard pudding contains no ingredient that is not in conformity with the Kashruth laws. It is Kosher. Like all other items, this one is Kosher provided it is prepared in kettles that have not been used for *trayfe* foods.

45. Can I serve borscht with both meat and dairy meals?

Answer: Borscht is usually *pareve* and can be served with both meat and dairy meals. However, to be sure read the label so that you will be certain that milk or milk products have not been added.

46. I am a baker. Recently a salesman offered for sale a product which is called "whey." What is this product?

Answer: Whey is a milk product, and therefore all products that are made with it are *milchig*.

47. Do coffee and tea require Kashruth supervision. If so, why?

Answer: Coffee and tea are products which usually do not have other ingredients mixed into them, and therefore they are Kosher without Kashruth supervision.

48. Is it permissible to cook a meat meal in the same oven where dairy foods have been cooked previously?

Answer: Yes, it is permissible to cook meat foods in the same oven in which dairy foods have been cooked. Although we make a careful separation between meat and dairy in a Kosher home, the Kashruth laws do not require separate ovens because, as the Talmud put it, "odors are not important." This means that if the aroma from a meat meal remain in the oven, it is still permissible to cook a dairy meal in this same oven. Provision, of course, must be taken to be sure that no particles of food from the dairy meal remains in the oven which could create Kashruth problems.

49. Are sour pickles, olives and relishes Kosher?

Answer: As a rule sour pickles, olives and relishes are Kosher. However, certain brands of sour pickles and olives contain casein, which is a dairy product, and therefore they are *milchig*. A further question in the preparation of these products arises from the fact that a *trayfe* glycerine may be used in bottling. It is, therefore, best to purchase only sour pickles, olives and relishes which have proper rabbinic supervision.

50. Does wax paper require Kashruth supervision?

Answer: No, the wax or paraffin coating used today on the paper is Kosher.

51. Is there any ingredient in shredded coconut which is objectionable?

Answer: Shredded coconut is usually Kosher. However, certain brands of shredded coconut contain glycerine to keep it moist. Such coconut is *trayfe*. It is best to inquire

about the Kashruth of the shredded coconut from the manufacturer.

52. Is halava Kosher?

Answer: Yes, halava is Kosher. It is made from nuts.

53. Is tapioca pudding Kosher?

Answer: Yes. Tapioca pudding is Kosher. Tapioca is a
farinaceous food extracted from the roots of cassava or
manioc plants. It is very digestible and used to thicken soups
and broths. It is more popularly used in making milk pud-
dings.

54. May black seedless raisin be used in a Kosher home?

Answer: Yes, black seedless raisins may be used in a Kosher home. They are a fruit. Be certain, however, that they
are not treated with glycerine which is *trayfe*.

55. Are Chinese bean sprouts questionable regarding
Kashruth?

Answer: No. They are a vegetable and therefore permissible.

56. Is Kraft American cheese a Kosher cheese?

Answer: No. Kraft American cheese is not usually a Kosher cheese. There are a number of Kosher cheeses available
in the markets. Most supermarkets carry them.

57. Do cereals like Wheatena and Cream of Wheat contain any questionable ingredients?

Answer: No, They are free of any non-Kosher additives
and are permissible.

58. Is wheat germ Kosher?

Answer: Yes. Wheat germ is the nucleus of the wheat
kernel which is used as a vitamin additive.

59. Is Bumble Bee brand salmon Kosher?

Answer: Yes. It is Kosher. The oil in the can is from the
salmon itself.

60. When I was child, my mother gave me cod liver oil for my health. Today this is no longer practiced. However, I am curious to know if cod liver oil is Kosher?

Answer: Yes, cod liver oil is Kosher. The cod is a Kosher fish and all products made from it are Kosher.

61. Is Russian caviar Kosher?

Answer: Russian caviar is usually *trayfe*.

62. Do canned juices such as tomato juice, contain any substance that would be contrary to the Kashruth laws?

Answer: No. Pure canned juices generally are in fact pure except for the addition of sugar in some instances. Tomato juice does not contain anything that violates the Kashruth laws.

63. When an advertisement appears in the Jewish newspapers as being Kosher is it correct to assume that the item being advertised has been investigated by the publisher and is in fact Kosher?

Answer: No. Newspapers, whether they be in the English or Yiddish languages accept advertisements from those able to pay the fee for such publicity. The publisher does not assume any responsibility whatsoever for the Kashruth of the products which are advertised in his newspaper.

64. May brown sugar be used on Passover?

Answer: Yes. There is nothing in the brown sugar that is in violation of the Passover laws.

65. What about Powdered (confectioners') sugar?

Answer: It should be free of starch if it is used on Passover.

66. Can you verify for me if corn starch is added to table salt?

Answer: To the very best of our knowledge, no one adds corn starch to table salt when it is being manufactured for home use. Calcium salt is added to table salt in order to prevent it from clogging in moist weather. Calcium salt is Kosher and may be used on Passover as well as all year round.

67. Is steel wool Kosher? Does it need Kashruth supervision in order to be permissible for use in a Kosher home?

Answer: Steel wool is Kosher. It does not require Kashruth supervision in order to be acceptable for use in a Kosher home.

68. Is Heinz mustard Kosher?

Answer: Mustard is made from a seed. It is generally Kosher. Heinz mustard has Kashruth supervision and is surely Kosher.

69. Is Del Monte tomato sauce Kosher?

Answer: Yes. It is Kosher. It does not contain any substance that would be contrary to the Dietary Laws.

70. Are all flours used in bakeries Kosher?

Answer: Regarding the flour used in bakeries, it may be assumed that the flour is chiefly wheat or rye. There are cakes like corn muffins, made from corn. All are Kosher.

71. May sour salt be used without a *hechsher?*

Answer: Yes, sour salt may be used without a *hechsher*. It may be used for Passover as well without a *hechsher*. However, care should be taken to take the sour salt on Passover from a previously unopened box which guarantees that the contents did not come in contact with any *chometz.*

72. What is the question surrounding dried cereals?

Answer: None. Except that if the cereal has been vitamin enriched it should be ascertained that the source of the vitamin is Kosher.

73. Someone raised the question recently regarding the

use of wax paper on Passover. Is wax paper permissible?

Answer: Yes, wax paper is permissible for use on Passover and during the entire year. It does not need a *hechsher*.

74. Why are some salts labelled as Kosher salts? Does this imply that there are Kosher and non-Kosher salts?

Answer: No. All salts are Kosher. The term Kosher used on a box of salt means that the salt is coarse and can be used for Koshering meats. The salting of meats to Kosher them requires a thicker grain salt than table salt in order that the salt when applied to the meat should not dissolve before the Koshering process has been accomplished. To assure this, a coarse salt is used.

75. I notice that pectin often appears on the packages of candies. What is pectin and is it Kosher?

Answer: Pectin is a synthetic manufactured from chemicals. It is Kosher and *pareve*.

76. Is sardine a Kosher fish?

Answer: Yes, sardine is a Kosher fish. When sardines are canned in oil or tomato sauce the whole product is Kosher.

77. Is Breakstones cream cheese Kosher?

Answer: Yes, it is Kosher.

78. Is there a question of Kashruth regarding packaged potato chips?

Answer: Most packaged potato chips are prepared in pure vegetable oil and are Kosher. There are a number of brands of potato chips which have a symbol indicating Kashruth supervision.

79. My children enjoy chocolate covered marshmallow cookies. May they be eaten in our home? We observe Kashruth.

Answer: The usual brand of marshmallows is made with

non-Kosher gelatin and therefore is not Kosher. There is available, however, a Kosher brand of marshmallow and it is used in making a Kosher chocolate marshmallow cookie.

80. I know that chicken eggs are Kosher. But what about duck and geese eggs?

Answer: Ducks and geese are Kosher fowl, therefore, the eggs which they produce are equally Kosher.

81. Is malted milk Kosher?

Answer: You must be referring to the malt put in milk shakes to thicken them. The malt used in this drink is Kosher.

82. Is Halibut a Kosher fish?

Answer: Yes, halibut is a Kosher fish.

83. Is goat's milk Kosher?

Answer: Yes, it is Kosher.

84. Is kippered herring Kosher?

Answer: Yes. It is the Kosher fish herring that has been cured.

85. What is *Shmura* Matzoh?

Answer: The words *Shmura* Matzoh means "Watched Matzoh," which is the appellation given to Matzoh which has been carefully protected so that no water came upon the wheat from which it was made that might have fermented it. Care is taken so that no question of the possibility of fermentation occurred from the time the wheat was cut until the final product, the Matzoh, came out of the oven.

Many observant Jews eat the special "*Shmura* Matzoh" on the first two Seder nights of Passover, in addition to the conventional Matzoh.

86. If eggs are found in a freshly-killed chicken must these be Koshered like the raw meat?

Answer: If the eggs are without the shell, or with the shell but still attached with veins, they must be Koshered like raw meat. If the eggs are completely developed, however, they need not be Koshered.

The Tragedy of Corruption

> "Unlike the con men of yesterday who were often so
> heavy-handed that they offended the law, today's modern
> bandits of the marketplace are the masters of the light
> touch. With their insidious misrepresentations, silver-
> tongued lies, half-truths, and exaggerated promises, these
> men can reach even deeper into our pockets without
> producing a rustle to disturb the law—or even the
> victim himself. From coast to coast we are exposed to
> their Pandora's box of selling tricks—some old, but
> handily adapted to modern circumstances, and some
> new, and carefully devised to outwit the law."
>
> ("THE DARK SIDE OF THE MARKETPLACE")
> by Senator Warren B. Magnuson and Jean Carper

7 The corrupt practices of those who sell their products on the Kosher food market are not limited, nor are
they unique to these businessmen alone. The incidents and
facts of fraud in Kashruth which shall be unfolded in the
following pages should be appreciated against the backdrop
of fake fronts and frauds which have crept into many other
economic areas as well as the Kosher-foods industry, where
a fast buck can be made. However, in order to grasp the
intensity of the attraction which draws the entrepreneur of
a Kosher foods establishment and urges him to sell a prod-

uct which is actually *trayfe* to the unsuspecting public, passing it off as the Kosher item, we must appreciate the inducement which traps him. It is the profit motive! Granted that this is no startling revelation, except that most people are shocked more deeply when they learn of fraudulent practices involving Kosher products than they are when they are apprised of fraud in the automotive or entertainment industries for examples. For reasons of naïvete, people do not imagine the Kosher-foods businessman in the same light as they behold and evaluate other businessmen. After all, he is involved in selling a product that has been hallowed by Jewish tradition. The Kosher foods purveyors, however, see *themselves* as no different from their colleagues who have invested their money, their abilities, and their hopes for success in a business venture. The Kashruth business is *strictly* business, and must return the highest measure of financial, not spiritual, success to the one who has undertaken it. To achieve this end, the unscrupulous Kosher-foods businessman is willing to cut the proverbial corners.

To begin with an example of this deliberate fraud, the following incident, involving a caterer of presumably strictly Kosher foods of the highest quality, will be instructive. Recently, a prominent rabbi in an eastern seaboard city came to the office of the executive secretary of a Kashruth supervising agency to lodge a complaint against a caterer who was under supervision of this agency for Kashruth. The rabbi expressed his suspicions that the caterer was cheating families in the congregation who were using his services by charging them for Kashruth supervision, but not in fact providing a Kashruth supervisor, a *mashgiach*.

The majority of the Kosher affairs at his temple had been

tendered without the service, of a *mashgiach*, a violation of Kashruth, in addition to the fact that the caterer was pocketing the money given him by the families involved as payment for the *mashgiach* fee. The rabbi had warned the caterer many times about his negligence, but had gotten no satisfaction; the corrupt practice continued. Now the rabbi was prepared to take serious action against the caterer and needed proof of the deliberate fraud. He requested of the secretary of the Kashruth agency that he check the record of this caterer to determine how many times a *mashgiach* had been assigned to him to supervise his parties. A review of the caterer's file revealed that the caterer had requested a *mashgiach* only three times throughout the entire year. The rabbi was shocked to learn that confirmation of his suspicion had gone far beyond his fears. The Kosher caterer had served forty families of the congregation during that year, and each had paid for the services of a *mashgiach*. But only three of them had actually had the Kashruth supervision they paid for. The caterer was under contract with this particular Kashruth supervising agency to employ only their *mashgichim* and none others, so no substitute *mashgiach* could have supervised any portion of the caterer's operation.

Having established this, it was a simple matter to compute the measure of fraud. A *mashgiach* at the rabbis temple usually received $35 for each party he supervised. This figure, multiplied by the thirty-seven families who paid for Kashruth supervision but never got it, amounted to $1,295 which the caterer pocketed without any effort or cost to himself whatsoever.[1]

The foregoing case is undoubtedly one out of hundreds that have not been revealed, and the stolen amount of

$1,295 is only a mere drop in a proverbial ocean of illegally-gotten wealth.

In unfolding the larger record of corruption in the Kosher food industry, it will prove edifying to look first at the national picture of abuses in the meat industry. Knowledge of fraud in meat plants across the nation came to light through congressional hearings in 1967, when the president called upon the congress to enact a "clean meat" bill to protect the consumer. The official investigations and the committee hearings brought to light shocking tales of practices in the meat industry that were dangerous to the health of the consumer. These acts, which resulted in health hazards, were motivated by greed and practiced by deception.

Nineteen sixty-seven was a momentous year for the housewife and for the meat industry. Lyndon B. Johnson, who was President of the United States at that time, signed into law a new federal meat-inspection bill to replace the outdated law of 1907. The original meat inspection bill, which had not been revised in the sixty-year period provided for the inspection of "all red meats prior to and after slaughter." [2]

A major flaw in the effectiveness of the law was that it provided only for the inspection of meats that were shipped *interstate*. Meats that were sold within the boundaries of the state were not covered by the law of inspection. Some states enacted their own inspection regulations, but these were often poorly administered due to the lack of both funds and community interest. Other states had no inspection laws at all, relying completely upon the integrity of the abattoir or meat-packing-house owners to set their own standards of voluntary meat inspection.

President Johnson made his original request for the new

law in 1964, telling the Congress that a housewife had the right to know that the meat she was buying had been inspected by federally trained personnel who performed their vital tasks with the backing of the powerful federal government. The framers of the 1907 law could not have anticipated the phenomenal growth of the meat industry and the broad advances in modern technology which brought about vast changes in the handling and processing of meats. As a result of both of these new conditions, many meat plants were left unsupervised, and innumerable shocking unsanitary and unhealthy practices were typical to their operation.

There are in this country 17,000 meat packing plants. Only two thousand of them are under federal inspection. Together, these two thousand plants produce eighty-five per cent of the meat consumed. The remaining fifteen thousand plants, which process from eight to ten billion pounds of meat, enough to feed thirty million Americans annually, are not under federal inspection, and in many instances receive no formal inspection at all! [3]

In his testimony before the House Agriculture Committee on June 26, 1967, Deputy Assistant Secretary of Agriculture, Rodney E. Leonard, reinforced the President's remarks when he noted some of the changed conditions in the meat industry since the original law was written. He noted, as an example, that the law did not provide authority for supervising certain independent types of meat plants that had appeared recently, such as boning plants, cold-storage warehouses, wholesaler, and jobber plants, where adulterations of meats could and do occur. Changes in meat packing procedures, bulk-freezing of meats and the modern uses of meat tenderizers, he said, had rendered the law outdated.[4]

A most serious flaw between federal and state programs of inspection, even for those states that had instituted meat inspection procedures, was the lack of coordination between the two. This resulted in a disparity between the meats marked under the federal system and those marked and sold under the generally looser standards of the state.[5]

Statistics on the actual state inspection programs that were in force revealed that forty-one out of the total fifty states had some kind of meat inspection laws. And of those forty-one states, only twenty-six provided for mandatory inspection of the animals before and after slaughter, which is the basic requirement for an effective meat inspection program. Miss Betty Furness, Special Assistant to President Johnson for Consumer Affairs, testified that investigators for the Department of Agriculture had found many meat-inspection laws of the states ineffective for guarding against contaminated meats, even in those twenty-six states which required mandatory inspection. She stated further that even where such inspection was state sponsored, thirteen out of the twenty-six states with such laws had varying degrees of success with their programs because of the indifference of government and community leaders. A major city such as New York had adopted its own inspection program because of the inability of the state office to monitor meat packing operations in the city.

A variety of witnesses described the many hazards to health which came out of meat packing plants because of the absence of a strong meat-inspection program. For example, Representative Neal Smith of Iowa, who had led the fight for a new meat bill for many years, provided concrete examples of conditions in certain meat plants that produced undeniable health hazards. He testified that, "uninspected plants can cut down costs of manufacturing sausages by introducing into the mixture of meat blood, lungs, detergents, hair, hides, antibiotics, and excessive amounts of flour and water without having to label the final product in such a way that the consumer would know what he is buying." [6]

Others who testified before the congressional committee pointed out that the existing law did not adequately preclude someone from buying meat that was substandard on the pretense that he was going to use such meat in the manufacture of a cheap brand of dog and cat food, and then process that meat for human consumption. A renderer might pick up a dead cow that had been lying in some farmer's barn, chop it up, and sell it for hamburger meat without fear of detection. [7] A state inspector testified that in one plant which he visited, he had found one hundred and fifty pounds of rancid beef, twenty pounds of rancid chicken breasts, and several hundred pounds of meat patties in containers that bore the label of a company no longer in existence. [8]

Stephen Kota, a federal meat inspector, reported that in a meat plant which he had inspected, he had observed sides of beef being dragged across a primitive floor on which there were vermin droppings. Meat was packed in rusty metal barrels. He found rodent harbors, abscessed beef and pork livers, and parasitic infested livers mixed with edible products.

Other problems which came to light during the committee hearings provided a long list of hitherto undetected fraudulent practices which had arisen through the new techniques now being employed in the meat industry. Some of the new processes which had given rise to fraud were the fast meat-curing procedures, artificial tenderizers, and smoking and bleaching agents that were used to hide the true identity of the condition of the meat that was released for public sale. The uses of excessive water and meat extenders hid equally the true nature of the meats being sold. Because of new techniques, meat could now be chopped and sliced while still in the frozen state, making meat inspection of the end-product extremely difficult. In all of these cases, if fraud was perpetrated on the public, serious injury to the public health could occur.

This was the shocking reality of conditions actually in existence in the meat packing industry. As the possibility of a new meat-bill loomed larger, the powerful meat lobby began to politic in an attempt to retain the old meat bill. Spokesmen for the Meat Packers Association protested the proposed changes in the existing law, pointing out that the old law had served very well to safeguard the consumer. Proof of the validity of the old law was in the fact that during the sixty-year period since the passage of the law, the legislature had not found reason to tamper with it. This fact, they claimed, was sufficient proof of the broad coverage which the present law provided. But there were other voices coming from within the ranks of the meat industry which spoke out in favor of the proposed changes. Leon B. Schachter, International vice-president of the Amalgamated Meat Cutters and Butchers Union, said in his testimony that "some very strange situations exist in the meat industry." [9] He confirmed the statement that under existing conditions it was virtually impossible for the consumer to know what meat was in the ground hamburger or processed salami he was buying.

Ralph Helstein, president of the United Packinghouse Food and Allied Workers Union, told the congressional committee that the union's own investigations had revealed many cases of unsanitary conditions. He related that when inspectors for the United States Department of Agriculture began reporting, in 1963, the filth and the tainted meats that were in some of the state's meat-packing houses, the leaders of the meat industry began at once to create a variety of state meat-packers associations, each of whom lobbied aggressively in the legislatures for state inspection rather than the more stringent federal inspection.[10]

Help for a new, stronger meat bill came from sources outside the meat industry. Ralph Nader, who gained national fame when he championed the cause of safer automobiles, jumped into the meat-inspection foray and crusaded for stronger meat inspection laws on both the state and federal levels. He chided the Department of Agriculture for "behaving in a manner that suggests submission to the powerful State Department and the pressures from the meat industry." [11]

Inevitably the old law had to be replaced by a new meat bill which took into account the existing abuses. A strong law was needed in order to remove the travesties from the meat industry by establishing proper guidelines that would reflect the advances of the meat industry and modern technology. The new "Clean-Meat Bill" was enacted into law in December 1967. It gave broad powers to the Secretary of Agriculture to establish new programs of meat inspection on both the federal and state levels. It provided that the federal government would match expenditures by the states in order to improve their meat inspection activities so that their standards were at least equal to those of the federal government. Emphasis was placed upon inspection of meats that were to be sold intrastate, which was the major lack and fallacy attributed to the old law. States were given two years to upgrade their meat inspection programs, allowing for a one-year extension if, in the opinion of the Secretary of Agriculture, a sincere effort was being made to improve and establish a strong inspection program. In such instances, where the state failed to act to tighten its meat-inspection program, the Secretary of Agriculture was now authorized to step in and establish a federally prepared inspection program.

The Secretary of Agriculture was given the power to act against any state plant found to be distributing adulterated meats dangerous to the public health. He could, henceforth, visit any state plant at any time, inspect the sanitary conditions there, review its records, and take samples of its products for laboratory testing.

Imported meat would also become subject to the same strict federal procedures and regulations as native meats. This too was a significant change from the old bill, which simply recommended that imported meats approach United States federal standards of inspection.[12]

The new law set high standards for labeling meats, defining what constituted adulterated and mis-branded meats. The wording of the law encompassed "all meat products capable of use as human food." [13] This extended the coverage of the new inspection procedures.

Soon after the passage of the meat bill, action was taken to extend the authority of the law to the poultry industry.

The most recent act affecting the poultry industry was the Poultry Products Inspection Act of 1957. The difficulties which arose from this law originated with the smaller producer of poultry who was exempted from inspection on the condition that he maintained "such sanitary standards, practices, and procedures as may be prescribed by the Secretary of Agriculture." [14]

This form of voluntary inspection along federally mandated guidelines was found to be ineffective by the federal inspectors, who reported finding contaminated and unwholesome poultry in certain state plants. Pressure for a more stringent law that would cover the small poultry-producer was brought about by the National Broiler Council, whose members complained that the larger producer of poultry was placed in a weakened competitive position to the smaller producer due to the strict federal inspection laws which were applied to him, but not to his smaller competitors. Frank Frazier, Executive vice-president of the National Broiler Council stated in his testimony, "In our opinion it is essential that in order for a poultry inspection system to be effective, it must assure the consumer of a uniformly wholesome and properly packaged and labelled product from all sources and at all levels (of the poultry industry)." [15]

On August 18, 1968 a new poultry inspection law was enacted to protect the consumer at all levels.

Significantly, just one year following the passage of the "Clean Meat Bill," on December 17, 1968, the New York Times reported that seven hundred meat plants had been shut down by the Department of Agriculture. The majority of the closed meat plants were shut down voluntarily by their owners, who found it too expensive to upgrade their operations to meet the federal standards of inspection. These plants operated wholly within their states, and were heretofore untouched by stringent inspection procedures. Fifty-nine plants were closed by the states, and ninety-eight others had their health and operating licenses revoked. The Federal Government itself took action against forty meat plants within various states which it felt were immediate health hazards. Of those forty plants against which federal inspectors moved, ten were shut down, twenty-one were cleaned up to eliminate health hazards, one was put under federal inspection, and action is pending against eight others, all of them in Puerto Rico. The Department of Agriculture refused to name the owners and locations of the plants it acted against.

At a news conference explaining the government's actions, Rodney E. Leonard, consumer and marketing administrator for the Department of Agriculture, said, "Thirty-seven states have taken substantial corrective action on their own to clean up meat plants since the law became effective on December 15, 1967. Twenty-eight states have entered into agreements with the Federal Government to upgrade their meat inspection programs to meet Federal standards, but that as of now no state had a program that met federal criteria." [16]

During the months of Congressional hearings prior to passage of the "Clean-Meat Bill," reports appeared daily in the press regarding abuses that were current in meat-packing plants. Few items regarding the Kosher meat-processing plants, however, appeared. One such item reported in the *National Jewish Post and Opinion* praised the Kosher meat plants for maintaining such laudable practices that they satisfied the most stringent inspection requirements. [17]

In a later issue of the same newspaper, however, a news article appeared stating that a state inspector had found deplorable filth in one meat provision plant "on the lower East side of New York." [18] It appears that the factual account of the meat plant story will continue to remain shrouded in some measure of mystery. Even Mr. Rodney E. Leonard of the Department of Agriculture at his news conference, on advice of counsel, refused to answer all the questions of the newsmen. When he was asked by newsmen whether the public was being protected from suspected meat, he replied that on the advice of his lawyers he could not disclose the names of the plants that received government action. He would obtain, if it became necessary, legal justification for withholding the names of those plants.

This devil-may-care attitude, which prevailed in the meat industry generally over the many decades until the enactment of the Clean-Meat Bill, has plagued the Kosher foods industry specifically, and remains to be cleaned up. To begin with, the civil laws governing Kosher foods and inspection procedures need to be upgraded. For example, the Kosher law which prevails in New York State, and which has served as a model for the other states which have enacted Kosher laws, is limited in its reach. In Circular 811 of the Department of Agriculture and Markets of the State of New York, issued in 1961, the law declares that,

"A person who, with intent to defraud, sells or exposes for sale any meat preparations, article of food, or food products, and falsely represents the same to be Kosher, whether such meat or meat preparations, article of food or food products, be raw or prepared for human consumption, or as having been prepared under, and of a product or products sanctioned by, the Orthodox Hebrew religious requirements, either by direct statement orally, or in writing, which might reasonably be calculated to deceive or lead a reasonable man to believe that a representation is being made that such food is Kosher or prepared in accordance with the Orthodox Hebrew religious requirements. . . ." [19]

This law, as quoted above in part, makes it very clear that the primary criterion for determining the Kashruth of a product is its conformity to the "Orthodox Hebrew religious requirements." The monopoly of control is thus given to the Orthodox Jewish attitude on matters of Kashruth. What does the law propose regarding the Conservative Jewish opinions about Kashruth? It may be readily granted that the Reform Jewish position on matters of Kashruth is laissez-faire, but the scholars and leaders of the Conservative movement claim to have as much interest and concern for matters of Kashruth as do the Orthodox Jews! Over the years, the Conservative rabbinate has differed with their Orthodox colleagues on a number of matters regarding questions of Kashruth.

Great injustices have already been committed against the innocent, helped by the law, because the wording of the law relinquishes the entire matter of Kashruth to the Orthodox Jewish community alone. For example, let us consider the case of Mr. Cohen, who was in the fish business. Mr. Cohen represented his business as being a strictly Kosher operation selling only Kosher fish products. Among the fish foods that a Kosher housewife could purchase from Mr. Cohen there was swordfish. Mr. Cohen belonged to a Conservative temple, and his rabbi had shown him the response which the Law Committee of the Rabbinical Assembly of America (Conservative) had issued regarding swordfish. According to Rabbi Isaac Klein, dean of the Conservative Rabbinic Law Committee, swordfish is Kosher. On the basis of this ruling, Mr. Cohen had included swordfish in the list of fish he was selling. Mrs. Ginsberg, however, belonged to an Orthodox Jewish congregation and lodged a complaint against Mr. Cohen for misrepresentation in selling swordfish as a Kosher fish when, according to her rabbi, who was Orthodox, it was not. Mrs. Ginsberg's rabbi had informed her that swordfish was a non-Kosher fish, and forbidden to Kashruth-observing Jews.

In presenting her complaint, Mrs. Ginsberg quoted the response of Professor Moses Tendler of the Yeshiva University, given her by her rabbi, in which it is stated unequivocally that swordfish is not Kosher.

Mr. Cohen was directed to appear in court to answer the charge. The judge was lenient, and merely fined him and sent him off with a warning not to continue to sell swordfish as Kosher. It was understood, however, that if Mr. Cohen continued to sell swordfish as Kosher, he would be called back into court and given a jail sentence.

All this can come about because the authority to decide matters of Kashruth has been rendered over *completely* to the Orthodox rabbinate. Other rabbinic viewpoints are of no consequence.

This law of New York State as well as many other states, which has given the monopoly of decisions regarding Kashruth to the Orthodox community, is outdated, and in effect unjust. Like the meat bill of 1907, it unwittingly encourages injustice, misrepresentation and similar abuses.

Other problems which exist in the Kashruth industry today however, cannot be blamed directly on the weakness of the law. Those who commit fraud and deception know well that they are doing wrong and would avoid the law even though it was stronger. For many years the Jewish community has complained about the incongruities between the vital *mitzva* of Kashruth as a religious precept, and the degradation which this holy commandment has suffered because of the brazen violation of the laws, both secular and religious. From the pettiness of the small shopkeeper who openly defies Kashruth by mockingly offering to place "Kosher-For-Passover" labels on a variety of unsupervised products in his store if the customer requests him to do so, to the large meat-packing-house owner who sells non-Kosher meats as Kosher, there are the unscrupulous who willfully violate the tenets of Kashruth. The glitter of the bright profit margin and the bribe have tripped many an otherwise honest layman, and caused many a rabbi to fall from the grace of both God and man. And once caught in the trap, neither has had the courage to pull out. How wise is the biblical admonition, "You shall not take a bribe, for bribes blind the eyes of the discerning and upset the plans of the just." [20]

The knowledge that so much corruption exists in the Kashruth industry has been wielded like a two-edged sword against observance of the commandment. Those who wanted to rid themselves of Jewish rituals generally pointed to the abuses going on in Kashruth, the gangsterism that had become a part of it, saying, "Could this be what God wants . . . a Jewish Mafia?" And those who wanted to extol it so that their children would accept it as a part of their Jewishness found it extremely difficult to do so when the corruption was known and ridiculed so openly. The result has been a loss of adherents to Kashruth over the years. This unfortunate condition was documented recently in a study by Dr. Marshall Sklare, the eminent sociologist, in his work entitled *Lakeville Jews*. He notes that the *mitzvah* of Kashruth, once held so dear by the older generation, has been rejected by a large number of younger Jews.[21]

The following details of Kashruth corruption are told not merely to expose them alone, but, more important by far, to arouse future generations of young Jews to vigilance in the cause of cleaning up the dishonesty which has beset Kashruth so that it shall be hallowed once again, and those who would receive it into their lives as a *mitzvah* may do so with pride.

In relating the story of deception in Kashruth it is necessary to have a description of how a company that is producing a food product obtains Kashruth certification. We will imagine that company X, which manufactures cookies, has decided to enter the Kosher foods' market. The company's management will turn to one of the Kashruth supervising agencies or to an individual rabbi to obtain Kashruth supervision for their cookies. After a preliminary discussion, the company will be required to submit to the rabbi a list of the ingredients which go into the manufacture of the cookies, describing in detail the method and place of production, and what other products, if any, are baked in the same ovens or mixed in the same vats and pans in which the cookies are prepared.

If this initial investigation presents no special Kashruth problems to the rabbi who will be providing the *hechsher*, then the next step requires that the rabbi make a personal visit to the baking plant in order to see for himself the actual production of the cookies. This will further enhance his decision-making. Prior to accepting the responsibility for supervising production of the cookies, the rabbi will make recommendations to the management based upon his knowledge of the production techniques as to how Kashruth supervision can best be implemented. An agreement is then reached between management and the rabbi or supervising agency to provide Kashruth supervision according to an established program which includes the fee for supervision. The fee can range from a few dollars to thousands, depending upon the size of the company, the product's market-potential and the time that the rabbi will devote to supervision.

The decision to "go Kosher" is in itself an important step because it is even at this initial juncture that financial considerations can cause corrupt practices to manifest themselves. For example, there is the case of the maneuvering of the ⓤ *hechsher*. The ⓤ withdrew its Kashruth supervision from the Barricini Candies in favor of Barton's Bonboniere and Candy because of financial considerations, according to an editorial by Dr. Trude-Weiss Rossmarin in the Jewish Spectator. She wrote:

"In order to land the Kashruth contract for Barton's Bonboniere and Candy, the Union (of Orthodox Jewish congregations) withdrew its (ⓤ) *hechsher* from Barricini Candy, arguing that Barricini kept its stores open on the Sabbath while Barton's stores are closed. Yet the Union of Orthodox Jewish congregations continue to give *hechsherim* to concerns (including Jewish-owned) that do not observe the Sabbath. Why then was the *hechsher* taken from Barricini? The answer is simple: Barton's made this the condition for paying the Orthodox Union for affixing its "ⓤ to the packages." *[22]

A common method of compelling a company to pay up once it has accepted Kashruth supervision, occurs in the

following way: A company that has been producing Kosher foods for some time may have achieved great success
with its product in the Kosher market. Quite apart from
any properly *deserved* increment of the fee for supervision,
the supervising agency or "rabbi" will approach the management and demand a new and higher fee, capriciously
established, wholly on the basis of "this is the fee I feel you
ought to pay me." The company is threatened that unless
the new fee is paid, the *hechsher* will be withdrawn, and
the product denounced in the Jewish newspapers as being
trayfe. This kind of pressure has been applied to many
companies, and in some cases where the company was small
and could not meet the new financial burden, it had to
leave the Kashruth market altogether.[23]

In one instance of this kind of corruption, the rabbi was
not so open as to insist that money for the new fee be paid
directly to him. Instead, he requested that the money be
sent as contributions to certain charities which he favored.
Investigation revealed, however, that the charities which he
listed were non-existent, and that the central office to
which the contributions were to be sent was actually the
rabbi's own home.

There is also a more delicate form of extortion associated
with Kashruth. This might be termed the "Silent Treatment," and it operates in a number of forms. For example, a
company will inquire about Kashruth supervision for its
product. The truth of the matter is that this product would
be acceptable even without supervision, as may be the case
with window cleaning liquid, toothpicks, aspirin, corn

---

* Note: Barton's candies are presently sold in stores that are open on
the Sabbath. The Ⓤ *hechsher* continues to appear on the wrapper.

starch, diaper detergents, etc. The company is not informed that they can sell their product in the Kosher market without supervision. Instead, the company is induced to
purchase Kashruth supervision.

Mr. Allan G. Feld, writing in the *Jewish Spectator*,
complained about the waste of Ⓤ energies in giving its
hechsher and its supervision to companies of this type,
while ignoring the possibilities of providing Kashruth supervision to places where a real service would be performed. He wrote:

"By all means let the Union (of Orthodox Jewish Congregations) make money and let the Kashruth supervisors make
money, if nobody is harmed. But what upsets me is that the
officials of the Union who admonish us, Always look for the
"Ⓤ"—it's your guarantee of Kashruth—don't look for the "Ⓤ"
where it's really necessary. After all, when you and I are traveling—or even when we eat out in our own home towns—we
don't look for Kosher diaper deodorants, or Kosher bleaches,
but for an honest-to-goodness Kosher restaurant. But the Union Kashruth Directory, unbelievable though it seems, does
not list even one Kosher restaurant! So how are you or I to
know where we may and where we may not eat? And tell me,
isn't it ridiculous—and perhaps you want to take a more serious
view of the matter and use a different term—for a group of
people who want to promote Kashruth to certify salt and
pepper and vinegar while not doing a thing about restaurants
and caterers (the "Directory" lists just one lone caterer) and
summer camps?" * [24]

When a responsible Kashruth supervising agency such as
the Union of Orthodox Jewish Congregations sells its

* Note: Since Mr. Feld's nudging of the "Ⓤ", matters have improved
somewhat. See the recent publications of the "Ⓤ" directory.

hechsher to companies that actually do not require Kashruth supervision, it is the kind of abuse that degrades the
prestige of Kashruth. To do so is to be on a par with those
who fleece the innocent by persuading them to purchase
home appliances they really do not need. And when such
activities are perpetrated under the guise of religious observance, the crime is greatly compounded!

The rationale behind such manipulation of Kashruth is
the realization that when a housewife who keeps a Kosher
home goes shopping, she will automatically be drawn to the
product that displays a symbol of Kashruth supervision,
especially the popular ⓤ symbol.

A variation of the "Silent Treatment" results from the
collusion of a number of responsible people to represent a
product to the public as being Kosher when in fact it is not.
Incidents of this variety of fraud are widespread in the
Kashruth industry, but it is especially so in the meat packing houses. An example of this brand of Kashruth misrepresentation was revealed a few years ago, as follows:

In December 1960 a delegation of two rabbis and a
layman from a community in upstate New York went to
investigate a Kosher sausage plant in a Mid-Western metropolitan city. Although the sausage had been advertised as
Kosher, and bore upon its casings the customary names of
the rabbis certifying the Kashruth, reports had been received from a number of places that the Kashruth of the
sausage was questionable. When the delegation arrived at
the plant, the owner graciously consented to take them on a
tour of his facilities. The *mashgiach* of the plant went along
to answer any queries that might come up. The owner
informed the committee at the outset that he had established a Kashruth procedure which was foolproof. He

explained that the Kosher department was restricted to one floor of the plant, the non-Kosher to another separate floor. Vats in which Kosher meats were moved about were clearly marked as "Kosher" so that no mistake could be made, while the vats in which the non-Kosher meats were moved had no markings whatsoever. The system sounded good enough, but much to the chagrin and dismay of the members of the delegation, the procedures which the system was supposed to guarantee were far from foolproof.

When the delegation arrived on the second floor of the plant, where only Kosher meats were processed and only vats marked "Kosher" would be found, they found ten vats of meat that had no markings on them at all. Presumably these vats were filled with *trayfe* meats. When the head of the delegation asked the owner to explain the presence of these unmarked vats on the Kosher floor, the owner apologized and assured the committee that this was a mistake which would not be repeated. He ordered the vats removed from the floor.

Subsequently, however, as they were talking, a worker came by pushing an unmarked vat that was now empty of its former contents. When the worker was asked what happened to the meat inside the vat, he replied simply and honestly that it was being packaged as usual for shipment out to the various Kosher delicatessen dealers. It was obvious to the delegation that a vat of *trayfe* meats had been processed and packaged as Kosher and sent out to market to be purchased by unsuspecting and trusting Kosher housewives!

All this was done with the full knowledge of the *mash-giach* and *rav hamachshir* who were responsible. As the delegation prepared to leave the meat plant the *mashgiach*

apparently sensed their disappointment in his faulty supervision and felt the need to make some kind of excuse for his
negligence. He turned to them and asked them to use their
influence with the owner of the plant so that he would
obey the *mashgiach's* recommendations.[25]

A favorite ruse used by the Kosher meat purveyors when
they are apprehended possessing *trayfe* meats, is to claim
that they are simply holding the meats for a Christian friend
who is in temporary difficulty. For example, a large meat
packing plant in an eastern city was reputedly engaged in
processing only Kosher meats. This particular meat plant
catered primarily to the Kosher trade, selling to Kosher
summer camps and to Jewish theological seminaries, all of
whom trusted the integrity of the owner of the Kosher
meat plant. Their trust, however, was shattered one day
when a committee representing a number of Kosher camps
visited the meat plant unannounced and found there a
variety of *trayfe* meats. The following is the report which
the committee filed with their institution following inspection of the meat plant:

> "When we arrived at the plant, the owner appeared
> delighted to see us. He asked the *mashgiach* to take us
> through the cooler and any other areas of the plant that
> we would want to see. When we entered the cooler we
> noticed a number of *trayfe* salamis on the shelves. The
> sight of these *trayfe* salamis in this plant, which has for so
> many years been accepted as Kosher, selling only Kosher
> meats, was for all of the members of the committee a
> shocking thing. However, we now alerted ourselves to
> the possibility of other *trayfe* products. We therefore
> made a very careful inspection of every carton of meat in

the cooler to determine if the meat in it was Kosher or not. One carton which was labeled for shipment to one of our Kosher camps contained meats which had no *plumba* testifying to its Kashruth. In view of this further misrepresentation which we found, we had no choice but to inform the owner that we would have to remove his plant from the approved list.

The owner begged for our patience and understanding, assuring us that a mistake had been made somewhere, and that all questions could be clarified. He then called in the *mashgiach*, who was asked to explain to us how it was possible for these *trayfe* salamis and meats to be in the plant. With much embarrassment the *mashgiach* explained that the salamis and the meats were in fact going out to a *trayfe* summer camp and should have been labeled so. The fault was with the worker, a Puerto Rican, who did not understand the instructions given him in English, and therefore mislabeled the carton. The *mashgiach* thanked us for catching this error. He would correct it immediately.

The *rav hamachshir* was also called in to explain the mixup, and he verified the *mashgiach's* excuse that a terrible mistake had been made, but he assured us that it was nothing more than a mistake.

When the committee asked how it was that the plant was suddenly doing business with *trayfe* summer camps, when to the best of everyone's knowledge the plant was selling to Kosher places only, the owner himself intervened and gave us an answer. He confessed that the salamis and the meats without *plumbas* were not being sent to a non-Kosher camp as the *mashgiach* and *rav hamachshir* had testified. The real truth of the matter was that he was merely holding on to them for a friend who asked him to help out temporarily. His friend was shipping meats via truck from one end of the city to the other when his truck broke down suddenly. This being mid-summer, and even though the meats were *trayfe,* they could not be permitted to sit in the hot sun and rot. Out of desperation, and at the risk of his reputation as a purveyor of Kosher meats, the owner permitted the *trayfe* meats to be brought to his plant for temporary safety."[26]

Though the story told by the owner of the meat plant sounded plausible, investigation into the facts revealed that there was not a shred of truth in it. The truth that came to light was that if the owner wanted to assist a friend in a moment of difficulty, he could have placed the meats in the *trayfe* meat plant next door to his own, in which he owned an interest. His excuse was obviously a hoax which had been concocted to confuse the members of the committee. An amazing confirmation of the truth of the matter came just a few days after the committee's visit to the meat plant, when the plant suddenly, and mysteriously had a fire which destroyed it completely. The owner now moved his entire operation to the *trayfe* plant next door, dealing only in *trayfe* meats. It then became known that he had more than a partial ownership of the *trayfe* operation next door—he was the sole owner of it and the *trayfe* meats discovered by the committee during its visit were in fact *trayfe* meats that would have gone to Kosher institutions had they not been discovered beforehand.

The guilt for such a flagrant, deliberate collusion to perpetrate fraud upon the unsuspecting public must certainly fall upon the religious functionaries involved—the *rav hamachshir* and the *mashgiach*. A large measure of the blame, however, must rest upon the owner, who in his lust for financial gain, contrived the plan to deceive his customers by selling them *trayfe* meats in place of the Kosher products they thought they were buying.

A recent exposé covering a broad scope of this kind of fraud was published by Rabbi Morris Casriel Katz, who is an expert on the particular brand of deception that goes on in Kosher meat packing plants. He described the tactics employed by some purveyors of Kosher meats who practice misrepresentation through the medium of the "Kosher-front." The "Kosher-front" kind of fraud is another shading of the "silent treatment"; it too relies on rabbis and *mashgichim* who are willing to stand by in silence while the proprietors of the plants they are supervising deceive the public.

The "Kosher-front" operation is a carry-over from the old days when an old man with a beard was hired to sit in front of a Kosher delicatessen to give it the image of a strictly Kosher place. Similarly, the "Kosher-front" rabbi or *mashgiach* hangs around the plant he is supervising, performing some menial functions there, while in reality his responsibility is to deceive the skeptic who might come around to question the Kashruth. He does this by saying the right words, having the correct answers, and performing the expected rituals. Many of the so-called rabbis who are functioning in this capacity are self-ordained; they cannot produce a *smicha* (ordination) from a responsible institution of higher learning. The *mashgichim* involved in this kind of fraud are usually unlearned and untutored in the high idealism that is integral to Kashruth. Thus the corrupt meat-plant owner and the make-believe clergy find each other, and the system of deception proceeds smoothly.

In his startlingly frank paper, Rabbi Katz made the following revelation: "More pickled and cooked briskets (corned beef and pastrami) are sold in the U.S. as Kosher than are obtainable from all the packing companies that are in the Kosher fresh meat business! More natural casings, especially of sheep and lamb, are being used in the Kosher-labeled products than are obtainable from Kosher sources!" [27] Rabbi Katz's allegations could undoubtedly be substantiated if the legal authorities of the state and federal government were alerted to this problem. What would then be the ultimate conclusion? That some of the Kosher meat packing plants are packaging *trayfe* meats and selling them as Kosher. How could such a travesty of Kashruth continue without being challenged?—only with the help of those responsible to supervise Kashruth and make certain that machinations of this kind do not go on. But they have been bribed and, as the Torah has already warned, they have blinded their own eyes so they do not really perceive what their eyes behold.

A particularly distressing type of fraudulent Kashruth practice is common to many hotels and resorts. Throughout the country there are hotels which advertise themselves as "Strictly Kosher," or "Dietary Laws Observed." Some few are honest and live up to their advertised Kashruth, but most others do not; they fool the public year in and year out. Their method of fraud is interesting.

There are two types of "Kosher-front" resort hotels. The first advertises "Dietary Laws" somewhere amongst the array of social and sports activities which are offered by the hotel. This is done in order to attract every potential vacationer, including those who prefer to be at a Kosher resort while they are on a holiday.

In other resorts, there appears to be a reverse psychology at work. These do not advertise Kosher, but will inform anyone who visits or calls on the telephone to inquire about Kashruth, that they are a Kosher hotel. The thinking that seems to motivate the management of such hotels is that the words "Dietary Laws" or "Strictly Kosher" appearing among a very exciting advertisement about a "Swinging Singles Weekend" would be very incongruous, and would hurt their business. The religious implications of the Kosher words might frighten away the swingers—the place would appear too holy for them. Nevertheless, whether they advertise Kosher or not, these hotels are representing themselves as Kosher to the public while they are actually *trayfe*. Some examples of their methods of deception follow:

One hotel that I investigated, hired a rabbi for the High Holy Days services and publicized widely that rabbi X would officiate. After the holy days were concluded, the hotel saved the brochures with the rabbi's name and picture on them so that should anyone inquire about Kashruth at the hotel, any time during the year, the affirmative answer could be given, reinforced by the name and picture of the rabbi who was at the hotel for the holy days. One such hotel gave me the name of their rabbi who was in charge of Kashruth. I looked him up in the telephone book, but could not find a rabbi with this name listed. I did find a lawyer with this same name, however. I took a chance and called the lawyer, inquiring if he was the rabbi at such a hotel. The lawyer admitted that his avocation was to function as rabbi at this particular hotel for the High Holy Days.

When I asked him if he was responsible for Kashruth at the hotel, he became quite angry and told me that he had warned the hotel a number of times not to use his name as *mashgiach* of the hotel. If the hotel continued to do so, he would be forced to take legal action against them. He assured me that he was in no way responsible for the Kashruth of the hotel. His only function there was to officiate as rabbi at the holy days' services and at such special occasions during the year when a rabbi's services were needed!

Another hotel provided me with the name of the cantor who, they said, functioned as cantor and *mashgiach* at the resort. When I called the cantor to confirm the fact that he was responsible for Kashruth at the hotel, he told me that he had not been in the employ of the hotel for more than two years now, and that even when he was employed by the hotel, his sole responsibility was to officiate as cantor. He never accepted any duties as *mashgiach* at the hotel!

A variation of this kind of fraud is the rabbi or cantor who is not functioning as mashgiach *at* the hotel but has an "arrangement" with the management permitting them to tell anyone who calls that he is the *mashgiach* at the hotel. Usually such a phony setup can be readily challenged because the "*mashgiach*" is living at home, many miles away from the hotel. Such long-distance supervision is worthless.

There are so many variations of the methods of deception that one can never estimate just what combination of devious plans will be encountered. At a large hotel I visited I was informed that the hotel employed a full-time rabbi who lived on the premises. I met the rabbi shortly after my arrival at the hotel. He was in fact an ordained rabbi, and he was living on the premises when I met him during the summer season. The rabbi consented to take me on a tour of the hotel's Kosher facilities. During our walk about the hotel, the rabbi told me that in addition to his responsibility to the hotel to supervise Kashruth, he had a congregation in another community, which I recognized as being over a hundred miles away. When I asked how it was possible to serve a congregation that was so far away from the hotel and still be responsible for Kashruth, the rabbi informed me that he was at the hotel during the summer months only, during the period of his vacation from his congregation. Another rabbi took over the Kashruth supervision during the remaining ten months of the year.

Doubts about the veracity of the rabbi's statements entered my mind when I asked him the name of his replacement, and he could not give it to me, saying that he did not know too much about the man who followed him. Surely, I thought, there would be some measure of contact between them as they "changed the guard" at the hotel. This fact was never clarified for me, and I left the hotel confused and suspicious of the integrity of the Kashruth setup. My curiosity, however, had been awakened and I made a memo to follow through by calling the hotel after the summer was over and ask to speak with the second rabbi.

I telephoned the hotel some months later during the winter and asked to speak with the rabbi supervising Kashruth at the hotel. The telephone operator gave me the name of the rabbi I had met during the summer. When I objected to this, insisting that according to the information given me, there was to be another rabbi at the hotel supervising Kashruth, she returned my persistence with equal stubbornness that the hotel employed only one rabbi who was responsible for rabbinic ministrations to the hotel, including Kashruth, and not two rabbis. In desperation I called the summertime rabbi and asked him to clarify the situation for me. At this point he had no choice but to admit that the story he gave me was a hoax. He was in fact the year-round rabbi at the hotel. His residence at the hotel was during the summer months only. During the remainder of the year he supervised Kashruth "long-distance."

There are some hotels which do not bother to hire Kosher-front rabbis or cantors to assume the mantle of legitimate Kashruth. They claim to be Kosher under the supervision of either the owner himself or his chief steward. Having experienced many variations of fraud at resorts, I was not overly surprised when I met some of the owners and stewards at these resorts and found that they were not themselves observant Jews and were not personally committed to Kashruth. They could not be relied upon to uphold the laws of Kashruth.

The first Kosher-front hotel that I visited made a lasting impression upon me. That single experience provided me with much of the information I would need to know about the corruption in resorts. Other hotels, which employed different methods of deception, were actually offering only variations of this original pattern.

I arrived at this hotel at the appointed time and was greeted by a member of the management. Before we began our tour of the Kosher facilities, I was told that the rabbi of the hotel regretted that he could not be present for my visit. He was in the hospital having some minor surgery and would be back at the hotel within a few days, upon his recovery. (I learned later that the hotel did not employ a rabbi at all, but that this was just another part of the game of deception.) I was asked to bear this in mind as we made our tour, and that any infractions of the Kashruth laws that I might find were present only because of the rabbi's absence and would be corrected immediately upon the rabbi's return. In the meantime a member of the management, who was a religious Jew, was serving as *mashgiach*.

No sooner had I entered the kitchen with my guide that I met the rabbi's replacement. He was an elderly gentleman. I noticed that he was not wearing the traditional *yarmulka* (skullcap) worn by religious men, especially those fulfilling the role of the *mashgiach*. He greeted me with no embarrassment or attempt to explain his bareheadedness. Some time later, however, just prior to my departure, I met him once again, and this time he had been told to put on a *yarmulka*. Some of the irregularities that I found began in the kitchen where I saw packages of *trayfe* Jello and cans of *trayfe* chicken soup. No one could explain how these *trayfe* items got there but they were there nevertheless, and would be used whether by accident or by design. I was assured that these *trayfe* items would be removed immediately.

My guide was called to the telephone for some important matter, and I was encouraged by her to wander the grounds on my own. I completed the inspection of the kitchen on my own initiative and proceeded towards the coffee shop, which was a few yards from the main entrance to the hotel. As I walked towards the coffee shop I looked for a sign that might tell me whether or not it was run as a concession by an outside company, as is sometimes the case at resorts, but I did not see any such notification. Therefore I assumed that it was under the auspices of the hotel and was Kosher.

I entered the coffee shop and asked the woman serving

the food from behind the counter if I could inspect the kitchen. She reacted immediately and said that I could not. When I informed her that I had been taken through the main kitchen by an executive of the hotel, she relented somewhat and said that she would call the main office to obtain permission to show me through, but she would do this after the customer who was already waiting had been served. I agreed to this.

She took the customer's order, which was for a hot dog and a chocolate milk shake. She served him both foods without the slightest hesitation, although to do so was a clear violation of the Kashruth laws. When she made her call at last, she returned to inform me that her instructions were that I should not be allowed to go through the coffee shop.

Perplexed over this change of attitude, I returned to the main building of the hotel to inquire of the manager why I was denied the opportunity of going through with the inspection of this final portion of my visit. But I was never to know the answer to this question because very suddenly everyone became extremely busy with important matters. I waited a reasonable amount of time, and when it became clear to me that none of the executives would be free to return to the coffee shop with me, I left the hotel.

Numerous other incidents of Kashruth violations became evident to me as I visited a cross section of hotels and resorts advertised as Kosher. Except for variations in kind, a large number function with basically the same purpose, which is to deceive the unsuspecting, naïve public. The common method of deception is the establishment of an acceptable Kosher-front. And the tragic truth is that all Kashruth violations are not so secreted that the trained

Kashruth inspector, who has even a minimal amount of practical experience in this matter, could not easily recognize the fraud that is being perpetrated. Why are these abuses permitted to continue? Perhaps those in authority have taken the path of least disturbance— "No one has raised the question, so we will permit things to go along as they are!" What is equally possible is that some of the financial gains that have blinded the eyes of the rabbis and *mashgichim* at the hotels and resorts have worked with greater success upon the secular authorities.

This unfortunate-for-Judaism attitude of laissez-faire regarding matters of Kashruth reaches across the country. The railroads in their own involvement in the Kosher meats business compound the problems of Kashruth violations. For example, The Kashruth law requires that if fresh meat is to be kept for more than three days without being Koshered, it must be "washed down," once every seventy-two hours in order to keep it fresh. A piece of meat which has not been refreshed during this period is assumed to have hardened so much that the salting method of Koshering it will no longer be effective. Henceforth, the meat must be Koshered by broiling only. Therefore, some cuts of meat become useless to the housewife if they have not been washed within the proper time limit. Because of this, when meat is shipped interstate over a period of time that is longer than seventy-two hours, it is "washed down" along the way by a rabbi or his surrogate who is someone well qualified because of his knowledge of the laws of Kashruth. The railroads rely upon and pay the rabbis en route to wash the meats properly so that they arrive at their destination Kosher, without religious limitations on their use. However, as the situation is today, the manner in which the

railroads pack the meats into the freight cars makes it
virtually impossible to wash the meat properly. Even a
dwarf could not crawl into most of the freight cars which
carry Kosher meats and have such freedom of movement
that he could wash each piece of meat properly and in
accordance with the laws of Kashruth.

When the meats that have been taken care of on the
freight cars finally arrive at the meat market, neither the
butcher nor the housewife can know that they were not
properly washed. The unsuspecting housewife will inno-
cently bring the meat home and salt it for Koshering, but
by now the salting process is unacceptable.

Here again the responsibility for negligence rests upon
the shoulders of those in authority who know the problem,
but have taken insufficient action to resolve it. The resolution of the problem is simple, and could be easily accomplished if those concerned with the maintenance of Kashruth turn their attention to it.

"Why do the prices of meats, poultry and certain fish
skyrocket to double the regular price, or more, just before
the Jewish holidays?", asks a Jewish housewife in dismay.
Each year, a few weeks before Rosh Hashanah and Passover especially, the prices of these food items double and
even triple. It is true that the demand for these foods
explodes during these times of the year because of the
traditional menus of the holidays, but it is a shocking thing
to realize that, except for unforeseen calamities, these foods
are always plentiful enough to meet the stepped up demand. Why, then, is the observant Kosher housewife punished because of her devotion to Judaism? The question has
been raised by officials in various city and state govern-
ments. The perpetrators of this abuse have heard the pro-

test, but have gone along as before. A solution in the near future does not seem likely.

Finally, although by no means the end of the record, the catering business, both within and outside the temples, holds its own large measure of sway over the shady side of the Kosher foods industry. One incident has already been noted in this chapter on corruption in Kashruth. It is a typical example of temple caterers who increase their profits by charging families for Kashruth supervision without actually providing it. Further machinations involve the Kosher-front type of deception—paying a rabbi for the use of his name, but employing very little of his services. Who knows what goes into the pot of this rabbi's Kosher caterer? Does he really use only Kosher meats? It would be interesting to interrogate the *mashgiach* and discover just how much he knows about his caterers' food purchases. If he will answer, let the *mashgiach* testify to his negligence by reporting how many times he has been present throughout when the caterer has done his cooking. Would the *mashgiach* dare to check the quantity of Kosher meats his caterer *tells him* he has bought against the actual shipment bills indicating the real quantity of Kosher meats purchased?

The problem of the *mashgiach*, if he is trying to be sincere in his work, is that he is not a free agent. His very livelihood depends upon the whim of the caterer. The caterer pays him his wages and can remove him at will if he so desires. The *mashgiach* knows this well and plays it cool in order to keep his job, although in addition to keeping his job he must also keep his mouth . . . shut tight!

In the last of a series of articles entitled, "Need for Kosher Catering Authority," which appeared in the *Na-*

tional Jewish Post and Opinion, Philip Finklestein revealed some of the problems created by the caterer in the following statement: "Having paid the piper, and perhaps continuing to pay on a regular percentage basis, the caterer gladly calls the tune. Too often he may have the last word on programs, schedules, and events throughout the center (temple), let alone what goes on in his kitchen." [28]

To elaborate on Mr. Finklestein's words, the caterer, who may well be a non-observant Jew himself, has the power to determine a good measure of synagogue policy, especially the standards related to Kashruth for these standards effect his business directly. Often he dictates to the rabbi, *mashgiach*, and members of the congregation what will and what will not go on at the affairs he caters. He has a free hand, and in most cases exploits his power to his own fullest economic advantage.

It is not only in the area of Kashruth that the caterer is lord and master, but also in the commandment of morality. Thus, much of ancient paganism's orgies have crept into temples via the backdoor of Kosher catering. The vogue at Bar Mitzvah receptions may yet be the scantily dressed go-go girls, which one very prominent Kosher caterer brought to his temple for such a *simcha*. After all, the Bar Mitzvah boy, having chanted his *Haftorah* portion (a selection from the prophets) has performed the traditional Rite of Passage, and who can help him pass more readily into manhood then a well-meaning and affectionate go-go girl?

And what of the catering halls outside the temples which are reputed to be Kosher, under the supervision of the rabbinate, and who desecrate the Sabbaths and festivals with all manner of violation? There one finds the holy and the profane dwelling side by side in sweet harmony blessed by the local rabbinate. Smoking, picture-taking, candle-lighting ceremonies, and a host of other abuses of the holy days, which these same rabbis would undoubtedly denounce from their pulpits, are permitted to continue in the catering places under their supervision. In ostrich-like fashion they hide their heads from seeing the dangers to Judaism which occur outside their synagogues. Perhaps, if one is to be generous to them, they have determined that Moses received two Torahs—one for inside the sanctuary, and the other for outside the sanctuary.

Ultimately, the question arises as to how all this came about, and how it can continue. A partial answer lies in the fact that in former days the buyer was told to beware, and he was somewhat alerted to the dangers of deception because the elements that were cheating him fulfilled the crude image of his expectations of them; those who dabbled in corruption lived the part. But today, matters have changed radically. Those most efficient in deceiving the public have donned the mantle of holiness and/or refinement. This is true in many areas of our economic life, but it is especially true of the Kashruth industry where psuedo-rabbis and phony *mashgichim* make a strong front for Kashruth fraud! For years such men have said the right words, have prepared right answers and smiled away questions that could not be answered without exposing the whole corrupt situation. And those who questioned sensed the cancerous growth on the flesh of Judaism which they might uncover if they pursued the matter further, and for reasons of misguided mercy often relented and turned away from it all in utter frustration.

Tragically, the issue of Kashruth does not trouble many American Jews very deeply. There are what many will call the "larger issues" of Jewish life, such as Israel and her enemies, the Jewish student on the college campus, anti-semitism, intermarriage, etc., etc. Those who attend syna-gogue regularly might possibly hear their rabbi preach a sermon about Kashruth once a year, if he is prodded by the Religious Committee to do so. Kashruth, like motherhood, is an aspect of traditional Judaism which everyone accepts and no one attempts to delve into until illegitimate forces enter it and endanger the sacred institution. Now that the foregoing lines have been written to testify to the deep corruption which has infected Kashruth, perhaps some courageous voices will find the *chutzpa* to raise some seri-ous questions and insist upon the answers to them. The result will inevitably be that the deceptions will end, or at least become greatly limited, and, hopefully a new era of Kashruth observance will arise within the Jewish commu-nity!

BOOK TWO

The information contained in this book follows very naturally from BOOK ONE. Based upon the previous chapters it is designed to answer some practical questions on, "How to keep Kosher." Three areas of modern Jewish life wherein Kashruth exists are given priority consideration are the home, the home-away-from-home, and the congregation. While it is a relatively simple matter for someone living in a metropolitan Jewish community to keep the Dietary Laws, for someone living off the proverbial "beaten path," of Jewish life, the challenge to "do it yourself" presents formidable problems that often become crises for the observant Jew.

While not every problem that could arise has been given consideration in this section, many of them have been anticipated and solutions recommended.

Sample Menus (How to Arrange a Good Kosher Meal)

8 Jews who observe Kashruth need not be deprived of all gourmet delights. For example, foods eaten in foreign lands such as Italy, France and Japan, also include meats that come from Kosher animals and fish. They can be prepared in a Kosher home to the delight of the most dedicated "balebusteh" (A Jewish homemaker par excellence) and her family. Simply obtain the cookbook of your favorite foreign country and with typical Yiddish *sechel* (ingenuity) prepare a delectable Kosher meal.

The suggested menus presented here are traditional, for the Jewish festivals.

SAMPLE SABBATH EVENING MENU

APPETIZER Chilled California Cranshaw Melon
Cold V-8 Juice Cocktail
Frosty Grape Juice

SALAD Assorted Pickled relish
Chiffonade salad, Thousand Island dressing

ENTREE Gefilte fish
Chopped fresh chicken livers Garni

SOUP Consomme Matzo Ball
Scotch Barley
Bouillon en Tasse

A VARIETY OF MEAT FAVORITES
Roast capon, Appleberry sauce
Braised pot roast of beef, barley and beans (Cholent)
Barbecued prime beef ribs, hot mustard
Stuffed breast of veal
Chinese pepper steak, steamed rice
Pickled Ox-tongue Florentine, raisin sauce
Boiled beef flanken, bouillon potatoes
Boiled spring chicken, matzo ball

VEGETABLES
Stuffed derma (*Kishka*)   Pineapple carrots (*Tsimis*)

DESSERT
Hungarian Apple strudel   Blueberry cream tarts
Maple chiffon cake   coconut macaroons
Fruit compote
Fruit Ices

BEVERAGES
Cafe noir (with *pareve* coffee lightner)   Orange Pekoe Tea

Sabbath *challah* bread is served as well as Kosher sacramental
wine.

SAMPLE ROSH HASHANAH EVE MENU

APPETIZER   Fruit cocktail
Apple segments dipped in honey
Iced New York State Apple Juice
Chilled grapefruit

SALAD   Salad bowl of mixed greens, French dressing

RELISH
Hearts of lettuce   California carrot sticks   Crisp Pascal celery

SOUP   Chicken broth en tasse
Old fashioned lima bean
Chicken soup with rice

A VARIETY OF MEAT FAVORITES
Roast spring chicken
Roulade of boneless shoulder of veal, pineapple ring
Broiled double baby lamb chops, mint Jelly
Barbecued turkey wings, Spanish rice
Fried calves brains with sauce Remoulade
Boiled young fowl *en pot*, Matzo ball

VEGETABLES
French fried potatoes   Mixed garden vegetables

DESSERT
Taiglach, sesame candy   Bowties   Sponge cake   Fruit ices

BEVERAGES
Orange Pekoe Tea   Cafe *noir*   Club soda

YOM KIPPUR EVE SAMPLE MENU
(Before the fast begins)

APPETIZER   Chilled grapefruit
Boiled northern yellow pike *en aspic*
Chopped liver garni
Chilled orange juice

SOUP   Consomme matzo ball
Chicken en tasse with noodles
Clear chicken Soup

A VARIETY OF MEAT FAVORITES
Boiled chicken, bouillon potatoes
Boiled beef flanken with horseradish
Braised pot roast of beef
Roast chicken with applesauce

VEGETABLES   Carrots and peas   Mashed potatoes

DESSERT
Sponge cake, strudel (Apple)   Fruit compote

BEVERAGES   Cafe *noir*   Tea   Sanka

SAMPLE SUKKOTH EVE MENU

APPETIZER   Chilled tomato juice
                 Chilled sliced orange
                 Iced pineapple juice

SALAD   Mixed vegetable salad, garlic dressing

SOUP   Chicken soup with noodles
                 Minestrone
                 Barley bean soup

A VARIETY OF MEAT FAVORITES
             Boiled beef tongue, sweet and sour
             Chicken cacciatore spaghetti *en casserole*
             Stuffed cabbage roll
             Roast prime ribs of beef
             Rolled boneless shoulder of lamb, mint jelly
             Boiled chicken with potatoes

VEGETABLES
         Potato pudding *(kugle)*   String beans   Baked potato

DESSERT
             Taiglach   Mocha layer cake   Egg *kichle*

BEVERAGES
             Cafe *noir*   Orange Pekoe tea   Sanka

SAMPLE PASSOVER EVE MENU
Following the Seder

     Charoseth   Hard-boiled eggs in salt water   Bitter herbs

RELISH   Hearts of crisp Pascal celery   Rose radishes
             California carrot sticks   Sweet red peppers
                     New dill pickles

FRUIT   Chilled imported Spanish melon

ENTREE   Boiled jellied norwood pike
                 Gefilte fish, horseradish

SOUP   Consomme noodle and mandle

A VARIETY OF MEAT FAVORITES
        Broiled prine New York rib steak, *au cresson*
          (except on the Sabbath)
        Roast Philadelphia capon, cranberry sauce
        Braised boneless shoulder of spring lamb
        Boiled spring chicken with fresh vegetables
        Roast turkey with Matzo stuffing

VEGETABLES
Passover potato pudding (*kugle*) Candied carrots (or Brussels
                          sprouts)

SALAD   Chef's green salad   Oil and cider vinegar

DESSERT   Passover honey cake   Coconut macroons
                    Passover spongecake
                    Raspberry fruit Ice

BEVERAGES   Cafe *noir*   Orange Pekoe tea
            Club soda (flavored Passover sodas)

SAMPLE SHAVUOTH MENU

*During Shavuoth the custom has arisen of serving foods made
of milk and other dairy products. The following menu reflects
this tradition.*

APPETIZER
        Marinated herring in wine sauce or sour cream sauce
        Chilled prune juice
        Chopped eggs and onions

SOUP   Green split pea soup
                Cold beet borscht with sour cream
                Iced *schav*

A VARIETY OF HOT MAIN DISHES
        Broiled fillet of halibut, lemon butter
        Cheese blintzes and sour cream
        Italian pizza pie

Sliced hard egg a la creole
Baked Elbow Macaroni and cheese *au gratin*

VEGETABLES
Kernel corn   Creamed spinach   Fresh cauliflower *polonaise*

COLD DISHES
Hawaiian fruit plate, sliced Kosher Jello
Tunafish salad sandwich on rye bread
Imported Brisling sardine salad, Pickled bean sprouts
Combination garden vegetable platter

DESSERT
Fresh strawberry shortcake   Babka coffeecake
Shadow ice cream cake

BEVERAGES
Coffee with cream   Tea Postum, Decaf.   Buttermilk

SAMPLE MENU FOR CHANUKKA

Since the main staple of traditional food on Chanukka is po-
tato latkes (pancakes) which are usually served with applesauce
and sour cream, the following is a dairy menu. Potato latkes
may, of course, be made pareve *and served with a meat as well.*

APPETIZER   Pickled lox in sour cream sauce
                 Vegetarian chopped liver
                 Chilled tomato juice

SOUP   Split green pea
                         Cold borscht
                         Fish chowder

HOT DISHES
Potato latkes, applesauce and sour cream
Scrambled eggs with kippers and onions
Kasha *Varnishkes* and stewed mushrooms
Broiled baby scrod, lemon wedge
Garden vegetable plate

VEGETABLES   Spinach   Baked potato   Peas

COLD DISHES
Hawaiian fruit plate wth cottage cheese
Tuna fish sandwich on rye bread, cole slaw
Tomato herring salad, Bermuda onion ring
Gefilte fish, horse-radish

DESSERT
Peach shortcake   chocolate chip cake
assorted butter cookies

BEVERAGES
Coffee with cream   Tea   Postum   Buttermilk   Sanka

SAMPLE MENU FOR PURIM

During the Purim observance it is customary to enjoy a special meal called the Purim Se'udah *(festive meal). The main staple of the traditional food on Purim is the* Hamantasch *(Popover), which can be made either dairy or* pareve.

APPETIZER
Chilled grapefruit half
Chopped chicken liver garni
Sauté of calves sweetbreads on *vol-au-vent*

SALAD   Tossed green salad   Russian dressing

SOUP   Beef vegetable soup
Chicken soup with noodles or rice
Clear consomme

A VARIETY OF MEAT FAVORITES
Roast duckling with orange slices
Broiled Rib steak
Suki Yaki with rice
Fricassee of chicken wings with corn meal
Barbecued turkey wings with potato pudding

VEGETABLES
 Broccoli   Sweet potato   Carrots and Peas
BEVERAGES   Cafe *noir*   Orange Pekoe tea   Sanka
DESSERT
 Hamantaschen   Marble Mandlebread   Bowties

Kashruth Observance
on the College Campuses

9   The patterns of our modern living have brought about trends not known to previous generations. New problems confront those who observe Kashruth because of these new ways of living. Young people who have been reared in Kashruth-observing homes and want to observe Kashruth on the college campus or in the armed forces have special challenges to consider. Especially today, when the trend among young people is to attend a college away from home, there is a need for information about Kashruth-arrangements on college campuses. The same thing holds true for the observant Jew who is serving our country in the armed services.

This chapter is devoted to the college student and the G.I. It contains a comprehensive listing of colleges throughout the country, noting which ones have Kosher facilities, and which do not. This information has been provided by the B'nai B'rith Hillel foundation, the organization which has been recognized as representative of Jewish interests on college campuses. The information on the military has been obtained from the National Jewish Welfare Board Chaplaincy Commission, which is the recog-

nized agency for providing Jewish chaplains and services to
Jewish military personnel.

Both sources of information have provided their most
recent (1968) publications. However, with the passage of
time, it would be wise to consult each of them for their
most up-to-date information. Their addresses are listed together with their information sections.

HILLEL FOUNDATIONS have full-time professional staff, many
with their own buildings and large numbers of Jewish students.
They will afford the greatest opportunities for the observance
of Kashruth.

College Campuses

National Office,
B'NAI B'RITH HILLEL FOUNDATIONS—2
1640 Rhode Island Avenue, N.W.
Washington, D.C. 20036

ADELPHI UNIVERSITY
HOFSTRA UNIVERSITY
B'nai B'rith Hillel Foundation
Adelphi University
Garden City, New York 11530

It may be possible for observant students to rent apartments
and do their own cooking. Kosher food and meat are available
in nearby Hempstead, Long Island.

ALABAMA, UNIVERSITY OF
B'nai B'rith Hillel Foundation
728 10th Avenue
Tuscaloosa, Alabama 35401

Hillel Facilities
  None.
Off Campus
  Arrangements may be made with private family.
University Facilities
  Dairy, fruit, vegetable substitutes available at all meals in dining halls.
Other Arrangements
  Students may cook privately in dormitory, fraternity or sorority houses.

AMERICAN UNIVERSITY, THE
B'nai B'rith Hillel Foundation
A. S. Kay Spiritual Life Center
Massachusetts and Nebraska Ave., N.W.
Washington, D.C. 20016

Hillel Facilities
  None.
Off Campus
  Students may live in own apartments or with private families.
University Facilities
  Dairy, fruit, vegetable substitutes available in dining hall.
Other Arrangements
  Students may cook in dormitory, fraternity or sorority houses.

ARIZONA, UNIVERSITY OF
B'nai B'rith Hillel Foundation
1245 East Second Street
Tucson, Arizona

Hillel Facilities
  Lunch served on scheduled basis, Monday through Friday, at 50 cents per meal.
Off Campus
  Arrangements may be made to eat and/or live with observant family.

University Facilities
  Dairy, vegetable, fruit substitutes available in University
  cafeteria.
Other Arrangements
  Students may prepare their own dinners in Hillel kitchen.
  Students may make their own arrangements in sorority and
  fraternity houses.

BOSTON UNIVERSITY
B'nai B'rith Hillel Foundation
233 Bay State Road
Boston, Massachusetts 02215

Hillel Facilities
  None.
Off Campus
  Students may live off campus. If student does not eat
  breakfast and lunch in University dining hall, he will be
  excused from dormitory and food contract. Consent must
  be secured from Hillel Director for this arrangement.
University Facilities
  Kosher TV dinners available at 50¢ per meal. This cost
  is in addition to University board contract. Such arrangement should be cleared with Hillel Director. Dairy, fruit,
  vegetable substitutes available at all meals.

BRANDEIS UNIVERSITY
B'nai B'rith Hillel Foundation
Berlin Chapel
Brandeis University
Waltham, Massachusetts 02154

Hillel Facilities
  None.
Off Campus
  Student may live in own apartment and do his own cooking
  or board or have kitchen privileges with private family.

University Facilities
Kosher meals, three times daily, every day, available in University dining hall on regular contract.

BRITISH COLUMBIA, UNIVERSITY OF
4837 Cambie Street
Vancouver, B.C., Canada

A commuter school with very few out-of-towners.
Hillel Facilities
None.
Off Campus
The out-of-town students may make arrangements to live with private families.
University Facilities
It may be possible for boarding students to make special arrangements with University cafeteria for special foods.

BROOKLYN COLLEGE
B'nai B'rith Hillel Foundation
2901 Campus Road
Brooklyn, New York 11210

A commuter school. No out-of-town students.
Hillel Facilities
Dinner served every Thursday as part of the Hillel Institute of Judaic Studies only. Cost is 90 cents per meal, or $9.00 per quarter.
College Facilities
Hillel has arranged to have a kosher sandwich and food machine installed in the College Lunch Room.

BROWN UNIVERSITY
PEMBROKE COLLEGE
B'nai B'rith Hillel Foundation
80 Brown Street
Providence, Rhode Island 02900

Hillel Facilities
Dinner served on a regular basis, Monday through Friday.
Students may deduct cost of this meal from University
dining contract.
Off Campus
Upper classmen may live off campus and do their own cook-
ing, or arrange to live with private family.

BUFFALO, STATE UNIVERSITY OF
B'nai B'rith Hillel Foundation
40 Capen Boulevard
Buffalo, New York 14214

Off Campus
Room and board available with private families.
Other Arrangements
Kosher food available at The Young Israel House, supported
and supervised by The Young Israel of Buffalo.
A small number of students may be accommodated for room
and board in The Young Israel House. In addition, students
living in dormitories or in private quarters may contract for
dinners either on a semester or a per-meal basis. Students
contracting for such meals do not have to make a food contract with the University.

CALIFORNIA, UNIVERSITY OF,
  AT BERKELEY
B'nai B'rith Hillel Foundation
2736 Bacroft Way
Berkeley, California 94704

Hillel Facilities
"Sometime" breakfast and dinner served on Sundays.
Regular Thursday dinner served at $1-$1.25 per meal.
Off Campus
Students may rent apartments or rooms with private families
with kitchen privileges.

University Facilities
  Dairy, vegetable, and fruit substitutes available in University dining hall.

CALIFORNIA, UNIVERSITY OF, AT LOS ANGELES
900 Hilgard Avenue
Los Angeles, California 90024

Off Campus
  Private apartments or rooms with private families with kitchen privileges.
University Facilities
  Kosher frozen TV dinners available at no additional cost. Dairy, vegetable or fruit substitutes available in University dining hall.

CITY COLLEGE OF NEW YORK (DOWNTOWN)
B'nai B'rith Hillel Foundation
144 East 24th Street
New York, New York 10010

A commuter school. No out-of-town students.
Hillel Facilities
  None.

CITY COLLEGE OF NEW YORK (UPTOWN)
B'nai B'rith Hillel Foundation
475 West 140th Street
New York, New York 10031

A commuter school. No out-of-town students.
Hillel Facilities
  None.

CHICAGO, UNIVERSITY OF
B'nai B'rith Hillel Foundation
5715 Woodlawn Avenue
Chicago, Illinois 60637

Hillel Facilities
   Student co-op provides Friday night dinners and Saturday luncheons.
Off Campus
   A dining room operated by Mrs. B. Stern serves Friday dinner and Saturday meals.
   Apartments available, and boarding with private families.
University Facilities
   Kosher TV dinner available at $2.00 per meal, or $114 per quarter. These fees are in addition to University boarding contract.
   Dairy, fruit, and vegetable substitutes available in University dining halls.
   Dormitory dining halls also provide dairy, fruit, and vegetable substitutes.

COLORADO, UNIVERSITY OF
B'nai B'rith Hillel Foundation
2795 Pennsylvania Avenue
Boulder, Colorado

Hillel Facilities
   Luncheon at 50¢ per meal; dinner at $1.00 per meal— served every Sunday.
Off Campus
   Kosher food readily available in Denver. Arrangements can be made for cooking in student apartments, or for boarding with private families.
University Facilities
   Dairy, fruit, and vegetable substitutes available in University dining hall.

CONNECTICUT, UNIVERSITY OF
B'nai B'rith Hillel Foundation
North Eagleville Road
Storrs, Connecticut 06268

Hillel Facilities
>Dinner served on scheduled basis, Monday through Thursday. Cost of $5.00 per week, which may be deducted from University board contracts. Subsidy from Rabbinical Council of Connecticut helps defray cost of Kashruth dining operation.

CORNELL UNIVERSITY
B'nai B'rith Hillel Foundation
Anabel Taylor Hall
Cornell University
Ithaca, New York 14850

Hillel Facilities
>Young Israel house serves Kosher food. University gives rebates to students if they eat at Young Israel during the year, and at Hillel during Passover.
>Female students who take a contract with Young Israel for at least seven meals a week will be released from board contracts.

Off Campus
>Private apartments for own cooking are available.

University Facilities
>Dairy, fruit, and vegetable substitutes available, but on an inadequate basis.

FLORIDA, UNIVERSITY OF
B'nai B'rith Hillel Foundation
16 N.W. 18th Street
Gainesville, Florida

Hillel Facilities
>On a scheduled basis: Dinner every Tuesday and Thursday at $1.50 per meal. Luncheon every Saturday at 75¢ per meal.

Off Campus
>Students may have their own apartments, but Kosher foods are not available except through Hillel.

University Facilities
Provide no opportunity to do own cooking.

GEORGE WASHINGTON UNIVERSITY
B'nai B'rith Hillel Foundation
2129 F Street, N.W.
Washington, D.C. 20037
Hillel Facilities

Dinner served on scheduled basis Monday through Friday
at $1.40 per meal. This charge is in addition to University
board contract.
National Council of Young Israel helps subsidize the Kosher
dining plan.
Off Campus
Upper classmen may rent apartments and do their own
cooking.
University Facilities
Dairy, fruit, and vegetable substitutes are *not* provided in
University dining hall.
Other Facts
There is a compulsory board contract for residents of the
Women's Residence Dormitory, and for all male and female
resident freshmen.

GEORGIA, UNIVERSITY OF
B'nai B'rith Hillel Foundation
1155 S. Milledge Avenue
Athens, Georgia 30601

Hillel Facilities
Dinner served on scheduled basis every Sunday at $1.00 per
meal.
Off Campus
Upper classmen may do their own cooking in their own
apartments.
University Facilities
None.

HARVARD UNIVERSITY
RADCLIFFE COLLEGE
B'nai B'rith Hillel Foundation
5 Bryant Street
Cambridge, Massachusetts 02138

Hillel Facilities
Dinner served on scheduled basis, Monday, Tuesday, Wednesday and Friday; luncheon on Saturday. $1.90 per meal, deductible from University board contract.
Associated Synagogues of Greater Boston provide a subsidy for the Kosher dining operation.
Off Campus
Students may have their own apartments and do their own cooking, or board with private families.
University Facilities
Kosher lunch and dinner available in University dining halls at 50¢ per meal. Cost is in addition to board contract.

HUNTER COLLEGE (Park Avenue)
B'nai B'rith Hillel Foundation
Roosevelt Memorial House
49 East 65th Street
New York, New York 10021

A commuter school. No out-of-town students.
Hillel Facilities
None.

ILLINOIS, UNIVERSITY OF
B'nai B'rith Hillel Foundation
503 E. John Street
Champaign, Illinois 61822

Hillel Facilities
Dinner served on scheduled basis Monday through Friday; lunch on Saturday. Cost of $1.50 per meal, payable in advance at the beginning of each semester for the entire

semester, and is deducted from University board contract. Chicago Rabbinical Council and the Rabbinical Assembly provide subsidies for Kosher dining operations.
University Facilities
Dairy, fruit, vegetable substitutes available in University dining hall.

INDIANA UNIVERSITY
B'nai B'rith Hillel Foundation
730 East Third Street
Bloomington, Indiana 47403

Hillel Facilities
Dinner on scheduled basis, served every Sunday and Friday at $1.25 per meal. Cost is in addition to University board contract.

IOWA, STATE UNIVERSITY OF
B'nai B'rith Hillel Foundation
122 E. Market Street
Iowa City, Iowa 52240

Hillel Facilities
Luncheon at 50¢ per meal, and dinner at $1.00 per meal served every Sunday on a scheduled basis.
Off Campus
Special permission is obtainable to live in apartments or with private families, in order to observe Kashruth.
University Facilities
Dairy, fruit, vegetable substitutes available in University dining hall.

LOS ANGELES CITY COLLEGE
B'nai B'rith Hillel Foundation
903 N. Heliotrope Drive
Los Angeles, California 90029

A commuter school. No out-of-town students.
Hillel Facilities
None.

MANITOBA, UNIVERSITY OF
B'nai B'rith Hillel Foundation
67 Edmonton Street
Winnipeg, Manitoba, Canada

A "streetcar" campus with very few students who do not live
in Winnipeg.
Hillel Facilities
  None.
Off Campus
  For the few students who may require it, Kosher boarding
  is available in private homes.
  Students may have their own apartments and do their own
  cooking.

MARYLAND, UNIVERSITY OF
B'nai B'rith Hillel Foundation
P.O. Box 187
College Park, Maryland

Hillel Facilities
  Three meals a day, Monday through Saturday, served on
  scheduled basis. Cost is $275 per semester, deducted from
  the University board contract.
Off Campus
  Apartments, as well as room and board with private families,
  are available.

MASSACHUSETTS INSTITUTE OF
TECHNOLOGY
B'nai B'rith Hillel Foundation
% Religious Counselors Bldg.
317 Memorial Drive
Cambridge, Massachusetts 02139

Hillel Facilities
  Dinner served on scheduled basis, Monday through Thursday, at $1.75 per meal; $2 for Friday dinner; and lunch

every Saturday at $1.25 per meal. Students are required to pay a week in advance. Cost is deducted from University board contract.

The Associated Synagogues of Greater Boston provide subsidy for Kosher dining facility.

Other Facts

MIT provides space for the Hillel Dining Club in the Walker Memorial Building.

Jewish students are excused from compulsory "commons meals" (University dining), provided Hillel Director certifies that they are getting a hot meal at least once a day. Students have refrigerators in their rooms, and may prepare cold food for themselves for breakfast and lunch.

MASSACHUSETTS, UNIVERSITY OF
SMITH COLLEGE
B'nai B'rith Hillel Foundation
Student Union Building
University of Massachusetts
Amherst, Massachusetts 01003

Hillel Facilities
None.
University Facilities
At University of Massachusetts, frozen Kosher TV dinners are served in dining hall at no extra charge.
No facilities for Kashruth observance at Smith College.

McGILL UNIVERSITY
B'nai B'rith Hillel Foundation
3460 Stanley Street
Montreal 2, Quebec, Canada

Hillel Facilities
Lunch served on scheduled basis, Monday through Friday at 90 cents per meal. Cost is in addition to University board contract.

Off Campus
  Arrangements can be made with private family. Kosher restaurant also available. Both are 1–1½ miles from campus. Students may have their own apartments and do their own cooking.
University Facilities
  Dairy, fruit, vegetable substitutes available in University dining hall, but with difficulty.

MIAMI, UNIVERSITY OF
B'nai B'rith Hillel Foundation
1100 Miller Drive
Coral Gables, Florida 33146

Hillel Facilities
  Dinner served on scheduled basis, Monday through Friday; breakfast every Sunday. Cost—$7.50 per week.
Off Campus
  Private apartments with cooking facilities available.
University Facilities
  Dairy, fruit, vegetable substitutes available at all meals in University dining halls.
Other Arrangements
  Students may arrange to do their own cooking in dormitories.

MICHIGAN STATE UNIVERSITY
B'nai B'rith Hillel Foundation
319 Hillcrest Avenue
East Lansing, Michigan 48823

Hillel Facilities
  Most Sundays and some Fridays dinner is served.
Other Arrangements
  Apartments available in which students can do their own cooking. Kosher meat is obtainable from Detroit. If freezer space not available in the apartment, it may be possible to arrange for use of some of Hillel's limited freezer space.

MICHIGAN, UNIVERSITY OF
B'nai B'rith Hillel Foundation
1429 Hill Street
Ann Arbor, Michigan

Hillel Facilities
> Dinner served on scheduled basis Sunday through Friday.
> Cost is $138.60 per semester deducted from University board
> contract.
> National Council of Young Israel provides subsidy for
> kosher dining facility.

Off Campus
> Apartments are available. Students may sign up for Sabbath
> meal and/or one or more mid-week dinners at Hillel.

University Facilities
> Dairy, fruit, vegetable substitutes available in University
> dining hall.

Other Arrangements
> Students may do their own cooking in some dormitories,
> and in fraternity and sorority houses.

MINNESOTA, UNIVERSITY OF
B'nai B'rith Hillel Foundation
1521 University Avenue, S.E.
Minneapolis, Minnesota 55414

Hillel Facilities
> Lunch served every Wednesday at 50 cents per meal; dinner
> served every Tuesday and Friday at $.75-$1.00 per meal.
> Sabbath dinner served every other Saturday.

Off Campus
> Observant students may make arrangements with nearby
> private families.

University Facilities
> Dairy, fruit, vegetable substitute available in University
> dining hall.

MISSOURI, UNIVERSITY OF
STEPHENS COLLEGE
B'nai B'rith Hillel Foundation
1107 University Avenue
Columbia, Missouri 65201

Hillel Facilities
 An auxiliary kitchen with hot plate, electric oven, and
 refrigerator has been set up for students who wish to cook
 their own meals.

NORTH CAROLINA, UNIVERSITY OF
B'nai B'rith Hillel Foundation
210 W. Cameron Avenue
Chapel Hill, North Carolina 27514

Hillel Facilities
 Kitchen available for students to cook their own meals.
 Weekly Sunday suppers served in connection with program.
Other Arrangements
 Students may find facilities for cooking in fraternity houses.

NORTHWESTERN UNIVERSITY
B'nai B'rith Hillel Foundation
1740 Judson Avenue
Evanston, Illinois

Hillel Facilities
 Dinner served on scheduled basis, Sunday through Friday;
 luncheon served every Wednesday and Saturday.
 Students are charged on quarterly basis. Cost deducted from
 University board contract.
 Students may arrange to do their own cooking in Hillel's
 kitchen.
University Facilities
 Dairy, fruit, and vegetable substitutes available in Univer-
 sity dining hall.

OHIO STATE UNIVERSITY
B'nai B'rith Hillel Foundation
46 East 16th Avenue
Columbus, Ohio 43201

Hillel Facilities
> Dinner served on scheduled basis, Monday through Friday, at $1.25-$1.50 per meal; breakfast served every Sunday at 50 cents per meal; lunch every Saturday.
> Students may pay daily, weekly, or quarterly. Costs are in addition to University board contract.

Off Campus
> Students may cook in some rooming houses.

University Facilities
> Dairy, fruit, vegetable substitutes available in University dining hall.

OHIO UNIVERSITY
B'nai B'rith Hillel Foundation
97 University Terrace
Athens, Ohio 45701

Hillel Facilities
> Students have the privilege of using Hillel freezer, refrigerator and kitchen facilities.

University Facilities
> Dairy, fruit, and vegetable substitutes available in University dining halls.
> Freshman students are required to live and eat in the dormitories and cafeterias of the University.

Other Notes
> Kashruth observance extremely difficult at this University.

OKLAHOMA, UNIVERSITY OF
B'nai B'rith Hillel Foundation
494 Elm Avenue
Norman, Oklahoma 73069

Hillel Facilities
No regularly scheduled meals except those served at special program events.
University Facilities
University apartments may be obtained for students who wish to do their own cooking.
Students under 21 who request apartments must have approval of Hillel Director.

PENNSYLVANIA STATE UNIVERSITY
B'nai B'rith Hillel Foundation
224 Locust Lane
State College, Pennsylvania 16801

Hillel Facilities
Dinner served on scheduled basis, Monday, Wednesday, and Friday at $1.75 per meal. Cost is in addition to University board contract.
Off Campus
Apartments may be obtained in downtown area for students to do their own cooking.

PENNSYLVANIA, UNIVERSITY OF
Hillel Foundation
202 S. 36th Street
Philadelphia, Pennsylvania 19104

Hillel Facilities
Dinner served on scheduled basis, Monday through Friday. Cost per semester is $135, which is deducted from University board contract.
Non-contract students may eat at Hillel at $2.00 per dinner. Small annual subvention from Women's League is made to Hillel for maintaining the Kosher facility.
Other Notes
Freshmen and all women students who live in dormitories must have meals there.

Students who sign contract to eat at Hillel are excused from eating dinner in dormitories.

PITTSBURGH, UNIVERSITY OF
CARNEGIE INSTITUTE OF TECHNOLOGY
B'nai B'rith Hillel Foundation
Y.M. and Y.W.H.A.
315 S. Bellefield Avenue
Pittsburgh 13, Pennsylvania

Hillel Facilities
  None.
University Facilities
  During the winter trimester of 1966 a trial system was initiated. A Kosher frozen dinner was served in the University dining hall. Cost is $100 for trimester per student, in addition to University board contract. Present indications are that the University is willing to make an adjustment in the room and board contracts for those students desiring Kosher food.

PRINCETON UNIVERSITY
B'nai B'rith Hillel Foundation
Murray-Dodge Hall
Princeton University
Princeton, New Jersey 08540

Hillel Facilities
  Kosher food served in Yavneh House, located one block off campus.
  Three meals daily, 7 days a week for full term, are served on a scheduled basis.
  The facility is under surveillance of Hillel. All students eating there must be certified by Hillel Director.
  Freshmen and sophomores save University dining cost if certified by Hillel and enrolled at Yavneh House.
  Graduate students may sign contract for dining at Yavneh House.

PURDUE UNIVERSITY
B'nai B'rith Hillel Foundation
912 State Street
West Lafayette, Indiana, 47906

Hillel Facilities
Dinner served on scheduled basis every Friday at $1.25 per meal.
May be possible for observant students to do their own cooking in Hillel House.

QUEENS COLLEGE
B'nai B'rith Hillel Foundation
154–29 65th Avenue
Flushing, New York

A commuter school. No out of town students.
University Facilities
College cafeteria serves Kosher sandwiches.

QUEEN'S UNIVERSITY
Hillel Foundation at Queens University
26 Barrie Street
Kingston, Ontario, Canada

Hillel Facilities
Dinner served daily on scheduled basis at $1.25 per meal.
The Kosher dining club is not located in the Hillel House.

ROCHESTER, UNIVERSITY OF
B'nai B'rith Hillel Foundation
Todd Union
River Campus Station
Rochester, New York 14617

Hillel Facilities
Kosher dining club (not in Hillel building) serves dinner, Monday through Saturday, at $1.35 per meal, or on a con-

tracted board plan. Cost deducted from University board contract.
Dinner served two Sundays per month in connection with program.
Off Campus
Students may make outside housing arrangements that include boarding, or with kitchen privileges.
University Facilities
Dairy, fruit, and vegetable substitutes available in University dining hall.

RUTGERS STATE UNIVERSITY
B'nai B'rith Hellel Foundation
341 George Street
New Brunswick, New Jersey 08901

Hillel Facilities
Dinner is served on scheduled basis Monday through Thursday. Students must sign semester contract at $90, which is deducted from University board contract. Friday-night dinner also served on scheduled basis, but is not part of Hillel dining contract. Meal is paid for separately.
University Facilities
Students may make arrangements to cook in fraternity houses.

SOUTHERN CALIFORNIA, UNIVERSITY OF
B'nai B'rith Hellel Foundation
1029 West 36th Street
Los Angeles, California 90007

Hillel Facilities
Luncheon served every Wednesday on scheduled basis at 75¢ per meal.
Off Campus
Arrangements can be made with private family.
Arrangements can be made with Kosher restaurant nearby.

Apartments for undergraduate and graduate male students and female graduate students may be obtained.

University Facilities

Dairy, fruit, and vegetable substitutes are available in University dining hall.

Negotiations are being held with the University by the Hillel Director and the Director of the regional office of the United Synagogue to provide frozen Kosher dinners for students living in dormitories. These may be available in the very near future.

STANFORD UNIVERSITY
B'nai B'rith Hillel Foundation
880 Emerson Street
Palo Alto, California 94301

Hillel Facilities

None.

Off Campus

All freshmen must live on campus, but all other male students may live off campus and make their own arrangements for Kosher boarding, or for cooking for themselves.

Graduate students live off campus, or in campus apartments, and may arrange to cook for themselves.

University Facilities

Dairy, fruit, vegetable substitutes available on an irregular basis.

It may be possible for students to obtain permission to cook in dormitory.

Other Arrangements

There are no Kosher restaurants in the area. Kosher meat may be ordered from San Jose.

SYRACUSE UNIVERSITY
B'nai B'rith Hellel Foundation
Hendricks Memorial Chapel
Syracuse University
Syracuse, New York 13210

Hillel Facilities
Lunch is served daily on a scheduled basis.
Dinner served on a scheduled basis Monday through Saturday.
Kosher dining club is situated in Young Israel House under Hillel auspices. Students are charged $260 on a semester basis. This contract replaces the University board contract. Young Israel provides subsidy for equipment.

TEMPLE UNIVERSITY
B'nai B'rith Hellel Foundation
2014 N. Broad Street
Philadelphia, Pennsylvania 19121

Hillel Facilities
Most students are commuters who live in Philadelphia.
There is no Hillel dining club, but there are kitchen facilities for students to use as needed.
A Kosher-sandwich vending machine is on the premises.

TEXAS, UNIVERSITY OF
B'nai B'rith Hillel Foundation
P. O. Box H, University Station
Austin, Texas 78705

Hillel Facilities
Kosher facilities are available only for special dinners, luncheons, and holiday observances.

TEXAS AGRICULTURAL AND MECHANICAL UNIVERSITY
B'nai B'rith Hillel Foundation
800 Jersey Street
College Station, Texas 77840

Hillel Facilities
None.
Off Campus
There are no available Kosher facilities.

TORONTO, UNIVERSITY OF
B'nai B'rith Hillel Foundation
186 St. George Street
Toronto 5, Ontario, Canada

Hillel Facilities
Dinner served on scheduled basis every Tuesday at $1.25
per meal.
Occasional Friday evening meals served.

Off Campus
It is possible for students to live with private families with
boarding arrangements or kitchen privileges. Students can
also rent apartments and do their own cooking.

TUFTS UNIVERSITY
B'nai B'rith Hillel Foundation
5 Bryant Street
Cambridge, Massachusetts 02138

Hillel Facilities
None.

Off Campus
It is possible for students to live with private families with
boarding arrangements or kitchen privileges. Students can
also rent apartments and do their own cooking.

TULANE UNIVERSITY OF LOUISIANA
B'nai B'rith Hillel Foundation
912 Broadway
New Orleans, Louisiana 70118

Hillel Facilities
None.

Off Campus
Arrangements can be made with private families nearby.
There is a nearby Kosher delicatessen.

VERMONT, UNIVERSITY OF
B'nai B'rith Hillel Foundation
389 College Street
Burlington, Vermont 05401

Hillel Facilities
  Students may obtain permission to use Hillel kitchen facilities in connection with pre-cooked frozen meals. Regular cooking not permitted in Hillel House.
Off Campus
  Possible arrangement with private families, but generally extremely difficult.
University Facilities
  Dairy, fruit, vegetable substitutes may be available in University dining hall.

VIRGINIA, UNIVERSITY OF
B'nai B'rith Hillel Foundation
1824 University Circle
Charlottesville, Virginia 22903

Hillel Facilities
  Students may use Hillel kitchen for storing and heating pre-cooked foods.
  Off Campus
  Apartments available where students may do their own cooking.
University Facilities
  Dairy, fruit, vegetable substitutes available in University dining hall.
Other Arrangements
  Students may be able to use kitchen facilities in fraternity houses.

WASHINGTON, UNIVERSITY OF
B'nai B'rith Hillel Foundation
4745 17th Avenue, N.E.
Seattle, Washington 98105

Hillel Facilities
  Hillel serves food only for brunches and dinners as part of special programs.

WASHINGTON UNIVERSITY
B'nai B'rith Hillel Foundation
6300 Forsyth Avenue
St. Louis, Missouri 63105

Hillel Facilities
None. Food served only during Passover.
University Facilities
Frozen Kosher dinners available in University dining hall.
Cost is $55 per semester in addition to University board contract.
Va'ad Hoeir may subsidized individual students on the recommendation of Hillel Director.

WAYNE STATE UNIVERSITY
B'nai B'rith Hillel Foundation
4841 Second Boulevard
Detroit, Michigan 48202

Hillel Facilities
Lunch served on scheduled basis every Thursday at 45 cents per meal.
Off Campus
Observant students may find apartments and do their own cooking. Kosher food shopping is no problem.
University Facilities
University has no dormitories and there is no boarding contract. University cafeteria serves fruit, vegetables, and dairy foods at all times.
Other Arrangements
Kosher restaurant off campus within 15 minutes by car or a half-hour by bus.

WEST VIRGINIA UNIVERSITY
B'nai B'rith Hillel Foundation
1420 University Avenue
Morgantown, West Virginia 26505

Hillel Facilities
  Hillel serves occasional Sunday brunches and suppers.
  Students may purchase Kosher food in Morgantown, Pitts-
  burgh or Uniontown, Pa.
  Storage space in Hillel freezer available.

WESTERN RESERVE UNIVERSITY
CASE INSTITUTE OF TECHNOLOGY
B'nai B'rith Hillel Foundation
11409 Bellflower Road
Cleveland, Ohio 44106

Hillel Facilities
  Dinner served on scheduled basis, Monday through Friday;
  luncheon every Saturday.
  Semester charge of $142.50 is in addition to University
  board contract.
Off Campus
  Apartments available in which students may do their own
  cooking.
University Facilities
  Dairy, fruit, vegetable substitutes available in University
  dining hall.

WISCONSIN, UNIVERSITY OF
B'nai B'rith Hillel Foundation
611 Langdon Street
Madison, Wisconsin 53703

Hillel Facilities
  Sunday dinner served on scheduled basis; Friday dinners
  served occasionally.
Off Campus
  Graduate students, men and women and undergraduate girls
  in senior year and/or 21 years of age may have their own
  apartments and do their own cooking.
  University will grant permission to students wishing to
  observe Kashruth to live in apartments. Hillel Director
  should be consulted about this.

Local Kosher butcher and baker both near campus and under supervision of the Va'ad Ha'Kashruth of Madison.

University Facilities

Fruit, vegetable, or dairy substitutes available in dormitory dining halls.

A private women's dormitory has made provision for Kosher meals at which male students are also eligible on basis of board contract. Campus Hall, 211 W. Gilman Street.

YALE UNIVERSITY
B'nai B'rith Hillel Foundation
265 Yale Station
New Haven, Connecticut 06520

Hillel Facilities

Lunch and dinner are served on scheduled basis daily.

Students are charged $307.50 on a semester basis, which is deducted from University board contract.

Students may also come for individual meals at $1.25 for lunch and $2.50 for dinner.

Local Young Israel Synagogue provides some subsidy for Kosher dining club.

Off Campus

Arrangements may be made with Kosher delicatessen nearby. Female graduate students and some law students who live in law-school suites may do their own cooking.

University Facilities

Kosher frozen dinners available for lunch or dinner at 70¢ per meal in the University dining hall. Dairy, fruit, vegetable substitutes are available in University dining hall.

UNIVERSITIES IN GREAT BRITAIN
B'nai B'rith Hillel Foundation
1 Endsleigh Street
London, W.C. 1, England

Hillel Facilities

Meals are served on a daily basis at University of London.

Off Campus
Arrangements can be made for students to live and board with private families.

Other Facts
There are Kosher eating facilities at the Universities of Oxford, Cambridge, Birmingham, Manchester, Leeds, and Sheffield. These are all subsidized by the B'nai B'rith Hillel Foundations.

The University of Glasgow also has Kosher meal facilities as part of the communal Kosher school meals service.

HILLEL COUNSELORSHIPS
Have part-time professional staff, usually a local rabbi or faculty member, have fewer Jewish students and no Hillel building. Kashruth observance presents some difficulties for the student. Where no address is given, students are advised to contact the National B'nai B'rith Hillel Foundations office in Washington, D.C.

Kashruth: B'nai B'rith Hillel Counselorships

ALFRED UNIVERSITY, Alfred, New York

Opportunity for students to cook privately in fraternity house.

BATES COLLEGE, Lewiston, Maine

Arrangements can be made with private family nearby.

BRIDGEPORT, UNIVERSITY OF, Bridgeport, Conn.

Off Campus
Arrangements can be made with private family nearby.

University Facilities
Dairy, vegetables, fruit substitutes available in University dining hall.
Students may arrange to cook privately in University dormitories.
The University has indicated its willingness to provide Kosher facilities if at least 200 students would be interested.

BROCKPORT, SUNY College at
GENESEO, SUNY College at
MONROE COMMUNITY COLLEGE
ROCHESTER INSTITUTE OF TECHNOLOGY
B'nai B'rith Hillel Foundation
Todd Union-River Campus Station
Rochester, N.Y. 14627

Off Campus
Students attending Monroe Community and Rochester Institute, may live in their own apartments or arrange facilities with private families.
University Facilities
Kosher TV dinner served in Rochester Institute of Technology dining hall at an additional 35¢ per meal above regular board charge.
At all schools, dairy, fruit, vegetable substitutes available in University dining halls.

BUFFALO, SUNY College at
B'nai B'rith Hillel Foundation
40 Capen Blvd.
Buffalo, N.Y. 14214

Off Campus
Arrangements may be made with private family nearby.

CALIFORNIA STATE COLLEGE
at Los Angeles

Predominantly a commuter school with very few students living away from home.
Students who do live in their own apartments or in dormitories may be able to make arrangements for private cooking.

CALIFORNIA, UNIVERSITY OF
at Riverside

Hillel Facilities
  Dinner served at rare intervals at $1.00-$1.50 per meal.
Off Campus
  Arrangements are made with private family nearby.
University Facilities
  Dairy, fruit, vegetable substitutes available in University dining hall.
  Opportunity for students to cook privately is available in University dormitories.

CALIFORNIA, UNIVERSITY OF
at Santa Barbara
909 Barcelona Drive
Santa Barbara, Calif. 93105

There are a few observant families who live far from campus. Possibility of making arrangements with them is very slight.

CARLETON UNIVERSITY
1378 Laperriere Avenue
Ottawa, Ont., Canada

Off Campus
  Arrangements may be made with private family nearby.
University Facilities
  Opportunity for students to cook privately available in University dormitories.

CINCINNATI, UNIVERSITY OF
Hebrew Union College
3101 Clifton Avenue
Cincinnati, Ohio

Hillel Facilities
  Lunch and dinner served on scheduled basis seven days per week.
  Students are charged $156.00 per quarter.
  The University rebates the $120.00 per quarter board fee.

University Facilities
Dairy, fruit, vegetable substitutes available in University dining hall.
Certain University dormitories are set up as apartment suites and students living in them can do their own cooking. Available only to upper-classmen.

DALHOUSIE UNIVERSITY
B'nai B'rith Hillel Counselorship
1480 Oxford Street
Halifax, N.S., Canada

Off Campus
Students are boarded with local families in the Jewish community.
Other students may rent their own apartments and do their own cooking.

DENVER, UNIVERSITY OF, Denver, Colorado

Off Campus
Arrangements could be made with private family nearby.

DRAKE UNIVERSITY, Des Moines, Iowa

Arrangements are made with private family nearby.

DUKE UNIVERSITY
NORTH CAROLINA, UNIVERSITY OF
at Greensboro
NORTH CAROLINA STATE
B'nai B'rith Hillel Foundation
210 W. Cameron Avenue
Chapel Hill, N.C. 27514

University Facilities
Dairy, fruit, vegetable substitutes available in University dining hall.

EASTERN MICHIGAN UNIVERSITY
B'nai B'rith Hillel Foundation
1429 Hill Street
Ann Arbor, Michigan 48104

Hillel Facilities
Dinner served on scheduled basis every other Sunday.
Off Campus
Students may live in apartments and do their own cooking.
University Facilities
Dairy, fruit, vegetable substitutes available in University dining hall.

EMORY UNIVERSITY, Atlanta, Georgia

Off Campus
Arrangements can be made with private family about two miles from campus.

FREDONIA, SUNY College at
B'nai B'rith Hillel Foundation
40 Capen Blvd.
Buffalo, N.Y. 14214

Off Campus
Students may rent their own apartments or rooms and do their own cooking.

GEORGE PEABODY COLLEGE
VANDERBILT UNIVERSITY, Nashville, Tenn.

Off Campus
There have been few cases in recent years where provisions have been made in private homes, but these homes are not

conveniently located. Such arrangements would be more a matter of accommodation than a business proposition.

ILLINOIS STATE UNIVERSITY, Bloomington, Ill.

Off Campus
Students who rent their own apartments could get Kosher meat from Chicago.

ITHACA COLLEGE
B'nai B'rith Hillel Foundation
Anabel Taylor Hall
Cornell University
Ithaca, N.Y. 14850

Kosher meals available at Young Israel of Cornell.

LAFAYETTE COLLEGE, Easton, Pa.

Off Campus
Students may rent their own apartments and do their own cooking.
University Facilities
Dairy, fruit, vegetable substitutes available in University dining halls.
Students may make arrangements to cook in fraternity house.

MASSACHUSETTS, UNIVERSITY OF
B'nai B'rith Hillel Foundation
Student Union Building
University of Mass.
Amherst, Mass. 01003

University Facilities
Frozen Kosher TV dinners served in University dining hall, lunch and dinner.

MEDICAL COLLEGE OF VIRGINIA
MARY WASHINGTON COLLEGE
VIRGINIA COMMONWEALTH UNIVERSITY
RICHMOND, UNIVERSITY OF
WASHINGTON & LEE UNIVERSITY
B'nai B'rith Hillel Foundation
1824 University Circle
Charlottesville, Va.   22903

University Facilities
  Dairy, fruit, vegetable substitutes available, but not always
  satisfactorily.
  Students at Washington and Lee may make arrangements to
  cook at fraternty houses.

NEW MEXICO, UNIVERSITY OF, Albuquerque, New
  Mexico

Off Campus
  Arrangements are made with a private family nearby.

OREGON, UNIVERSITY OF, Eugene, Oregon

Off Campus
  Sophomores and up may have their own apartments and do
  own cooking. Meat comes from Portland.

OSWEGO, New York, SUNY College at

Off Campus
  Arrangements can be made with private family nearby.
  Presently, there are only three observant families in Oswego.

PLATTSBURGH, New York, SUNY College at

Off Campus
  Students housed in private homes may have opportunity for
  Kashruth observance.

University Facilities
   Alternate choice offered in University dining hall when
   pork products are served.

RENSSELAER POLYTECHNIC INSTITUTE
RUSSELL SAGE COLLEGE, Troy, New York

Off Campus
   Private apartments are available with cooking facilities.
   Bet Atid in Troy accepts a limited number of guests for
   meals.

RICE UNIVERSITY
HOUSTON, UNIVERSITY OF, Houston, Texas

University Facilities
   Opportunity for students to cook privately available in
   fraternity houses.

RIDER COLLEGE
TRENTON STATE COLLEGE, Trenton, New Jersey

Off Campus
   Arrangements are made with private family nearby.
   Arrangements are made with Kosher restaurant nearby.

SAN FRANCISCO STATE COLLEGE
SAN FRANCISCO, CITY COLLEGE OF

Off Campus
   Arrangements can be made with Kosher restaurant nearby.
   Students may do their own cooking in their own aparments.
   Kosher food readily obtainable in San Francisco.
University Facilities
   Dairy, fruit, vegetable substitutes available in University
   dining hall.

SAN DIEGO STATE COLLEGE, San Diego, Calif.

Off Campus
   Students may live off campus and do their own cooking.
   Arrangements may be made with private family nearby.

SIMMONS COLLEGE
Temple Sinai
50 Sewall Avenue
Brookline, Mass. 02146

University Facilities
  Dairy, fruit, vegetable substitutes available in University
  dining hall.
  Students may find limited opportunities to do their own
  cooking in University dormitories.

SOUTHERN METHODIST UNIVERSITY
Dr. Harold A. Blum
Southern Methodist University
P.O. Box 136
Dallas, Texas 75222

Off Campus
  Students may make arrangements with private family
  nearby.
  Both Shaerith Israel and Teferith Israel Congregations may
  be able to help students work out Kashruth arrangements.

SPRINGFIELD COLLEGE
AMERICAN INTERNATIONAL COLLEGE
Sinai Temple
1100 Dickinson St.
Springfield, Mass. 01108

Off Campus
  Arrangements may be made with private family nearby.

TENNESSEE, UNIVERSITY OF
Mr. Louis Brown
2016 Court Avenue
Memphis, Tenn. 38104

Off Campus
　Arrangements are made with a private family nearby.
　Students may cook in their own apartments.

TUFTS UNIVERSITY
JACKSON COLLEGE
Please contact the
National Office in
Washington, D.C.

Off Campus
　Arrangements are made with a private family nearby.
University Facilities
　Dairy, fruit, vegetable substitutes are available in University dining hall.
　Students may cook privately in fraternity houses.

TRINITY COLLEGE, Hartford, Conn.

Off Campus
　Arrangements can be made with private families, but it would usually require considerable travel as the bulk of the Jewish community of Hartford is not located near the College.

UNION COLLEGE AND UNIVERSITY, Schenectady, N.Y.

Off Campus
　There are two delicatessen stores both one-half mile from campus, which can make up Kosher sandwiches for students.
University Notes
　Occasionally a student has inquired whether permission can be granted to live off campus in order to prepare his own Kosher meals.
　These requests have been so uncommon that no permission has ever been granted by the Dean of Students.
　If a sincere request will come from a student to live off campus due to his desire for Kosher meals, "then we shall attempt to work it out."

UTICA COLLEGE, Utica, New York

Off Campus
Arrangements can be made with Kosher restaurant nearby.
University Facilities
Dairy, fruit, vegetable substitutes are available in University dining hall.

WATERLOO LUTHERAN COLLEGE, Kitchener, Ontario, Canada

Off Campus
Arrangements can be made with a private family nearby.
University Facilities
Dairy, fruit, vegetable substitutes available in the University dining hall.
The University purchases kosher meet for students upon request but doesn't have separate cooking utensils.

WESTERN MICHIGAN UNIVERSITY KALAMAZOO COLLEGE, Kalamazoo, Mich.

Off Campus
If needed, arrangements can be made with private family.
Facilities are available for students to do their own cooking in their own apartments.
University Facilities
Dairy, fruit, vegetable substitutes available in University dining hall.

WESTERN ONTARIO, UNIVERSITY OF, London, Ont., Canada

Community Facility
Local fraternity serves dinner Monday through Friday.
They serve lunch Saturday and Sunday on regular scheduled basis.
Students are charged on a quarter basis.
Local community provides subsidy.

WILLIAM AND MARY, COLLEGE OF, Newport News, Virginia

Off Campus
Arrangements are made with private family and nearby restaurant.

University Facilities
Dairy, fruit, vegetable substitutes available in University dining hall.

Female students may cook in sorority houses.

Hillel meetings held in University Student Center; food served at meetings and at Sunday brunch every other Sunday.

WISCONSIN, UNIVERSITY OF
at Milwaukee
Jewish Vocational Service
207 E. Buffalo St.
Milwaukee, Wis. 53202

Off Campus
Students may have own apartments and do their own cooking.

Kashruth Observance in the Military

Kashruth observance in the Military is difficult, but not impossible

10   It is not easy to be a Kashruth observer in the military situation, but then, most things we regard as worthwhile do not come easily. The root of the difficulty, obviously, stems from the fact that each of the armed forces undertakes to feed its members—generally in a common mess hall. Jews constitute a small fraction (about 3½ per cent) of the American people, and a correspondingly small proportion of its military force. Kashruth observers are a still smaller group. Accordingly, the Department of Defense, although it understands the problem and is sympathetic, has repeatedly rejected as unfeasible requests by the JWB and by other interested agencies that the government provide Kosher food to those servicemen who are observant of Jewish dietary practices. We hope that at some time in the not too distant future the military will provide for the needs of Kashruth observers. Until then, however, such servicemen must find other means of securing an adequate supply of food. This is admittedly difficult, but it is not impossible. It has been done in times of war and periods of peace by thousands of Jewish members of the armed forces. They may not have eaten as well as they did at home. They made sacrifices and used some of their spending money for food—but they had the inner satisfaction of remaining true to their convictions and of strengthening the kind of Jewish life in which they believed.

Levels Of Observance

No serviceman should lightly discard the standards of observance to which he is accustomed. On the contrary, he should make a tremendous effort to maintain them. It is, however, gross ignorance to argue, for example, that since one may be forced by circumstances to use non-Kosher dishes, one may as well disregard the laws of Kashruth completely. One's guiding principle should be that under all circumstances he will observe as many cherished religious practices as possible. A stubborn determination to abide by all of the regulations of Kashruth may lead some men to total abandonment of Jewish dietary patterns. On the other hand, steadfast resolution to maintain a maximum practice will in all likelihood be successful.

In this connection, we cite "Israel in the Ranks, a religious guide of faith and practice for the Jewish soldier," by Rabbi Moses M. Yoshor, a guide based on the Hofetz Haim's "Mahneh Yisrael." It was published in 1943. On pages 70 and 71 one reads:

"When Kosher meat is unavailable, it is well to remember that one can frequently subsist on a purely vegetarian diet, and that people who live on a meatless diet prove to be no less strong or courageous, than those who dine on meat. Even a soldier may at times select a variety of vegetables and other healthful foods on which he can subsist.

"However, there are different degrees in the prohibition of non-Kosher foods. Some food articles are under a more stringent ban than others. In reference to animal food, the eating of meat of a forbidden animal is considered a more severe transgression than the meat from animals allowed for food, but prepared in a non-Kosher manner; or the drinking of *trayfe* soup is less a violation than the eating of *trayfe* meat.

"Hence, when the soldier is in a condition that he cannot subsist on a restricted diet, he should try to minimize as much as possible the violation which he feels compelled to commit.

"It is advisable for him to consult a person well-versed in the Jewish ritual whenever he has the opportunity."

PRACTICAL SUGGESTIONS

Use the Mess Hall

There are various foods which a Kashruth-observer can eat in a military mess. For example, the morning meal ordinarily includes fruit and juice, dry cereal, eggs in the shell, milk and other beverages—all of these may be eaten freely.

For other meals, it should be possible (with the help of a chaplain, if necessary) to secure at the mess hall canned tunafish, salmon or sardines, fruit and vegetables, boiled eggs and other permitted foods. At some installations permission may be obtained for bringing cans of food to the mess, and even for heating such food.

Know your Post Exchange (PX)

Most military exchanges carry *nash* items such as ice cream, candy and pop, which are Kosher. It is impossible to live on such items alone, but they can be an important supplement to an otherwise meager diet.

Know the Commissary

For families that are observant, commissary resources should be used to the full. On request, commissary officers often will stock Kosher delicatessen and other Kosher items. Even non-observant Jews may want to avail themselves of these Kosher foods.

Your Chaplain is a Resource

If you are stationed at a post or base to which a Jewish chaplain is normally assigned, he will have at his office a supply of canned Kosher food distributed by the National Jewish Welfare Board. This food (gefilte fish, chicken dinner, matzoh, etc.) is provided, without cost, as a further supplement to the diet of Jewish military personnel (and VA hospital patients) who are observant of Kashruth and who have no households of their own at the post or base. At some places, the chaplain's assistant will, in the absence of the Jewish chaplain, let you have this canned food. If no Jewish chaplain is assigned, a non-Jewish chaplain will order this food for you from JWB.

There are posts at which the Jewish chaplain's office has facilities for heating Kosher food and for refrigeration. At such posts, you are likely to find a group of Kashruth observers who will welcome you as a member. Occasionally, such a group eats together, especially on Shabbat and Yom-Tov.

The chapel program opens up still other possibilities to

the Kashruth observer. It is JWB policy that food contributed or purchased for an Oneg Shabbat, break-the-fast
meals after Yom Kippur, Sedorim, and other Passover
meals be Kosher. Some chaplains attempt to serve Kosher
food at other holiday seasons as well. The Jewish chaplain
is the key figure in enabling a Jewish serviceman to observe
the traditional dietary practices.

Community Resources

Many military stations are located not too far from organized Jewish communities which have Kosher butchers
and delicatassens. A serviceman, particularly after he has
completed basic training, can get into the community from
time to time and stock up on fresh baked goods, melba
toast, delicacies, and canned staples which he can then
bring back to the post to store at the chapel kitchen, or
even in the barracks. Some of these items may be available
at ordinary supermarkets close to the post.

Many traditional men are invited for a meal to the home
of a civilian rabbi or some other observant family with
considerable regularity. A hearty Kosher meal, once a
week or so, helps immeasurably in enabling a man to remain observant. Often, JWB Armed Services Committees,
organized by USO-JWB workers, can be helpful in ar-
ranging such hospitality.

Packages from Home

The most obvious source for Kosher food which will
delight an observant serviceman is the food sent him from
home. Even if he has to share some of it with his barracks

companions, packages of cake, cookies, and more substantial foods can help provide the calories, proteins, and other food values that an active serviceman requires.

No one of these suggestions will, of itself, provide an adequate solution to the problem of the Kashruth observer in the armed forces. Taken together, they do point to the solution.

A QUESTION OF MONEY

The Additional Costs

If a traditional serviceman had unlimited funds, it is probable that Kashruth would be no great problem to him. The reality of the situation is that most of the suggestions noted above involve the soldier in extra costs. PX items, store-bought food, reciprocating hospitality, packages from home—all of these are costly. Sooner or later most observant servicemen feel the pinch and look for means of avoiding the extra expenditures.

The magic door they seek to open is termed "separate rations." The armed forces, under special conditions, make available a small daily allowance (about $1.10) to certain men who do not live on post. There is, however, no directive which urges commanding officers to grant separate rations to Kashruth observers—living either on post or off. In some instances, as a matter of local determination, Jewish chaplains have succeeded in securing separate rations for strict observers of Kashruth. This is, however, not a widespread practice. It involves many administrative difficulties —choosing among applicants, questions of adequate diet and preparation, total exclusion of the serviceman from the mess hall, etc. Often the food he may eat in the mess hall on any given day is worth more than anything he could buy outside with a rations allowance.

You may want to ask about separate rations, through proper channels, but do not be disappointed if your request is rejected. (If granted, it is well to investigate the possibility of using commissary privileges.)

RELATIONSHIP TO THE JEWISH CHAPLAIN

Orientation

It is important to establish a pattern of observance early in one's military career, otherwise officers tend to ask when did the man suddenly get religious. We noted above that the Jewish chaplain is a resource for Kosher canned foods provided by JWB. In general, it is very important that a Kashruth observer secure the assistance of his Jewish chaplain, if there is one at his post. A Jewish chaplain is assigned to most large installations, including induction centers. During their first two or three days at a post, most men have an opportunity to meet their chaplain. He will generally deliver an "orientation talk," describing the total religious program at the post, or in particular, the Jewish program. It is important that a Kashruth observer introduce himself to the chaplain at this time, or even sooner. Some men take the added precaution of writing the chaplain in advance. (His name and address are available at the office of the National Jewish Welfare Board, 15 East 26 St., New York 16, N.Y.) It is well, too, when reporting at a new post, to have a letter of introduction from your former Jewish chaplain, or from a civilian rabbi who knows you.

If one is asked to complete a "religious identification card," he should be certain to note his interest in Kashruth and other observances.

Disposition Forms

At large installations, some Jewish chaplains have prepared a special message on behalf of traditional servicemen which they send to unit commanders. Such forms are generally honored, and they help ease the way for the observant soldier.

Establishing Contacts

The Jewish chaplain, unofficially, can be helpful in introducing observant men to other people of like mind—servicemen, civilians, and religious leaders in nearby communities. The military unit often seems to be an impersonal kind of organization. The chaplain, ideally, humanizes and brings warmth to this machine-like operation. He is, moreover, available when he is needed. Through channels, a soldier can get permission to see him whenever a personal problem arises and the chaplain has the authority to request that the soldier be sent to his office whenever he feels he can be of help.

ABOUT SPECIAL SITUATIONS

Anticipating the Unusual

To the normal problems of the Kashruth observers, circumstances occasionally add new obstacles. Passover, war games and maneuvers, changes in assignment, and travel overseas can put the traditional Jew in a special situation which compounds the normal difficulties he encounters. As a general rule, such situations do not arise before a serviceman has had an opportunity to become oriented to military life, to learn the ropes.

Passover or the High Holidays, it is true, may occur early in a man's tour of duty, but almost always a liberal leave policy is applied for such holy days—particularly for men who have saved up whatever leave-time may be due them, so that they may get away during Yom-Tov. (Even when servicemen cannot afford to travel home, or are not permitted to travel far, hospitality can generally be arranged in a nearby organized Jewish community.) If need be, with some forethought and effort, and with the help of a chaplain, holidays can be properly observed even on post. Your chaplain can give you the regulation number of your branch of the service entitling Jewish service personnel to leave time for holiday observances.

ON BEING DIFFERENT

Theory and Practice

We live in a society which gives lip-service to individualism but is, in practice, marked by a high degree of conformity. In the military, conformity has the sanction of necessity. Every one in the unit wears the same uniform. Outwardly, only his name plate marks him as an individual.

Living as a Jew in a non-Jewish environment means being different. It means, too, striving to set a worthy religious and moral example. Every Jew is, to some extent, set apart as a member of a minority group, but the observant Jew is set apart, much more and therefore is an object of curiosity, and sometimes even of derision or hostility.

Religion an Exception

Fortunately, however, there is in our society a healthy balancing trait—respect for and acceptance of religious differences. This respect is commonly granted to religious convictions when these are honestly held, and to religious practices when they are firmly adhered to. When it becomes clear that the Jewish soldier is not using religion in general, and Kashruth in particular, as a tool to help him duck out of unpleasant tasks or normal duties, his practices will become a matter to which his buddies will either be indifferent, or which will arouse their interest, and perhaps their admiration. Their basic interest in any soldier, however, is that he be a good soldier (or airman or sailor), someone who can be relied upon to do his share in time of need. The American sense of fair play, of live and let live, may not always spare one ridicule or hostility, but in the long run, it tends to make for general acceptance of any consistant pattern of religious behavior (other things being equal) on the part of anyone who is a "good Joe,"—fair, decent, and effective.

CONCLUSION

Jews have always been members of a "stiff-necked" people. It takes some sacrifice and great determination, but one can remain an observant Jew in the Army, the Air Force, or the Navy. Many have done it. Maybe it takes a bit of yielding on minor matters, but the well-informed Jew will know when, where, and how much he is permitted to yield —in the particular circumstances in which he finds himself. When in doubt, consult the Jewish chaplain, or your home-town rabbi.

The traditional Jew does not stand alone. His chaplain, JWB workers, local families, organizations, and folks at home—all are interested in helping him. Above all, he can rely upon his Heavenly Father who "neither slumbers nor sleeps" and Who knows the intentions of his heart.

Chemistry and Kosher Foods

11 Modern living has provided the homemaker with many packaged foods which ease the burdens of preparing meals for the family. The days when mother personally put all the ingredients into the food mixtures served her family are gone; they have been replaced by numerous ready-to-eat foods that are tempting as well as nourishing. While state laws require that the packaging on the foods list the ingredients that are included in the preparation of the item, the terminology used is chemical, and thus very confusing to the average housewife.

The housewife who observes Kashruth has a special problem in trying to understand the chemical terms, to determine which of them are Kosher, and which are not. One way out of this dilemma is to buy only Kosher foods, prepared under proper Kashruth supervision. However, this is not always possible. In many instances the housewife will have to decide for herself whether she may purchase a product or not. In such instances the following information should shed much light on the matter:

Shortening and Vegetable Shortening

Whenever the word "shortening" appears alone on a label, it must be assumed that it contains, at least in part, lard (pork fat) or tallow (beef fat). Any product containing plain shortening is therefore forbidden. Such items as roll mixes, cakes, cookies and crackers usually display the shortening ingredient on the wrapper of the package. When the term "vegetable shortening" is used, the interpretation may be that the product is wholly vegetable, but this depends upon the food laws of the state. In New York State, for example, the term "pure vegetable shortening" and "vegetable shortening" are synonymous. A product which represents itself as having vegetable shortening in New York State must contain pure vegetable shortening with no animal fat mixed into it. This is not true, however, in other states. "Vegetable shortening" appearing on a packaged product does not necessarily mean that it is pure vegetable shortening. It is best to write to the company producing the food item and inquire.

Artificial Sweetening Agents

A number of low calorie artificial sweeteners in small paper envelopes have appeared in the last few years. These almost always contain lactose. Lactose is milk sugar and made commercially only from milk. Such artificial sweeteners cannot be served at a meat meal. Saccharin and cyclamate tablets may contain lactose as a binder, and are therefore also forbidden for a meat meal unless marked "pareve." Liquid sweetners are the best assurance that no lactose has been used in the production of the artificial sweetner.

Non-Dairy Coffee Creams

Many of the so-called "non-dairy" coffee creams contain sodium caseinate, which is a milk protein, derived from milk, which makes the cream a dairy product. As such it should not be used at a meat meal. There are, however, completely non-dairy creams which are tasty and as good as or better than the real cream.

Mono and Di-glycerides

These are chemicals derived from fats which are helpful in emulsifying properties and they are widely used in dress-ings, baked goods, etc. Mono and di-glycerides may be derived from animal or vegetable fats but there is no way of telling the origin from the name given on the label. Here again, it is best to buy only Kashruth endorsed foods, or else to write to the manufacturer directly to ascertain the source of the emulsifier.

Vitamins

A large number of foods, especially breakfast cereals and milk, are enriched with vitamins which are usually identi-fied by their chemical names. While most vitamins are produced synthetically and are Kosher, vitamins A and D are obtained from fish-liver. Cod-liver oil and halibut-liver oil are Kosher, the liver oil obtained from the shark is not.

Therefore, it is necessary to write to the manufacturer to determine the source of the oil used as the vitamin.

Cheeses

In the making of hard cheeses such as Swiss, Gouda, or Munster, it is necessary to introduce a curdling agent. In most instances an ingredient known as "rennet" is used because it speeds up the process and results in a finer product. Rennet is obtained from the stomach of an animal. If the rennet comes from a Kosher animal that has been slaughtered Kosher, then the cheese is Kosher. However, the package label does not indicate the source of the rennet, therefore, unless the housewife is purchasing Kosher cheese, it is wise to write to the manufacturer for information regarding the source and kind of rennet used.

Dressings

Many salad dressings contain whey, a product derived from milk. Therefore, if "whey" appears on the label of the salad dressing, the dressing should be limited to dairy meals.

General Information

Algin, which is often used in making Kosher gelatin-type desserts, is derived from seaweed. An example of the presence of Algin is the gelatin found in jars of gefilte fish.

Pectin is derived from fruits. It is often used in preparing jams and jellies. "BHA," "BHD," and "EDTA" are initials frequently found on food packages. These are synthetic chemicals and are Kosher.

Standardization of Foods

The federal Food and Drug Law provides that foods may be standardized. This means that the recipe and procedures for making the food item is standard for all companies which manufacture the one item of food. For example, ketchup, mayonnaise, white bread, etc., are standardized foods. Because they are standardized, the manufacturer does not have to put the ingredients on the package. Nonstandardized foods must list their ingredients. Those who want to inquire about the ingredients of standardized foods can write to the bureau of food and drug administration to obtain a list of the ingredients. It is important to know the contents of standardized foods. For example, the standard for white bread and rolls permits the use of milk as an ingredient. Most manufacturers will put milk into their bread and rolls because it provides a better, richer flavor. Therefore, in using bread and rolls for hamburgers or frankfurters, it is necessary to make sure that they are *pareve* and Kosher.

The same is true for margarines; most are made with milk products. One should also bear in mind the origin of the fat used in the manufacture of margarine. Unless the package is labelled *All Vegetable Margarine*, it probably contains some meat fat or whale oil.

ADIPIC ACID—manufactured from chemicals. Kosher-*pareve*.

ALDEHYDES—chemicals usually found in flavoring extracts—always made synthetically from other chemicals. Kosher-*pareve*.

AGAR AGAR—a gum (thickening agent) derived from a seaweed Kosher-*pareve*.

ALGINATE—same as agar agar, but from a different variety of seaweed. There are also various salts of alginic acid, such as sodium alginate, potassium alginate, and propylene glycol alginate. All are Kosher-*pareve*.

AMMONIUM CARRAGEEN—manufactured from chemicals—Kosher-*pareve*.

BICARBONATE OF SODA—a chemical used as a leavening agent (baking powder). Kosher-*pareve*.

BACILLUS ACIDOPHILUS and BACILLUS BULGARICUS—bacterial cultures used in making cheese, sour cream, yogurt, etc. These are living organisms which metabolize milk and produce lactic acid, etc. Manufacturers usually remove a portion of each batch to use in starting the next batch. Kosher-dairy.

BENZOATE OF SODA—a chemical preservative made synthetically. Kosher-*pareve*.

BETA CAROTENE—manufactured from carrots—a vitamin. Kosher-*pareve*.

BENZOIC ACID—the acid from which sodium benzoate is made. It is not used much because it is insoluble. Made synthetically. Kosher-*pareve*.

CALCIUM ASCORBATE and CALCIUM PROPIONATE—included in foods to prevent molding. Kosher-*pareve*.

CITRIC ACID (called "sour salt" when in a solid form)—an acid which is present in citrus fruits. Nowadays it is made synthetically, usually by fermentation. Kosher-*pareve*.

CALCIUM CARBONATE limestone, a very weak alkali—it is usually used as a filler in low caloric foods because it has no calories. A mineral. Kosher-*pareve*.

CHICORY—a vegetable which, when dried, ground and roasted, can be used to make a beverage similar to coffee. Kosher-*pareve*.

CALCIUM DISODIUM EDTA—a chemical made synthetically. Use as a "sequestering agent"—that is, it removes iron, copper and heavy metals from solution. Kosher-*pareve*.

CARBONATE Y CELLULOSE—Made from wood. Kosher-*pareve*.

CELLULOSE—the basic constituent of fibrous plants such as cotton, wood, etc. almost always made from wood. Kosher-*pareve*.

CARBOXY METHYCELLULOSE—a synthetic gum (thickening agent) derived chemically from cellulose. Kosher-*pareve*.

CONFECTIONERS GLAZE—a sugar shellac. Kosher-*Pareve*.

DEXTROSE—a common sugar found in corn syrup, always made from corn syrup or other plant materials. Kosher-*pareve*.

ESTERS and ETHYL OENANTHATE—Esters are organic compounds, formed by the combination of an alcohol and an organic acid. Ethyl oenanthate is an ester (from ethyl alcohol and oenanthic acid). These are always either synthetic or isolated from natural materials such as apple essence. They are Kosher-*pareve*—A problem might arise regarding the Passover law if the Esters used in flavors are derived from grain alcohol. They would then be *chometz*. A rabbi should be consulted.

FURFURAL—is an aldehyde derived from corn hulls. Would be synthetic. Kosher-*pareve*.

FERRIE ORTHOPHOSPHATE—A vitamin manufactured from chemicals. Kosher-*pareve*.

GUN TRAGACANTH, GUM ARABIC, GUAR GUM, VEGETABLE GUM, and LOCUST BEAN GUM—vegetables gums, all derived from plant sources—nuts, trees, etc. They are thickening agents and are Kosher-*pareve*.

LECITHIN—an emulsifying agent derived from soy beans, eggs, or made synthetically. It is an oil or fat-like substance lipid, but is not found in animal fats. It is Kosher-*pareve*.

LACTIC ACID—a common organic acid, orginally found in sour milk. Nowadays, it is made synthetically. Kosher-*pareve*.

MONOCALCIUM PHOSPHATE—a mineral substance used in baking powders as an acid. Normally would be made from phosphate rock and limestone, but could be made from bone meal, which is largely tricalcium phosphate. It is necessary to inquire as to the source.

MONOSODIUM GLUTAMATE—A vegetable derivative used to bring out flavors in foods, Kosher-*pareve*.

OREGANO—A spice made from plants—used as a flavor—Kosher-*pareve*.

OIL OF CLOVES—an aromatic oil expressed from cloves, which is a spice. Used as a flavor. Kosher-*pareve*.

NIACIN—A 'B' vitamin manufactured from chemicals, Kosher-*pareve*.

OIL CASSIA—Cassia is a spice similar to cinnamon. Oil of cassia is the volatile oil found in this spice. It is derived from the bark of a tree. Kosher-*pareve*.

PROPYLENE GLYCOL—a chemical similar to glycerine, but always made synthetically. It is used as a solvent and as a Heumectant. Kosher-*pareve.*

POTASSIUM CHLORIDE—a chemical of mineral origin. Kosher-*pareve.*

PECTIN—a vegetable gum (sometimes declared on the label as vegetable gum) derived from either citrus fruits or apples. Used in making jams or jellies. Kosher-*pareve.*

POTASSIUM SORBATE—a chemical used as a preservative (has anti-mold properties). Synthetic. Kosher-*pareve.*

PYROPHOSPHATE—Manufactured from chemicals. Kosher-*pareve.*

PYRIODOXINE HYDROCHLORIDE—manufactured from chemicals. Kosher-*pareve.*

RUM—a product of the distillation of cane sugar into fermented sugar. A name extended to the product of the distillation of molasses. Kosher-*pareve.*

ROSEMARY—a spice similar to thyme, sage, etc. Vegetable. Kosher-*pareve.*

RIBOFLAVIN-VITAMIN B2—made from chemicals. Kosher-*pareve.*

SODIUM CYCLAMATE SUCARYL—Sucaryl is the Abbott Company's trade name for the cyclamates. Cyclamates are synthetic sweeteners used in artifically sweetened diet foods and sodas. Synthetic. Kosher-*pareve.*

SODIUM PROPIONATE—Trade name is "Mycoban." An anti-mold chemical used in breads and cakes. Synthetic. Kosher-*pareve.*

SODIUM SILICO GLUMINATE—Manufactured from chemicals. Kosher-*pareve*.

SOY PROTEIN—the soy bean contains much protein and very little starch. This is a vegetable protein. Kosher-*pareve*.

SULFUR DIOXIDE—a preservative used in dried fruits, etc. Mineral origin. Kosher-*pareve*.

SODIUM BISULPHITE—a chemical used as a source of sulfur dioxide in foods. Mineral. Kosher-*pareve*.

SODIUM IRON PHOSPHATE, SODIUM HEXAMETA-PHOSPHATE, and TRI-CALCIUM PHOSPHATE—These are inorganic chemicals used in foods for various purposes. Almost always of mineral origin. Kosher-*pareve*.

THIAMINE MONO NITRATE—a water soluble form of vitamin B1. Vegetable origin or synthetic. Kosher-*pareve*.

TURMERIC—the root of a plant, used for its coloring properties. Kosher-*pareve*.

TORULA—a species of yeast. Kosher-*pareve*.

VEGETABLE GUM—plant derivatives used for their thickening properties. Kosher-*pareve*.

VANILAN (VANILLIN)—an artificial vanilla flavor. Kosher-*pareve*.

VEGETABLE PROTEIN (HYDROLYZED)—Made from vegetables. Kosher-*pareve*.

A Selected List of Kosher Foods**

* APPLE SAUCE
Mussleman's
Veryfine
Lucky Leaf

BABY FOODS
Heinz
Beechnut

BEVERAGES
Cott
No-Cal
Hoffman

BLINTZES
Daitch
Golden
Milady's

BORSCHT
Mother's
Rokeach
Gold's

BREAD CRUMBS
Jason
Stella D'Oro
Tante's Flavored Bread Crumbs

* BREAD
Grossinger's Rye
Pechter's
Thomas

BUTTER
Ann Page
Fairmont

* CAKES
S. Gumpert Co. Cake Mixes
Deer Park Elite
Educator
Stella D'Oro

* CANDY
Ann Page
Barton's Bonbonniere
Barracini

** The foods listed bear some type of Kashruth certification—either that of an individual rabbi or of an agency such as the Ⓤ or the O.K. laboratories. The selected foods in no way are meant to indicate that these and none others are Kosher. The intent here is merely to indicate the wide variety of Kosher products which are available to the home-maker.

CEREALS
Cream of Rice
Instant Hot Ralston
Maltex

CHAMPAGNES
Carmel
Manischewitz (Monarch)

CHEESE
Dellwood
Miller's
Raskas

* CHOCOLATE DRINKS
Bosco
Fox's U Bet
Great Shakes

CATERERS
Astorian Manor, Astoria, L.I.,
N.Y. Huntington Town House,
Huntington, N.Y. Louis Ca-
terers, No. Bellmore, N.Y.

CLEANSERS
Ajax
Bab-O
Dutch

* COFFEE
Maxwell House
Yuban
Tasters Choice

* CRACKERS
Horowitz-Margareten Kosher
  Crackers
Streits Unsalted Top Kosher
  Crackers
Sunshine Unsalted Kosher Crack-
  ers
Tam Tam Crackers

* DATES
Betty Baker
Bordo-Iranian Dates
Dromedary

* DESSERTS
D-Zerta
Gel-A-Tone
Victor-Victor Gel Dessert
Kojel
Jello
S. Gumpert Co.

DETERGENTS
All
Fab
Mr. Clean

* DRESSINGS
Ann Page
Cain's
Daitch Salad Dressings
Mother's

* FALLAFEL
Telma-chi-chi

* FISH PRODUCTS
Mrs. Adler's
Rokeach
Vita

* FLAVORINGS
Ann Page
Burnett
S. Gumpert Co.
Waldbaum

* FROZEN FOODS
Crosse and Blackwell Frozen Con-
  centrates
Grossingers Frying Chicken
  Breasts
Empire Kosher Hors D'oeuvres

* FRUIT BUTTER
Simon Fisher-Lekvar-Prune
  butter
Golden Apricot Butter

* GRAPE JUICE
P Lipschutz Grape Juice

* HONEY
Ann Page
Horowitz-Margareten

HOTELS
P Concord, Kiamesha Lake, N.Y.
P Gibber, Kiamesha Lake, N.Y.
P Grossinger's, Liberty, N.Y.
P Lebowitz Pine View, Fallsburg, N.Y.
P Tanzville, Livingston Manor, N.Y.

ICE CREAM
P Dolly Madison
P Barton's Bonbonniere
P Dairy Barn

* JAMS, JELLIES and PRE-SERVES
Crosse and Blackwell
Polaner
Ann Page

* JUICES
Crosse and Blackwell
Lucky Leaf
Sunsweet

* KETCHUP
Crosse and Blackwell
Heinz
Rokeach

LIQUERS
Leroux

LIVER (CHOPPED)
Mrs. Weinberg's Kosher (Frozen) Chopped Liver Spread

* MARGARINE
Chiffon
Mazola
Parkay

* MAYONNAISE
Hellmann's
Mother's
Shopwell

* MEAT TENDERIZER
Adolph's

Ann Page
Accent

MEDICINE
Products of Freeda Pharmaceuticals Co.

MILK and CREAM SUBSTITUTES
Mocha Mix
No-Lac

* NOODLES-MACARONI
Butoni
Gioia
Mueller

* NUTS (Roasted Peanuts)
Carlton House
Planters
Skippy

* OLIVES
Ann Page
Sultana

* PEANUT BUTTER
Shop Rite

* POTATO CHIPS
Pantry Pride
Weston's
Wise

* PUDDINGS
Ann Page
Royal
Junket

* RELISHES
Heinz
Shopwell
Sweetmixed

* SALT and SALT SUBSTITUTES
Adolph's Salt Substitutes
Morton's
Sterling

* SHORTENINGS—OILS
Crisco
Mazola
Nutola

* SOUPS AND SOUP MIXES
Carmel
Croyden House
Mother's
Lou G. Siegel

* SAUCES
Croyden House
La Choy Soy Sauce
Polynesian Chinese Style Mustard
  Sauce

* SWEETENERS
Ann Page
Par-Ev
Sucaryl

* TEA
Nestea
Salada
Tetley

TOPPINGS
S. Gumpert Co.
Lucky Whip
Rich's Whip Topping

* VEGETABLES (PROCESSED)
Chow-Mein Vegetables With
  Water Chestnut
Lohmann

WINES
Carmel
Kedem
Manischewitz
Schapiro

P—Passover
* —Pareve unless label on package indicates a dairy ingredient. Always look for a Kashruth Certification.

Enter the Congregational Caterer

1 3 The presence of a caterer in congregations as an endorsed member of the official staff of the temple, is an accepted fact in modern times. In many synagogues it is the revenue from the caterer rather than from the congregation's membership that is paying off the mortgage on the new sanctuary, or the addition to the Hebrew school building. Unfortunately, however, the relationship of the caterer to the congregation has been warped out of focus in many instances because the catering business in congregations today is very lucrative, and overshadows the real purpose for his presence in the synagogue. Realistically, a caterer should be accepted as part of the congregational family because he is needed to help enhance the rabbi's religious program; i.e., if families cannot celebrate their weddings, Bar Mitzvahs, or anniversaries in the temple, they will be compelled to seek some other place to hold these special occasions in their lives, and often their choice may not be a Kosher place. Thus the caterer helps the rabbi encourage his members to keep Kashruth because now the rabbi can offer his members an alternative that is Kosher. They can celebrate their *simchas* in the temple with all their needs of

food, entertainment, etc. cared for in the finest Jewish
tradition.

Many people, however, who are in leadership positions
in congregations appear to be interested primarily in the
financial practicalities of the catering industry. Their business acumen causes them to envisage the caterer through
different eyes—they see his image covered over by a large
dollar sign. Let us give these dedicated workers proper
credit—their thinking is undoubtedly motivated by sincere
altruism. What harm can there be in mixing a little good
business with religion so long as it will help prosper the
congregation? And a successful caterer can indeed bring
much prosperity to the congregation, because the extra
income he will provide will defray a good portion of the
expenses of running the synagogue. The percentage pay-
ments from the caterer will offset much of the congregation's indebtedness, depending on how large is the caterer's
volume of business, and will help pay for a number of
improvements for which the congregation cannot find the
money. There is one caution, however, which should be
brought to the attention of those congregational leaders
who will be making the decision about a caterer, and that is
that great care must be exercised in welcoming a caterer
into the congregation. Especially in a large congregation,
the decision to bring in a caterer has many ramifications
which must be thoroughly investigated and carefully
weighed. This problem and suggested solutions will be
discussed in the following paragraphs.

For some strange reason a high wall of secrecy has
grown up around the contents of contractual agreements
which have been arranged between congregations and their
caterers. Many a novice catering-committee chairman has

been surprised to find that even his best friends who are his counterparts in their own congregations, will not divulge any except the most elementary details of the agreement, which their congregation has with the caterer. Apparently, there is the fear that if the details of the congregation's contract with the caterer become public knowledge, it will somehow have an adverse and damaging effect upon the existing agreement, and possibly even ruin a good thing. Therefore, obtaining information about such matters is as difficult "as the splitting of the Red Sea." The following information and recommendations regarding the relationship between a congregation and a caterer should prove very valuable.

Appointing a Catering Committee

The first action which a congregation should take when contemplating the addition of a catering service is to appoint a carefully selected committee. While such caution may be advised for every activity that is undertaken by the congregation, it is especially necessary in respect to the catering committee because they will ultimately commit the congregation to a contract that will probably be binding for a period of from five to ten years, or possibly longer. The members of the committee should include at least some men and women who have been long-time members of the congregation; they will be able to judge best the type of catering service the congregation will appreciate and use.

The rabbi of the congregation should be a member of the catering committee in order to insure that his religious scruples are satisfied. Much aggravation will be avoided by everyone concerned if the caterer is approved by the rabbi as the kind of person who will not, because of personal religious convictions or a lack of them, deny the particular religious setting of the congregation. If the congregational roster reveals a member who is in the food business, he should be put on the committee, for obvious reasons. On the other hand, while it is not always possible to deny the request of a member of the congregation to serve on a committee if he chooses to do so and is qualified for it, experience has shown that if at all possible, a member of the congregation who is a *caterer* himself should not join this committee, however much he may desire it. Although in certain instances such a person on the catering committee may prove to be of great help, this is the exception rather than the rule. In most instances, the caterer's personal involvement in the catering business, one way or another, interferes with his ability to maintain an objective attitude.

The real value of the committee's work will be revealed some months after the congregation has signed the contract with the caterer. If the committee has done its job carefully, the congregation will enjoy and benefit from the presence of the caterer. If, however, the choice of a caterer has been made carelessly, and with only superficial consideration, endless difficulties will prevail until the end of the long contract. One example of a committee's foible in choosing a caterer is the following: The committee set itself the heroic and glamorous goal of getting the fanciest caterer in town to sign up with the temple as its exclusive caterer. In their zeal they overlooked the financial capacity of the congregation. They were successful, after many months of negotiating with the caterer and the board of trustees, in achieving their goal. It soon became evident, however, that the congregation had purchased a magnificent jewel which very few members in the congregation could appreciate because his fancy prices were just not within the reach of the average member's pocketbook. Many families were compelled to take their *simchas* outside the temple. In the end, the caterer was unhappy because he did not do the anticipated business, in spite of a substantial investment. And the congregation was equally unhappy and disappointed because the anticipated revenue never materialized.

Such is the disappointment that can arise when a catering committee is not oriented to appreciate the broad significance of its purpose.

Catering Arrangements

There are three types of catering arrangements which a congregation might consider.

1. In smaller congregations, the Sisterhood of the synagogue might render the catering service to the congregation. This often proves to be a good fund-raising project for them. In addition to being a good fund-raiser, the control of the catering service by the Sisterhood has been a means of stabilizing the costs of such usually elaborate and costly functions as Bar and Bas Mitzvah receptions, limiting the lavishness of them, and reducing the economic competition among families of the congregation. Some Sisterhoods have used their handling of the catering service as a teaching tool, instructing young brides in the recipes of traditional Jewish cooking and the Kashruth laws.

2. For the larger congregation it would be impractical for the Sisterhood to undertake the mammoth job of cater-

ing the various functions of the congregation. Dedicated though the women may be, they could not possibly deal effectively with all the demands that would be made upon them. Therefore, the professional caterer is the only practical solution.

In selecting a professional catering service the congregation has two choices—an exclusive caterer, or a panel of several caterers. There is merit in both, however, and the pros and cons should be weighed carefully. Without a doubt the exclusive caterer represents a greater potential of benefits to the congregation. The exclusive caterer can be controlled, he can be monitored, because he is the only one to focus attention upon. In addition, the caterer also feels more at home in a synagogue where he is exclusive, and he is willing to participate more fully in the programs of the congregation. The caterer who is exclusive may be expected to decorate the areas of the synagogue building which he will use for his affairs. The synagogue kitchen supplies, chairs, tables and other types of equipment that the congregation might normally purchase will be purchased by the caterer, to be used as well by the congregation, as prearranged between the caterer and the congregation. Because the caterer is exclusive in the congregation, he will be willing to assume a larger financial burden in payment to the congregation for the privilege given him.

The caterer who is one of a panel of caters, however, cannot be expected to share in more than a minimal amount of financial obligation to the congregation. He is primarily a visitor to the synagogue, and undoubtedly has commitments to other congregations where he caters also. No one congregation can make too many demands upon him. However, the advantages inherent in the selection of a panel of

caterers is that such an arrangement provides the congregation with a number of choices for a variety of catering patterns. If one particular caterer does not suit certain families
in the congregation, they are free to choose another caterer,
and there are no resentments. This is not the case with an
exclusive caterer. The congregants have no other choice.
No one else may cater in the congregation. If families
choose to go out of the temple for their affairs, there is
much resentment. In some congregations where the caterer
was not satisfying the needs of the membership there developed a bitter resentment not only towards the caterer
but also toward the temple itself. The families who felt
strongly about celebrating their *simchas* in their temple
were compelled to use a caterer who was undesirable. Naturally, this was not a happy situation! This is the risk that a
congregation takes in contracting the services of an exclusive caterer. It is important for the catering committee
to be alert to this problem and its ramifications.

The Catering Contract

The contract between the caterer and the congregation is
like any other business document and such should be prepared by the legal counsel for the congregation. However,
the following are some suggestions as to what should be
included in the contract:

1. Name the congregation and its location, the caterer and
his address.

2. Specify the length of time the contract will be in effect.
Congregations that are contracting with a caterer for the
first time would be wise not to bind themselves with a
long-term contract. The most frequent time period for a

contract to run is ten years. Contracts between caterers and congregations, however, have run from 3 to 15 years.

3. The rooms and other facilities that are to be used by the caterer should be clearly noted in the contract.

4. Responsibility for maintenance of facilities used by the caterer should be clearly stated.

5. Sufficient insurance should be purchased by the caterer so that the congregation is not liable for any mishaps resulting from an affair served by the caterer at the temple. The usual amount for personal injury is $10,000.

6. Dates for affairs should be granted to families on a first-come, first-served basis. Once a date is given to a family, it should remain firm unless, by mutual consent, all parties involved in a change concur to it.

7. Where there is a panel of caterers, conflict is avoided by assigning the temple's facilities to one caterer at a time per day.

8. The caterer must employ union help.

9. Food poisoning insurance should be purchased by the caterer in the amount of between $100,000 to $300,000. All matters of insurance coverage are very important especially because the caterer is in a temple. The temple as such is expected by the community to display special compassion. In the event that some mishap occurs at a catered affair, ample insurance provides an immediate remedy, and no one can speak derogatorily of the temple.

10. Caterer should assume all risk for property he stores in the temple building. He should also be responsible for maintenance of his equipment.

11. If the caterer should attach to the synagogue building any permanent structure, such structure should remain as

a part of the edifice for all time and should be considered as belonging to the congregation.

12. Should any of the utilities fail to function during a catered affair, the congregation must not be liable for any damages which the family might decide to claim against the caterer. This release of such responsibility should, of course, be contingent upon the fact that the congregation can show evidence that it has not been delinquent in paying its bills for the continuation of the utilities. In some contracts the caterer assumes partial responsibility for payment of the utility bills.

13. The caterer must submit to the temple office copies of all contracts which he signs with a family for an affair. The copy of each contract for an affair should be in the temple office no later than seven days after it is signed. Final approval for an affair must come from the chairman of the catering committee. This is an important factor in insuring that no affair takes place in the temple which is offensive to the standards of the congregation.

14. The congregation should reserve certain dates for its own use. In many instances the caterer, as a courtesy, will serve these congregational affairs gratis.

15. A dairy kitchen should be maintained by the congregation for its own use. In addition, the *congregation* should reserve the right to serve small *Kiddushes* and similar collations.

16. The rabbi of the congregation must retain the right to approve all matters of a religious nature. If Kashruth is an important factor, then the rabbi must be the final authority on all matters of Kashruth. For example, the rabbi must approve the qualifications of the caterer's *mashgiach*.

The caterer must see to it that sleeping quarters are provided for the *mashgiach* especially during the summer months when the sun sets late in the day, and Saturday affairs in the temple cannot begin until a late hour. In this way the *mashgiach* can sleep over Friday night when necessary, and be available to the caterer immediately after sunset.

The *mashgiach* should be paid by the congregation and not the caterer, so that his income is secure, and he feels free to direct the Kashruth of the caterer without compromise of principle. Experience has shown that if the caterer pays the *mashgiach*, much of the *mashgiach's* independence is jeopardized.

To safeguard the Kashruth of the congregation, it would be wise for the catering committee to keep watch over the *mashgiach's* schedule to be certain that he is in fact present at every affair that is catered.

17. The revenues which the caterer returns to the synagogue are based upon a percentage of his income. The arrangements vary, however. The following are a few samples of the kinds of agreements that might be consummated.

In most instances the caterer returns to the congregation 10–15 percent of the gross food bill.

Another agreement required the caterer to pay the congregation 25 percent of the gross food bill until such time as the income to the synagogue from the caterer for the year reached $15,000. Then the percentage was dropped to 5 percent for each additional $10,000 business done by the caterer.

An agreement reached between one congregation and its caterer required that the synagogue receive 25 percent of the gross food bill where the charge per person was $10 or less. Where the charge was more than $10, the fee paid the synagogue was 30 percent.

The synagogue should receive monies as well from the checkroom, flowers, photographer, and any other additional services which the caterer provides.

18. Catered affairs which take place outside the synagogue building for members of the congregation should be included in the contract. Since the caterer does not use the synagogue building, it would be fair to require that he return a smaller percentage of the profit than usual to the congregation.

19. Provision should be made for arbitration of disputes in the event such a problem should come about.

20. Provision should be made for termination of the contract by either party prior to the expiration date, should such a circumstance arise.

21. Caterer should not incur any obligation in the name of the synagogue, and the synagogue should not incur any debt in the name of the caterer.

22. The caterer may use the synagogue's name in any advertising, but, he must first obtain approval from the congregation for such advertising.

A Brief Guide For The House Committee:

The house committee of the congregation must decide:

1. What facilities are available.
2. What are the maintenance rates for the rooms. Based on this, the room-fee schedule will be established.
3. When the building will be open, and when it must be closed.
4. What will be in the rooms—storage space, linens, dishes, etc.

5. Who may use the facilities—i.e., outside organizations.

6. Whether staff services will be available. Specific rules can be made, such as:

a. Instructions may be given to the superintendent or maintenance staff *only* if prior approval is obtained from the house committee chairman or the executive director.

b. The staff shall be available only for the normal services rendered for the facility that is used. Special services, such as the preparation of refreshments, washing dishes, parking, shall be handled by help provided by the executive director or house committee chairman, to be paid for by the lessee.

c. Any committee chairman or affiliated organization needing the assistance of the clerical staff should be requested to contact the executive director. No work may be assigned without his permission.

7. A master calendar is prepared and kept by the executive director or the house committee chairman. Entries may be made at their direction only.

Procedure

1. All on-going synagogue groups are asked to submit their programs for the year well in advance.

2. The committee confirms the dates by letter to the organization. A copy of the house rules is included.

3. A week prior to a meeting, the organization must clear, in writing, all arrangements with the house committee.

4. If the building has a gym, then an athletic committee should be responsible for scheduling and supervising related activities. A representative of the athletic committee should sit with the house committee, and vice versa.

Statement of Policy

1. The sanctuary, chapel, and classrooms, social hall, auditorium, kitchen and grounds, are provided primarily for the members and their families, and for affiliated member organizations of the congregation to serve their spiritual, educational, and social needs.

2. These facilities may be made available to such other organizations and institutions of a religious, educational, and philanthropic nature as may be requested, but only at the discretion of the house committee and with the approval of the board of trustees. The facilities are available to those non-members and outside groups only at such times as are not in conflict with the synagogue's own program.

3. The house committee reserves the right to check on the conformity with established rules of the congregation at the time of the function, and to take immediate action to correct any non-conformity. It shall also be the right of the house committee or any of its authorized agents to ask any person or persons to leave the premises because of unseemly conduct.

4. In the event of a dispute, the house committee will authorize or reject the use of the synagogue's facilities. Three or more members of the house committee constitute a quorum.

5. These rules may be amended with the approval of the board of trustees, or changed without notice upon the recommendation of the house committee for the purpose of maintaining the building for the greatest benefit of the majority of the congregation's membership.

General Rules

1. No organization may use the synagogue's name in publicity materials without the consent in writing of an authorized representative of the synagogue.

2. Organizations are requested to mail to the synagogue copies of invitations and other publicity for all functions held at the synagogue.

3. Facilities needed for other than regular purposes (rehearsals and special events) must be booked in the same manner as meetings.

4. If an outside organization or party cancels a booking for synagogue facilities or services, charges will be made unless such notice of cancellation is given at least two weeks prior to the scheduled event.

5. The congregation is not responsible for any personal-property loss suffered by any individual using its facilities.

6. All persons will use the synagogue building or equipment with due care. Any damages to synagogue property or equipment shall render the person or organization liable for damages.

7. No person or organization may tape or tack anything to the building, or move furniture about without specific authorization from a member of the house committee or the executive director.

8. Synagogue property or equipment may be loaned only with the permission of the chairman of the house committee.

9. Dishes, silverware, kitchen utensils, and supplies may be used only with specific written authority of the house committee. This applies to caterers, individuals, and organizations.

Ritual Observances

1. Smoking is prohibited in the sanctuary or chapel at all times. On the Sabbath, smoking is not permitted in any part of the building, or on the synagogue grounds.

2. Before entering the sanctuary, men are requested to cover their heads. Women are also requested to wear hats and to dress in a dignified manner.

3. No photographs or motion pictures may be taken of any religious service or ceremony in the synagogue, or in any place in the building where religious services or ceremonies may be held unless special permission is granted by the rabbi. No photographs or motion pictures may be taken at any luncheon, dinner, reception, or gathering held on the Sabbaths or festivals.

4. In preparing for an affair, caterers, florists, etc. must not violate the Sabbath or festivals. Decorations must be up by Friday, early in the afternoon prior to candle-lighting time. All deliveries must be made by that time, nothing may be removed until after the Sabbath or festival.

5. What can or cannot be brought into the synagogue:

   a. No prepared foods from private homes.

   b. No cooking or baking utensils from private homes.

   c. Only paper cups and plates for coffee and cake should be used at a non-catered function.

   d. All foods prepared or to be prepared must be Kosher and from stores approved by the rabbi. For strict control, the purchaser can be requested to submit the store's receipt to the synagogue office.

   e. If a non-catered *kiddush* is to be prepared, the office must be notified as to what foods are being served.

Notes

KASHRUTH AS A MORAL FORCE

1. Medrosh, Bereshith Rabbah 33:3, Talmud Sabbath, p. 119a
2. Maimonides, Moses, "Guide to the Perplexed" part 3, chapter 8, p. 253
3. Grünfeld, I., "The Dietary Laws: A Threefold Explanation," *Tradition* Magazine, Vol. 4, no 2, p. 24, 1962
4. See Rashi's commentary on the Torah, Book of Numbers, 19:1
5. Genesis, 18:8
6. Genesis, 32:33
7. Exodus, 23:19, Exodus, 34:26, Deuteronomy, 14:21
8. Genesis, 2:17
9. Exodus, 16:4
10. Leviticus, 25:55
11. Isaiah, 11:6, 7, 9
12. "The Dietary Laws," Dresner, Rabbi Samuel H., Seigel, Rabbi Seymour, Burning Bush Press, 1966, p. 47
13. Proverbs, chapter 3, verse 6
14. Genesis, 5:9
15. Psalms, chapter 34, verse 9
16. Talmud, "Ethics of the Fathers," chapter 4, lesson 1
17. Zachariah, chapter 4, verse 6
18. Talmud, Baba Metziah, p. 24a
19. Exodus, 23:19, Exodus, 34:26, Deuteronomy, 14:21
20. Maimonides, Moses, "Guide to the Perplexed," part 3, chapter 8, p. 253
21. Deuteronomy, 12:16, Leviticus, 17:4 also

HUMANE SLAUGHTER

1. *Guide of the Perplexed*, Moses Maimonides, Friedlander Translation, Part 3, Chapter 8, p. 253, The University of Chicago Press, Chicago, Ill.

2. *Talmud, Baba Metzia,* p. 85a
3. *The Dietary Laws,* Friedman, Rabbi Sol B., doctoral dissertation for Yeshiva University, p. 35
4. *Yoreh Dayah,* Hilchos Shechita (Laws of Kosher Slaughter) Chapter 23, 24, also *Talmud Hulin,* p. 2b
5. *Shechita,* Berman, Rabbi Jeremiah J., Bloch Publishing Company, New York, New York, p. 236
6. *Reichgesetzblatt,* Vol. 1, 1933, p. 203
7. *Shechita,* Berman, Rabbi Jeremiah J., Bloch Publishing Company, New York, New York, p. 249
8. *Friends of Animals,* statement by president of a national humane society, February 15, 1967, name furnished by Friends of Animals, New York, New York
9. *Teitz, Rabbi Pinhas,* New York Times, January 7, 1966
10. *A.S.P.C.A.* pamphlet reporting use of the holding pen

A SHORT HISTORY OF KASHRUTH ORGANIZATIONS

1. *The Records of New Amsterdam,* edited by Berthold Fernow, New York, 1897, Volume 7, p. 259
2. *Shechita,* Berman, Rabbi Jeremiah J., Bloch Publishing Co., New York, New York, p. 279
3. *Ibid:* p. 279
4. *Ibid:* p. 284
5. *Publications of the American Jewish Historical Society,* Baltimore, Maryland, 1913, Volume 21, edited by Samuel Oppenheim
6. *Ibid:* Volume 25
7. *A Century of Judaism in New York,* Israel Goldstein
8. *The Occident,* May 1863
9. *Ha Yehudim V'hayadut B' New York,* Moses Weinberger, New York, 1887, p. 17
10. *Ozar Zikhrotainu,* J. D. Eisenstein, New York, 1929, p. 350
11. Notes from an interview with Rev. Eli Meltser, President, *Shochetim* Union, Also: "*Shechita,*" Jeremiah J. Berman, Bloch Publishing Company, New York, New York, p. 305
12. *Ibid:* Rev. Meltser
13. *Ibid:* Rev. Meltser
14. *Shechita,* Rabbi Jeremiah J. Berman, Bloch Publishing Company, New York, New York, p. 323
15. *Ibid:* p. 329
    Article in "*Jewish Morning Journal,* December 1, 1939
16. Notes from an interview with Rev. Eli Meltser, President, *Shochetim* Union
17. *Ibid:*
18. *Shechita,* Berman, Rabbi Jeremiah J., Bloch Publishing Company, New York, New York, p. 343
19. *New York Law Journal,* January 28, 1936

20. *Miscellaneous Report*, New York, March 1933, Case #290, Volume 147, p. 25
21. *Shechita*, Berman, Rabbi Jeremiah J., Bloch Publishing Company, New York, New York, p. 336
22. *Ibid*: p. 334 and U.S. Reports, p. 497, "Hygrade Provisions Co. vs Sherman, Attorney General, State of New York, Appeal from U.S. District Court for So. District of New York, No. 104. Argued November 20, 1924, Decided, January 5, 1925
23. *Ibid*: Berman, p. 344 also, *New York Law Journal*, January 28, 1936
24. *Ibid*: p. 344
25. *Kosher Kitchens Weren't*, Long Island Press, April 2, 1963
26. Notes from an interview with Rabbi Sheppard Baum, director, Kosher Law Enforcement Bureau, State of New York
27. Notes from an interview with an inspector from Dept. of Markets, City of New York
28. Notes from an interview with Mr. George Goldstein, former Director, O.K. Laboratories, New York, New York
29. *New York Times*, February 24, 1966
30. *Kosher Food Guide* published by O.K. Laboratories, New York, New York, March 1935
31. *Builders and Creators of My Generation*, Liebman, Isaac, Volume 2, Grenich Printing, New York, New York, 1955
32. Notes from an interview with Rabbi Chaim J. Hurwitz, Executive Secretary, Kashruth Supervisors Union, New York, New York
33. *"A Short History of the Kashruth Department*, the New York Metropolitan Region of the United Synagogue of America," p. 2
34. *Ibid*: p. 2
35. *Ibid*: p. 2

THE DIETARY LAWS

1. *The Universal Jewish Encyclopedia*, Vol. 6, p. 240
2. *Ibid*: p. 241
3. *Ibid*: p. 242
4. *Genesis*, 6:1
5. *Ibid*: 7:2
6. *Leviticus*, 11:20
7. *Ibid*: 17:14, also Deuteronomy, 15:23
8. *Exodus*, 23:19, Exodus, 34:26, Deuteronomy, 14:21
9. *Ibid*: 12:19-20
10. *Shulchan Aruch*, Laws of Kashering
11. *Genesis*: 15:5
12. *Passover Haggadah*, p. 2

GLATT KOSHER MEAT—JEWISH MILK

1. *Shechita*, Berman, Rabbi Jeremiah J., Bloch Publishing Company, New York, New York, p. 78

2. *Ibid:* p. 78
3. *Ibid:* p. 79
4. *Ibid:* p. 79
5. *Ibid:* p. 80
6. *Ibid:* p. 82

THE TRAGEDY OF CORRUPTION

1. A case of fraud known to the author
2. *Congress Weekly Report,* July 28, 1967
3. *New York Times,* December 6, 1967
4. *New York Times,* October 31, 1967
5. *Congress Weekly Report,* June 26, 1967, also July 28, 1967
6. Smith, Senator Neal, D. Iowa, testimony before House Agriculture Committee, 90th Congress, HR 6168, July 17, 1920, 1967 *Congress Weekly Report,* July 28, 1967, p. 1298
7. *Ibid:* p. 1298
8. *New York Times,* May 3, 1967
9. *New York Times,* November 14, 1967
10. *Ibid:*
11. *Ibid:*
12. *Congress Weekly Report,* November 24, 1967
13. *Congress Weekly Report,* November 3, 1967
14. *Ibid:* p. 13
15. *New York Times,* February 20, 1968
16. *New York Times,* December 17, 1968
17. *National Jewish Post and Opinion*
18. *Circular 811* published by New York State Department of Agriculture, Albany, New York, 1961 (to replace circular 780)
19. *Deuteronomy,* 16:19
20. *The Lakeville Studies, Jewish Identity on the Suburban Frontier,* Vol. 1, Sklare, Marshall, Greenblum, Joseph, Basic Books Inc., New York, New York
21. *Jewish Spectator,* November 1957
22. Incident of fraud reported to the author by a colleague
23. *Jewish Spectator,* January 1958
24. Incident of fraud reported to the author by a colleague
25. Incident of fraud known to the author personally
26. *Deception and Fraud with a Kosher Front,* Katz, Rabbi Morris Casriel, Midstate Litho Inc., Endicott, New York, 1968

Index